The One and Only Law

James R. Martel presents a radical critique of contemporary legal practices and understandings based on a new consideration of an apparent paradox in Walter Benjamin's "Critique of Violence," widely considered his final word on law. While Benjamin proposes that all manifestations of law are false stand-ins for divine principles of truth and justice that are no longer available to human beings, he also suggests that we must have law and that we are held under a divine sanction that does not allow us to escape from our responsibilities. Martel argues that this paradox is resolved when one considers that, for Benjamin, there is effectively only one law that we must obey absolutely—the Second Commandment against idolatry. Martel argues that, quite unlike our current system based on consistency and precedent, the form of law that would remain when its many false bases of authority are undermined would be a form of legal and political anarchism, one that would still retain the ability to enable and shape our polity.

Throughout the book, Martel engages with the thought of several key authors including Alain Badiou, Immanuel Kant, and H. L. A. Hart in order to revisit common contemporary assumptions about law and to reveal how, when treated in constellation with these authors, Benjamin offers a way for human beings to become responsible for their own law, thereby avoiding the false appearance of a secular legal practice that remains bound by occult theologies and fetishisms.

James R. Martel is Professor of Political Science at San Francisco State University.

THE ONE AND ONLY LAW

*Walter Benjamin and the
Second Commandment*

James R. Martel

University of Michigan Press
Ann Arbor

Published in the United States of America by
The University of Michigan Press
Manufactured in the United States of America
♾ Printed on acid-free paper

2017   2016   2015   2014   4   3   2   1

A CIP catalog record for this book is available from the British Library.

Library of Congress Cataloging-in-Publication Data

Martel, James R., author.
    The one and only law : Walter Benjamin and the second commandment / James R. Martel.
        pages   cm.
    Includes bibliographical references and index.
        ISBN 978-0-472-07230-9 (hardcover : alk. paper) — ISBN 978-0-472-05230-1 (pbk. : alk. paper) — ISBN 978-0-472-12050-5 (e-book)
        1. Law—Philosophy.   2. Benjamin, Walter, 1892–1940—Criticism and interpretation.   3. Ten commandments—Images.   I. Title.

K235.M3745   2014
340'.1—dc23

2014010712

Contents

Acknowledgments

I want to thank two editors, Robert Dreesen at Cambridge University Press and Melody Herr at University of Michigan Press for their help in making this book happen (and Melody for her help more generally with two books now). I also want to thank Austin Sarat for bringing me to Amherst to give a talk that became the basis for chapter 1 in this book, along with his colleagues, Tom Dumm, Martha Umphrey, Lawrence Douglas, Adam Sitze, Andrew Poe, and many others who asked many difficult but vital questions. Nasser Hussain is part of that group too, but my thanks to him are for all kinds of reasons.

Peter Fitzpatrick set up a similar chance for me to present my work at Birkbeck College, and so I thank him as well as many others in the Birkbeck community: Elena Loizidou, Maria Aristodemou, Julia Chryssostalis, Başak Ertür, Patrick Hanafin, Costas Douzinas, Patricia Tuitt, and Marinos Diamantides.

I want to give a special thanks to two wonderful critics, Marc de Wilde (who also presented on Benjamin at the same panel at Birkbeck, along with Patricia Tuitt) and Illan rua Wall. I could not have asked for two better readers. I also want to thank my writing group in the East Bay: Keally McBride, Kate Gordy, Sarah Burgess, and Darien Shanske, the latter who was instrumental for help with questions about legal positivism.

I gave several iterations of other chapters too; thanks to Bonnie Honig at Northwestern and also to Peter Fenves; Michaele Ferguson at University of Colorado, Boulder; Megan Thomas, Vanita Seth, and Dean Mathiowetz at UC Santa Cruz; Erik Doxtader, Jill Frank, and Justin Weinberg at University of South Carolina; Linda Ross Meyer at Quinnipiac Law School.

I also owe thanks to various friends and colleagues for their advice, work on panels, and support: Jodi Dean for helping to keep the Left both fun and alive, Jimmy Casas Klausen for being a fellow (and avowed) anarchist, the aforementioned Bonnie Honig for her inspiring example as a thinker, reader, and writer. Shalini Satkunanandan and Andrew Poe were both very helpful and generous with their time and thoughts for the Kant chapter. Thanks are also due to Andrew Dilts, Charles Barbour, Andrew Poe, Mark Andrejevic, Jennifer Culbert, Ben Wurgaft, Jackie Stevens, Ron Sundstrom, Miguel Vatter, Ben Golder, Brian Bernhardt, Antonio Vázquez-Arroyo, Kevin Olson, Robyn Marasco, Banu Bargu, Jill Stauffer, Christina Tarnopolsky, Paul Passavant, Wendy Brown, Panu Minkkinen, Stacy Douglas, Ayça Çubukçu, Samera Esmeir, Mark Antaki, Vicky Kahn, David Bates, and many others. Thanks also to my terrific students in my fall 2012 seminar on Walter Benjamin and especially to Tatsuya Goto with his excellent help and advice about Kant. Above all thanks to my wonderful and ever supportive family: Carlos, Jacques, Rocio, Nina and Kathryn, Elic and Mark, Ralph, Huguette, Django, Shalini and Shaan.

Earlier versions of a couple chapters, or parts of chapters, appeared in other publications. A portion of chapter 1 is based on my contribution entitled "The One and Only Law: Walter Benjamin, Utopianism and the Second Commandment" that appears in Austin Sarat, ed., *Law and Utopian Imagination* (Stanford University Press, 2014), published with permission. Part of the conclusion appeared as "Can the Law Transcend Its Own Violence?" 31 *Quinnipiac L. Rev.* 551 (2013), also published with permission.

The cover art is a painting by my mother, Huguette Martel. It is a painting of Walter Benjamin's passport photo, which is held by the Walter Benjamin archive at the Academy of Art in Berlin.

Introduction

A Slight Adjustment

Numa's Lie

How do we know when or if a law is legitimate? On what basis can we judge the functioning of a legal system that effectively inscribes us and produces us as subjects? Tradition and "nature," "reality" and "procedure" are the usual answers to these questions, but they seem to beg the question in the very way they posit something hazy and indefinable, or perhaps just tautological, in place of a hard and fast source of judgment. Because of this, law has a tendency to ask us not to look at it too closely, not to see "how the sausages are made." Asking too probing questions of law threatens its very basis for authority, its quality of definitively answering and moving on from vexing questions of conduct and justice. We feel that we need the law in order to make a society possible at all and therefore are generally willing to suspend a certain degree of legal skepticism.

Such a suspension of skepticism has long roots in the Western tradition. Machiavelli famously tells us in his *Discourses on Livy* that the true founder of Rome was not Romulus but Numa, the king who pretended to receive laws from a goddess and, by that ploy, established Rome as a credible and sustainable polity.[1] Without law, Machiavelli tells us, the Romans were "savage."[2] He also tells us that "Numa mistrusted his own authority, lest it should prove insufficient to enable him to introduce new and unaccustomed ordinances in Rome."[3] By resorting to his fable about the origins of the law, Numa was able to assert his own laws and have them be accepted by the Romans, allowing the city to flourish and expand.

Machiavelli goes on to argue that all political foundings necessarily resort to some version of Numa's trickery. And yet, even in his telling of this story, there is something subversive afoot. By telling us this story, Machiavelli is implicitly pointing us to the false and arbitrary roots of Roman law, thus unmasking the trick in the guise of merely reporting and commenting on it.[4] And the effect of this unmasking is not limited to Rome alone. Insofar as Roman law is the source of much of contemporary law, not only in the West but, by dint of export and imperialism, in much of the rest of the world as well, Machiavelli has let us in on quite a secret.

If Numa is a liar, and if the laws he offers us—the laws that much of Western, and arguably global, jurisprudence is based on—are just his invention, what does this say about the source and authority of law? Must we rely on such phantasms in order to have law at all? Can we ever come to trust our own right or ability to make law without such disguises? Would such law ever be authoritative? In this book, I will be arguing that Walter Benjamin supplies us with answers to these questions. Benjamin is famously critical of all manifestations of law. He deems them to be instances of what he calls "mythic violence," that is, a form of power that is rooted in phantasm. In his view, all attempts to base law in authoritative sources such as God, nature, or the state amount to a practice of legal and political idolatry or fetishism—the projection of human artifices onto false screens of both the secular and the theological variety.[5] These practices lead to what Benjamin calls "the phantasmagoria," a miasma of misrepresentation that passes for reality in our world.

For all of this, Benjamin does not suggest that we must give up on law altogether. On the contrary, he tells us that we are bound by law; God's divine law applies to us even as we have no way of knowing what it is, nor do we have any access to the truth or justice that it speaks for. For Benjamin, we must, in effect, legislate in the dark, even as we remain responsible for what we do. Rather than being paralyzed by this position, I will argue that Benjamin shows how we do have the power to make and engage with law in such a way that defies and subverts the phantasms that law is usually associated with. As subjects of law, we have the duty, Benjamin argues, to disrupt and subvert these false projections, not in order to give us access to "true" law—since we can never have that—but rather to assert our own power to decide, our own responsibility to law. Benjamin tells us that we must "wrestle . . . in solitude" with the implications of divine law and make whatever decisions we opt for accordingly.[6]

Thus, Benjamin offers us another way to understand what Machiavelli is doing in his discussion of Numa. Even as the story of Numa suggests the false basis of law, it also suggests something else, the fact that Numa was able to effectively take responsibility for making law even as he appeared to pass that responsibility onto some other, false, figure. While in telling Numa's story, Machiavelli exposes the phantasmic disguise of law, he also shows that it is possible for a single actor or a collective set of actors to determine what law will be with the full knowledge—as only Numa could then have had—that there is no *deus ex machina*, no "big Other" who is going to come into the world in order to tell us what to do.[7]

But, a reader might object, if we knew that Numa made up all of his laws, that would seem to lead to anarchy, to an unmaking of law as the basis of a polity insofar as any one law seems arbitrary and alterable. Why would people obey a law that one person simply made up? Isn't that why a good and decent king like Numa resorted to lying in the first place? In this book, I will argue that such a disenchanted and denuded view of law does indeed lead to anarchy but not in the sense of the lawless free-for-all that is often invoked by liberal renditions of that term. The tricks of Numa—the very ones that Machiavelli exposes—are indeed necessary for the kinds of false forms of politics, the states and kingdoms and empires and even the republics and democracies that dominate our world. These polities are all examples of "archism," a system of organization in which the majority of subjects are not involved in their own self-determination, in which authority is produced via dictate or by representation as opposed to direct participation. No such archist polity could exist or perpetuate itself with the full knowledge that its laws are based on nothing but the local and contingent decisions of a single person or a group of people.[8]

But what would it mean to eschew such tricks? What would our relationship to law become if we looked at it straight in the face and saw our own reflection? What if we saw ourselves as being bound by law even if we know nothing at all about what law requires of us? Although exposing the phantasms that law is generally based on is anathema to archist forms of politics—political systems like Rome and like our own contemporary polities—it does not mean that human communities have to choose between duplicity and lawlessness.

In *The One and Only Law* I will argue that in Benjamin's theory we find a way to think about law that avoids being anchored by such political fetishism even as it also avoids falling into a lawless meaninglessness, what Arendt calls an "abyss of freedom."[9] We do this, I argue, by obeying just one law: the Second Commandment against idolatry. One standard version of this commandment reads, "You shall not make for yourself a graven image, or any likeness of anything that is in heaven above, or that is in the earth beneath, or that is in the water under the earth."[10] Taken broadly, this commandment forbids fetishism or false representation, not only of God but of any other thing on, in, or under the earth. In Benjaminian terms it can therefore be read as a challenge, above all, to the phantasmagoria that envelops us all.

While all other commandments are, for Benjamin, unknowable and inscrutable—including the commandment against killing—from a Benjaminian perspective we can safely obey the Second Commandment without (much) fear of fetishism insofar as this law is itself oriented against fetishism in all forms.[11] By obeying this commandment, we cease to obey the laws that normally render us complicit with the phantasmagoria. At the same time, we are also given a way to regain a connection to law itself. The exploration of how we can obey only one law and, at the same time, enjoy what law—in its mythic variants—promises but never usually delivers is the basic purpose of this book.

To obey only one law may seem, once again, like a recipe for anarchy, and so it is. The anarchy that is produced by obeying the one law—the anarchy that is envisioned by Walter Benjamin, consistent with what he also calls "communism"—is a set of legal and political practices that resists the recourse to myth and fetishism. Crucially, in order to avoid replacing one set of myths with another, this anarchism accepts that it has no access to truth, to divine or natural law. Instead, it is based on local, specific, and contingent practices. It always has the one and only law to guide and maintain the coherence and authority of the community as it discovers for itself what it is, and has always been, capable of when it is not framed and organized by the phantasmagoria.

The One and Only Law is the third and last of a trilogy of books on Walter Benjamin's political and legal theory. The first two books, *Textual Conspiracies: Walter Benjamin, Idolatry, and Political Theory* and *Divine Violence: Walter Benjamin and the Eschatology of Sovereignty*, set up, respectively, an overview and application of Benjamin's methodologies to various literary and political texts, and a critique of sovereignty based on that method.[12] This book represents an application of Benjamin's methodology to the field of legal theory and philosophy. Each book is written in such a way that it can be read on its own and, for that reason, there are a few (hopefully short and rare) redundancies between them. But they also share a vocabulary and build upon one another. Collectively, they attempt to have Walter Benjamin speak to central questions of political and legal theory, to directly engage a thinker who is often seen as mystical and esoteric with some of the most critical issues of our time.

Benjamin's Cosmology

In order to better make my argument, and to situate this inquiry in Benjamin's larger opus, I will give a brief overview of some of Benjamin's basic cosmology, a much more expansive version of which occurs in *Textual Conspiracies*. To understand the basis of Benjamin's theologically inflected political theory not only improves our grasp of his legal theory, but it also serves to better our understanding of how, for Benjamin, any change, any form of resistance at all, is possible given how complicit we all are in political and legal forms of fetishism.[13] Benjamin's key insight in this regard comes from his notion—one that is itself rooted in traditional Jewish doctrine—that the Messiah "will merely make a slight adjustment in [the world]."[14] That is, for Benjamin, the difference between a world that is redeemed and one that is not is only a hair's breadth, hence requiring only a "slight adjustment." Every moment of damnation in his view is simultaneously a moment of redemption.

In his well-known work "On the Concept of History," Benjamin elaborates on this viewpoint when he famously concludes that "for [the Jews] every second was the small gateway in time through which the messiah might enter."[15] In other words, for Benjamin, every moment is at once a banality that reinforces the status quo of the phantasmagoria ("a fact," to use Alain Badiou's term) and at the same time a moment ripe with the potential for revolution.[16] For Benjamin, it is critical to note that the moment of messianic redemption and the moment of revolutionary self-delivery are simultaneous and interrelated, although not identical.

It is important to keep this cosmological insight in mind when thinking about Benjamin's law and what we are and are not capable of, because it explains a peculiarity about Benjamin's thought more generally, namely Benjamin's openness to redeeming even the most compromised, the most deluded of subjects, the subject of law very much included. In his interest in figures like Charles Baudelaire, for example, Benjamin evinces a very high tolerance for someone who, by his own standards, has bought in to the phantasmagoria hook, line, and sinker. For Benjamin, no subject is so compromised that she is beyond recuperation and redemption; on the contrary, the more a subject is compromised, the more effective and spectacular her act of subversion may be if the "slight adjustment" is realized in her. This is true not just for Baudelaire, but for all the losers of history, the failed revolutionaries, the stooges, braggarts, and drunkards that litter the larger history of leftist defeat. Indeed, these are the very subjects that most interested Benjamin. His life's work is, in many ways, a study, a rereading, and a recuperation of these marginal and failed characters.

Benjamin is open to failure, to compromise and loss, because in his view the world is fundamentally good. He tells us in the *Origin of German Tragic Drama*:

> It is said of God after the creation: "And God saw everything that he had made, and, behold it was very good." Knowledge of evil therefore has no object. There is no evil in the world.[17]

For Benjamin, then, there is no such thing as objective evil. Evil is a purely subjective force, stemming from the Fall of Adam (and the rarely mentioned Eve). In paradise, Benjamin tells us that Adam had an unmediated relationship to the objects of the world; his task was to name them. Since the Fall, humans have had no recourse but to representation, to the doomed attempt to reproduce that original relationship with the objects of the world. For Benjamin, because it is disconnected from God's truth, representation is inherently idolatrous; it is merely a projection, marked by the hubris that human beings can know things on their own terms, without God's sanction. Benjamin calls such activity "satanic" because it is produced by, and reflects, Satan's own rebellion against God.[18]

For Benjamin, we are therefore to some extent all fetishists; all our claims to knowledge are merely substitutes for the truths we have lost access to. Benjamin calls such knowledge "the triumph of subjectivity and the onset of an arbitrary rule over things."[19] This arbitrary rule is the hallmark of the phantasmagoria, a state of being where we seek to control the world, ourselves, and one another via the promulgations of truths that have no actual basis in reality. The promulgation of mythic law is just one—but a key—example of this process. For Benjamin, under conditions of capitalism, and hence of commodity fetishism, our mass practice of idolatry takes on its most pernicious form, but since the Fall, human beings have never been innocent of it.

In Benjamin's view, the key distinction between a fetishist and an antifetishist is not that the antifetishist gets "the truth" and the fetishist does not. Such a position would itself be a kind of ultimate idolatry. Instead the antifetishist seeks out and welcomes the failure of representation; only the failure to "know" the false truths that make up our world can give us a position that is not totalized or determined by fetishism.[20]

Thus, for example, Benjamin is highly appreciative of the failures of Franz Kafka as a writer. Through Kafka's failures, his inability to convey the (false) truths that he himself may have sought to promote, Benjamin tells us that "no other writer has obeyed the commandment 'Thou shalt not make unto thee a graven image' so faithfully."[21] Here, Benjamin quite explicitly connects failure with the injunction to obey the Second Commandment. The failure to "know," the rejection of truth as it appears to us is, from a Benjaminian perspective, the essence of iconoclasm, and hence obedient to the Second Commandment.

In his *Origin of German Tragic Drama*, Benjamin also favorably compares the failed works of the German Baroque dramatists to their contemporaries like Shakespeare and Calderón. While the latter were able to transcend the impossible task of representing divine and state power through the sheer force of their talent, the former wrote such clumsy, clunky plays that impossibility itself—and hence the failure of the representation of what they sought to convey—is what we read in them. In this view too, we can say that because they failed as playwrights, the German Baroque dramatists obeyed the Second Commandment in a way that Shakespeare and Calderón did not. This is the case despite their own complete buy-in to fetishism in all of its forms.

Two Perspectives

Thus, for Benjamin, antifetishism often comes in strange, unexpected, and even accidental forms. What looks like failure, impotence, and defeat is, at least potentially, the subversion of the phantasms that we all subscribe to whether we wish to or not. In order to think further about how failure may not be what it appears—that is, how it may in fact possess a force of its own conforming to what Benjamin would call a "*weak* messianic power"—it is helpful to think of two separate perspectives.[22] First, there is the divine or messianic view that sees the true world, knows divine law, and sees us in all of our hubristic fumblings.[23] From this perspective, even the fetishist is redeemed; in all of her frantic attempts to control and have truth, she is simultaneously also pointing to and piecing back together the broken bits of paradise. The problem is that she does not realize this; thus she is condemned by her own subjective faith (her faith, that is, in "objectivity").

The other perspective is the human one. As human beings we are utterly denied any real access to the God's-eye view. Critically, an act when seen from the human perspective has an entirely different meaning than it has for the divine. So Kafka's "failure" in this (human) realm is a "success" in the other (divine) view, as are the "failures" of the German Baroque dramatists. Passivity and loss here are simultaneously active and positive movements there.

Fittingly, Kafka—arguably Benjamin's greatest muse—supplies us with a short parable that helps us understand this dual perspective a bit better. In his parable "The Invention of the Devil" ("Die Erfindung des Teufels"), Kafka writes:

> It simply goes without saying that the falling of a human hair must matter more to the devil than to God, since the devil really loses that hair and God does not. But as long as many devils are in us that still does not help us arrive at any state of well-being.[24]

Here, the same act, the falling of a human hair, occurs in two registers. In God's register, the hair is not lost. In the devil's register, which is to say the register of human beings after the Fall of Adam, the hair loss is "real." But this reality is, once again, purely subjective. It is only real according to our own fetishistic reading of the world; it conforms to what we project as being true. Thus, as God alone knows, we suffer from loss even though it has not actually happened. Critically, Kafka tells us that the knowledge of the God's-eye view does not "help us arrive at any state of well-being" insofar as "many devils are in us." In other words, so long as we hold onto the fetish, to the phantasmagoria more broadly, we will continue to suffer; our continuing violation of the Second Commandment will have an immediate, perceptible affect on us.

Since it is entirely denied to us, all that the notion of a God's-eye view can do for human beings is to call into question the reality we subscribe to, to enhance the possibility of our own failure to represent. The suggestion of such an unreality may be the grounds for a larger subversion, for a recognition of the failure of truth all around us. Such a revelation will not make us "free" or safe from phantasm; it only gives us an opportunity—but one that is critical nonetheless—to not be completely determined by fetishism.

Thus we can see that for Benjamin, the fetishist and the antifetishist are engaged in fundamentally the same activity: both engage in representation, in the attempt to piece together once again the broken fragments of paradise. The one real advantage that the antifetishist has is that her knowledge has been turned, as it were, against itself. She benefits from the fact that every assertion of fetishism is also, and at the same time, a denial of that fetish, an exposure and failure of representation. In this way, every incident of fetishism potentially becomes a weapon to be wielded against the phantasmagoria.

Messianism and Revolution

How then do we go from one relationship with representation to another? How do we learn to disobey the fetishes that structure and order our world? Here we meet what seems to be a quandary. Insofar as the "slight adjustment" that Benjamin calls for is actually an act of God, such a sublime vision of antifetishism might seem to disable our own response; unlike God, we are not guided by a sure view of truth, nor are we immune to the seductions of the fetish. Yet, for Benjamin, as we have already begun to see, the divine serves not to overwhelm our own antifetishism but to undergird it, to make it possible in the first place.

This is true, not only in terms of taking on the idea of God's perspective as an instrument of antifetishism, but even more directly in terms of Benjamin's vision of a messiah that forcefully intrudes into the world in order to destroy the fetishes that are associated with it. He describes this phenomenon in his "Critique of Violence" as an act of divine violence, an answering force that undermines and obliterates mythic violence. In that description (to be discussed further in the next chapter) Benjamin shows that after the messiah removes its own idolatry, it withdraws from the world, leaving us utterly on our own. Such a notion of messianism offers us no "truth" at all, no guidance for how to properly engage in law. What it does do is to give us the possibility of being free—at least relatively so—from fetishism. Such an act of divine violence serves as a model for us; it permits but is not identical to our own response (something I will argue at much greater length in the conclusion to this book).[25]

In his notion of a "*weak* messianic power" that he sees as inhering in every generation, Benjamin coordinates the external, divine destruction of idolatry and our own response, our own acts of resistance.[26] In some ways, for Benjamin we must *abandon* God, or at least what passes for God—including, as we will see further, some of God's commandments—in order to preserve God as an aporia. It is between these forces, the messianic and the revolutionary, between the sense of God as an active force in the world and a God that we absolutely cannot know (and hence we must rely on ourselves) that we find the terrain of Benjamin's legal theory.

The "Slight Adjustment" and the Law

With this brief discourse on Benjamin's cosmology, we can return to the question at hand, that of the status and possibility of the law in terms of how we can come to obey one single law without giving up on law itself. If we think of the practice of antifetishism in legal terms, we can see that it might appear oxymoronic to speak of "law" in the same breath as we discuss abandonment, failure, or anarchism. Law, after all, seems by definition to be the antidote to such dangers, or at least what is perceived as dangers from a particular, generally liberal, viewpoint.[27] It surely cannot be considered lawful to disregard or disobey all laws but one. Law, by definition—or at least by a prominent definition that will be addressed at greater length in chapters 1, 3, and 4 and the conclusion—seems to require a systematic, regular, and even application. Without recourse to some fundamental basis of authority, law appears to risk becoming utterly untethered. Its most basic functions seem jeopardized: its ability to protect us, to regulate and order our lives, to subject us to its neutral and discerning eye.

Perhaps even more troubling, we could further ask why such a recourse to one law does not become its own fetish? Since the commandment against graven images was inscribed on Moses' tablets, one could argue that the commandment was violated—that is, represented—even before it was articulated to human beings; we can see here a risk of reproducing fetishism in the guise of avoiding it. Why is *this* commandment different than other ones? How is it too not "mythic," not based on a theology—such as the one already described for Benjamin—that is itself entirely speculative, not based on any actual truth (even a truth that Benjamin scrupulously separates from the human realm)?

Much of this book will be a response to these concerns, but for now let me offer a few preliminary responses. The first thing I'd say—and this is not itself a terribly original thought—is that our current practice of law, one that is based on falsities, that claims to be neutral and fair when it is not, is an example of the "arbitrary rule over things" that Benjamin speaks of.[28] Such a law does not deliver us justice and fairness but only the appearance of those things, an appearance that itself can be the basis of much that is unjust and unfair. We are thus at the very least no worse off following a form of law that appears to break with so much of what we expect or demand from law in general insofar as ordinary forms of law do not give us these things either.

A second, perhaps slightly more original claim—one based on Benjaminian principles—is that a law that recognizes its own failure, that is anchored in no truth at all but merely in fighting off the falsities that are normally attributed to it, is the closest thing to a "true" law that we can have in this world. Such a law *can* be trusted, can be authoritative, because it harkens to the only thing we know for sure: that we don't know anything truly. That is the antifetishist stance in a nutshell. To obey only one law, the Second Commandment, serves as the basis for a new understanding of positive law (as I'll argue further in chapter 4) by asserting the only positive that we know: the failure of law to be true.[29] With this basis, new orderings are not only possible but in some ways already present to us. When the law becomes our own way of reaching out toward a messianic figure who in turn reaches back toward us, we see the parameters of the "slight adjustment" that is continually made in the world for Benjamin. We also see the chance for a sustained and antifetishistic political practice as well, a practice that I will argue throughout this book must be anarchist to reflect the statutes of the one supremely antiauthoritarian law that it obeys.

As for the danger of the fetishism even of this antifetishistic commandment, I'd say that indeed we can never be free of fetishism and thus cannot expect this commandment to completely save us from an engagement with fetishism, including its fetishization of itself. All we can ever do for Benjamin is to struggle with and resist the fetish; that struggle has to be enough. The day that we think we have triumphed over the fetish and can yield representation—taking this term in all its theological, linguistic, and political senses—in an unproblematical way, or even dispense with representation and just "be" what we are, is the day that we give ourselves over to the fetish in a way that would be much more difficult to address. Feeling as though we had "faced down" the fetish, we would be unaware of the way that fetishism continues to form and dominate us.

We must also distinguish between the Second Commandment when it is set in its usual context as one of the Ten Commandments as inscribed by Moses, and the Second Commandment as it is understood via a Benjaminian reading. When it is part of its usual, traditional context, the Second Commandment does indeed potentially become part of the apparatus of fetishism (in this case, of the divine); it becomes a support for the kind of rigid monotheism that we associate with divine law—taken as a human projection—more generally. But when we think of the Second Commandment when it is unmoored from the other nine, when we treat it as the one law that is based entirely on failure—and, in particular, on the failure of representation—we can revisit the Second Commandment as being a kind of anticommandment, a law that undoes law (in chapter 3, citing Badiou, I will call it the "law of the break with law").[30] In such a context, although it too is not free of fetishism—because nothing is—it becomes, I'd say free*er*; as a law, it changes from a universal truth that is to be applied uniformly in all cases (as it would be for Kant, whose distinction from Benjamin when it comes to legal theory will be taken up in chapter 3) to a local engagement that is contingent, subjective, and temporary.

Thinking about such a treatment of law more generally, we can see that, although he engages, to a great extent, in Jewish tradition, as well as in conversation with a long tradition of legal theory, philosophy, and theology, Benjamin's reading of the Second Commandment and law—at least in the ways that I have interpreted and applied them to Benjaminian thought—is often at odds with the very traditions that he takes them from. Consistent with his own style of reading, Benjamin upends our expectations and turns our own subjective reading into a tool against itself. Benjamin batters away at our fetishism with more of our fetishism, using our own belief in truth as a way to undermine its own possibility, and allowing its failure to become legible to us. What he draws us toward might seem too awfully nihilistic and itself fetishistic were it not for his political theology that gives us the courage to make what he himself calls a "faithless . . . leap" away from all the false assurances that constitute our world and toward something truly unknown and unknowable.[31]

Even before we get into the substance of the arguments I will make about Benjamin and law, it may already be apparent that there are some potential benefits to thinking along the lines I have proposed. For one thing, if this analysis is correct, we do not need to wait for revolutionary moments (what Alain Badiou calls "the event)" to occur.[32] For Benjamin, in our relationship to law, as with everything else that we do, we are already resisting idolatry (albeit in ways that are generally unrecognized by us) even amid our general subservience to myth.

Furthermore, Benjamin's stance shows us the ongoing value of law even in the face of his charge that all law, with one critical exception, is mythic. Law itself can be seen as the mechanism by which it becomes possible for us to imitate or gesture toward the messianic "slight adjustment." Just as God's acts of divine violence challenge mythic law in all of its forms, so too do our own acts of disobedience and failure—that is, our acts of obeying one law instead of many—undermine the myth and unreality we all subscribe to.

Finally, such an exploration may help us to better understand what law is when you remove all of the certainties and "authorities" upon which it is based, that is, when you return that authority to the legal subject herself (or, to put this in terms of the way I began this chapter, what Numa's act becomes when you expose his lie). This analysis will examine what happens to law when such obfuscation is brought into open question, directly challenged. What remains may be the "pith" of law, that excess—to cite Badiou once again—which survives the removal of everything else.[33] As already noted, this notion of law also depends on a kind of external authority. It requires some concept of a God's-eye perspective, a notion that there *is* a divine law even though we know nothing of it and never will. Yet the authority that is produced out of such a basis is turned in on and against itself. When human beings find ways to resist their own fetishization via law, when divine law/violence cancels out mythic law/violence, we are left with our own law and our own form of authority. This is an authority that we exercise without plunging into the nihilism and relativism that is threatened by such a reduction of law; our tether, what keeps our own authority over law from becoming random and just more violence, is our engagement with the Second Commandment.

Chapter Overviews

To give a better sense of how this argument will unfold, let me give an overview of the various chapters that make up this book. Chapter 1 deals directly with Benjamin's understanding of law. In that chapter, I engage in an analysis of three writings that are perhaps most critical for understanding Benjamin's notion of law. The first is Benjamin's essay "On Language as Such and the Language of Man." The second is the very famous "Critique of Violence." The final essay is an earlier companion piece to the "Critique" entitled "The Right to Use Force." Together, these texts offer us a broad understanding of Benjamin's seemingly perverse argument that law as we know it is mythic and false even as law remains valid and, indeed, that there is divine law that obligates us despite our knowing nothing more about it. In this chapter, I seek to reconcile these claims by looking at Benjamin's treatment of the Second Commandment as well as of other Commandments. In particular, I will examine his claim, made in the "Critique of Violence," that we must "wrestle in solitude" with the Sixth Commandment against killing and at times, if necessary, we must "abandon" it. I will align his notion of a divine violence that eliminates all fetishes—the fetish of law very much included—with the possibility for human action and resistance as exemplified by Benjamin's discussion of the revolutionary general strike. Without collapsing the two, I will seek to show how for Benjamin the divine and human responses to fetishism remain in perpetual tension. This tension produces the possibility for resistance to—if not escape from—fetishism, hence serving as the basis of what might be called "Benjamin's law."

Chapters 2 through 4 examine specific writers and thinkers who have some similarities to Benjamin's theory when it comes to legal iconoclasm. By looking at three key thinkers in turn (Alain Badiou, Immanuel Kant, and H. L. A. Hart), I try to show that, when read on their own, these think-ers do not offer as pure an iconoclasm as at first appears, but, when read in conjunction (or "constellation") with Benjamin, their more radical poten-tial becomes apparent.

Chapter 2 begins to look at the ethics of obeying one law only. By engaging with the ethical theory of Alain Badiou, I will ask how a law that does not offer a cookie-cutter answer or model for all situations, a model that involves personal struggle and the possibility of abandoning basic principles such as the condemnation of killing, could possibly be ethical. In looking at Badiou's ethics, I will draw from his own reading of how ethics must be individual and local. In my view, Badiou's analysis helps us to think further about the implications of Benjamin's own theorizing. Ultimately, I will distinguish Benjamin's understanding of ethics from Badiou by argu-ing that Badiou's direct engagement with an idea of the "universal," as well as his particular understanding of time and the future, risks some of the very fetishisms that both thinkers set out to oppose. Thus Badiou's own work must be seen as an aid in grasping, but not the final expression of, what a Benjaminian ethics—one that springs directly from his understand-ing of law—might look like. At the same time, at the end of the chapter, I look at what a Badiouian notion of ethics can do for Benjamin (once its own iconoclasm has been intensified via a connection with Benjaminian theory). I argue that Badiou shows us a great deal about what happens to law (taken in its human sense) after its encounter with the Second Com-mandment and also how the legal subject is altered by their encounter with this form of law.

In chapter 2, I also turn to the work of Slavoj Žižek, treating his criti-cism of the prominent role the Second Commandment plays in Jewish thought, specifically in terms of the work of many twentieth-century Jew-ish thinkers such as Levinas, Derrida, and Benjamin himself. For Žižek, the idea of the wholly other, of the unrepresentable that comes from a promi-nent reading of the Second Commandment, distorts the possibility of a radical practice of politics insofar as it makes an actual political relationship impossible. In arguing against this reading, I will seek to distinguish Benja-min's iconoclasm from Levinas's (at least Žižek's reading of Levinas). I will show that even the commandment against idolatry can potentially produce idols ("the wholly other"). Rather than seek out a pure nonidol, Benjamin's practice is to subvert and upend the idols we otherwise worship. In this way, a Benjaminian practice of the Second Commandment helps to guard even against its own self-fetishism. When it is properly applied, I argue, against Žižek, the Second Commandment not only makes a radical politics possible, but is necessary for such a politics to occur at all.

In chapter 3, I engage with Kant's idea that the "most sublime" passage in Jewish law is the Second Commandment. I consider the extent to which Kant himself is an antifetishist insofar as he too is very suspicious of truth claims and insists that any truth claim he is making is only an ideal, purely metaphysical concept. In this chapter, I focus mainly on two works of Kant, his *Critique of Judgment* and *Religion within the Limits of Reason Alone*, arguing that in the two years that passed between the publication of these works, Kant appears to compromise his iconoclastic stance to the point of seeking transcendence through ordinary forms of religion in the later work (an idea he rejects quite explicitly in earlier works). Yet even in the *Critique of Judgment* I find Kant's iconoclasm to be only partial, perhaps incomplete. Through the experience of the sublime—the encounter with some object or set of objects that is too vast to adequately grasp with the human intellect—the subject is meant to feel the extent of her own inability to understand the universe. This humbling sensation is for Kant at the same time a premonition of a higher, moral law that we intuit even as our empirically based senses retreat from their grip on our conscious minds. For Kant, this inkling of a higher, moral law is transformational, but I argue that such a conviction disguises the ways that even the sublime experience itself can be idolatrous. By trusting that the negative experience of the sublime is sufficient to overcome the idolatry of the world of sense—and, in the process, ignoring the way the sublime experience itself is a relationship with the sensual world—Kant fails to completely protect against the ways that even this experience, even this intuiting of the moral law, potentially preserves the very idolatry it is meant to combat

I argue further that if we read Kant in constellation with Benjamin, we emphasize that iconoclasm cannot be the attempt to intuit truth (even negatively) but only a way to enhance the failure of representation. In juxtaposing Kant's legal theory to the work that Benjamin does in his "Critique of Violence," we come closer to the kind of nonidolatrous relationship to law that Kant seeks via the exercise of the sublime but does not quite achieve. Such a rereading, wherein we take Kant's esteem for the Second Commandment more seriously, offers us a more radical Kant. Reading Kant in this way (with some help from Peter Fenves) offers us a glimpse, I argue, of an anarchic form of law, one that does not abandon law entirely—since there is always the one law we must not disobey—but which frees us even from the self-imposed "autonomy" that comes with more ordinary Kantian readings of the moral law.

Chapter 4 engages with legal positivism, a system of jurisprudence that, on the surface of things, may appear to have a great deal in common with what I have been ascribing to Benjaminian law. Legal positivism formally denounces all moral systems and engages instead in a language of efficiency, pragmatism, and the kinds of authority that stem from ongoing legal and social practices and traditions. I focus especially on the work of H. L. A. Hart as offering an especially cogent and reasonable-sounding articulation of legal positivism. In this chapter, I argue that Hart's legal positivism is not as unconnected to moral conceptions as he seems to suggest. Legal positivism formally distances itself from moral laws but in fact covertly relies on a kind of Kantianism, what Linda Ross Meyer has called "kanticism," a pared-down sense of rational and moral values that come from the uniform application of basic principles.[34] I argue that Hart relies on such a moral tradition when the law fails to be just. Hart is thus much less of an iconoclastic legal figure than he appears to be. In a sense, his concept of law itself serves as a covert way to smuggle in further—and unseen—anticipations of Kantian moral law; by assuming that his formal disavowal of moral law renders him "free" of it, Hart allows unseen connections to such forms of moral reasoning to persist. Yet, here, once again, I attempt to read Hart in constellation with Benjamin, emphasizing another form of "positive" law that is far more iconoclastic than what Hart normally proposes insofar as it reflects a notion of law that follows after "law" as a concept has been deflated and subverted, hardly recognizable as law at all.

Chapter 5 and the conclusion are attempts to think out the ramifications of a single, Benjaminian law in terms of our actual application of such a theory to the world in which we live. In chapter 5, I apply my analysis of a Benjaminian concept of law to the Haitian Revolution at the turn of the nineteenth century. I argue that the Haitian Revolution offers a concrete example of following the Second Commandment. When the French Revolution produced the Declaration of the Rights of Man and Citizen, among other "radical" declarations, the Haitian slaves mistakenly thought that its call for freedom applied to them. Seeing themselves as having been called, they rose up and ended their slavery and the French were unable to reenslave them. The Haitians' radical resistance to reenslavement in turn (as C. L. R. James tells us) set an example for and radicalized the French workers so that a false, liberal—and idolatrous—revolution was subverted via the mistaken self-inclusion of Haitian slaves. In turn, by becoming the model of revolution more generally, the French Revolution spread this radicalism—at least potentially—to the rest of the world. This is an example of turning an idolatrous concept, in this case the "freedom" promised by the Declaration, into a weapon against itself so that the slaves' own experience of freedom was something radically different from the concept that inspired them. In their resistance, the masses of former slaves were far more radical than their leadership: Toussaint Louverture and even Jean-Jacques Dessalines, his main general (who is often considered more radical than Toussaint) both attempted to impose a plantation, wage-based system in Haiti instead of classical slavery. The Haitian ex-slaves resisted both this imposition and Toussaint's more general accommodations with white planters. Left to themselves, the former slaves organized into smallholding farmer communities that resisted the various levels of slavery and exploitation that others sought to impose on them; that is, they resisted both state and market. The position of the former slaves—stark as it was—proved itself almost immune to the blandishments of liberal capitalism and so offers a model of resistance that goes well beyond what is generally attributed to that revolution. In the hands of the former slaves of Haiti, the idea of freedom became simply the conviction not to be reenslaved. Guided by that conviction, they were able to follow the Second Commandment; the idol of freedom became, for them, a weapon that they wielded against all forms of phantasm (and most prominently, phantasms of freedom). For this reason, I argue that we might think of this revolution not only as an event (in the Badiouian sense) but perhaps even *the* event—the event whose own coming into possibility made future events less impossible. Although the power the Haitians wielded can be considered what Benjamin calls a "*weak* messianic force," the case of Haiti shows that it can actually be a very strong "weakness": here, a group of former slaves defeated Napoleon's armies when all of Europe could not. Most critically, this chapter argues that the example of Haiti shows that not only is obedience to the Second Commandment theoretically possible but that it can be read as having actually happened.

In the conclusion, I engage with the question of what makes a law "lawlike" when it has been stripped of its veneer of divine, natural, or other mythic fonts of authority. Insofar as Benjamin's understanding of law seems so contrary to any conventional understanding of law, why even persist in calling it a law at all? In this concluding chapter, I try to imagine what the ongoing practice of obeying only one law might look like, how decisions would be made, and whether they'd be adhered to. In doing so, I seek to portray an anarchist community united only by the common purpose of obeying the Second Commandment.

In this chapter, I discuss (in conversation with Simon Critchley) whether such a community can ever break with violence, with its own origins in mythic law and also whether human beings are themselves capable of divine violence, as many writers from Žižek to Agamben imply; my own answer is a firm no.

I also look at the kind of subject that such a relationship with law produces. Drawing from my discussion of Kant and Hart and also the example of the Haitian Revolution, I argue that the subject of the Second Commandment is a misinterpellated one; she hears the call of the law even though it is not addressed to her. As such, these subjects are able to subvert the original, idolatrous intention of law in the name of some other kind of law (the Second Commandment) using, here again, their own fetishism in order to fight further fetishism.

Ultimately, I argue that a community that follows only one law does not entirely abandon law, but that the basis for legal authority, the basis for the force of law itself, is entirely altered. When subjects of the Second Commandment break the one and only law, their punishment is instant; the reemergence of idolatry and, thus, a form of slavery to phantasm. When, however they continue to obey the Second Commandment, their reward is, if not a perfect freedom, then at least a space that is deprived of the certainty of phantasm, a space that was briefly discovered by the Haitian revolutionaries and which has reemerged from place to place (the Paris Commune of 1871, anarchist Spain in the 1930s, the streets of Tunisia and Egypt in 2011, the tents of Occupy Wall Street that same magical year, Turkey and Brazil at the time I am writing this).

The One and Only Law

Many readers who are familiar with Derrida's "Force of Law: The Mystical Foundation of Authority" may be puzzled as to why it seems that we need to revisit Benjamin's notion of law when Derrida himself has already plumbed that subject so well.[35] In *Divine Violence*, I argued that for all his glossing of Benjamin, Derrida actually comes out with a very different reading than I think can be found in Benjamin's own work.[36] The main difference between these authors, as I see it, is that although Derrida shares and appreciates Benjamin's focus on the idolatrous nature of law, he, unlike Benjamin, does not offer as much in the way of recourse.

As I argue in that book, Derrida's understanding of the Messiah is one that is both much *less* and much *more* present in the world than Benjamin's. It is much less present because Derrida does not emphasize or share Benjamin's view of divine violence, a force that actively interferes in the world to remove its own idolatry. At the same time, it is more in the world because Benjamin's God is absolutely and utterly unknowable while Derrida's Messiah "trembles" at the boundaries of the world, always nigh but never quite arriving. The salvation such a figure offers is always "to come," never here.

Accordingly, I see Benjamin as offering a much more tangible, actual plan for combatting idolatry than Derrida. For Derrida—especially the later Derrida—the fact of our position of being absolutely responsible but also unable to know what God asks of us can be terrible and paralyzing.[37] From a Benjaminian perspective, as I've argued in this introduction, the solution to this dilemma is to scrupulously follow the Second Commandment; by imitating God's own acts of divine violence—an imitation that can never actually be identical to divine acts—we can act in the world, not only in ways that are "to come" but in ways that are already here and now. In fact, I will argue, we have been acting in this way, resisting fetishism, all along, even if we are not usually aware of this. In any case, the point for Benjamin is to act in ways that are more coordinated, more strategic, more visible to ourselves as such.

Accordingly, this book is not about Derrida's version of Benjamin but constitutes a return to Benjamin's own text(s). Instead of treating with Derrida, my prime interlocutors will be authors including Badiou, Kant, Hart, Critchley, and Žižek. All of these authors offer visions of law that I will argue at times look similar to Benjamin's own ideas about combatting fetishism (with the exception of Žižek, who places himself, as already noted, in opposition to the iconoclasm of Benjamin, among other thinkers). Yet it is Benjamin himself, I suggest, who uniquely offers a way to struggle with fetishism, who shows us how we can engage with law in ways that do not replicate the problems of authority that motivate each of these other thinkers in turn.

In making these claims, I am not trying to say that Badiou and the rest are fetishists. Or, rather, they are, but so are we all, including me, including you, including Benjamin. In a world marked by phantasm, we have no choice but to engage with fetishism to some extent. The question is not so much "Are we fetishists?"—since the answer is always yes—but rather how committed are we in our simultaneous antifetishism or iconoclasm? In this way I do not seek to cast aspersions on any of the authors that I treat (on the contrary, I see each of them as contributing something valuable and vital to a Benjaminian legal and political project) but only to suggest that, when read in constellation with Benjamin, their commitment to antifetishism becomes stronger, reinforced, and therefore more subversive to the phantasm we all (still) subscribe to. By extension, it is to be hoped that in engaging with these ideas our own commitment to antifetishism might similarly be bolstered. That at least is the hope—surely a "hope [that is] . . . not for us," to cite Kafka yet again—that animates this book.[38]

Insofar as this book too is, inevitably, a work of fetishism, I would urge on the reader a style of reading that Benjamin sought to promote as well;

the reader is meant to resist the authority of the text, the siren call toward truth and meaning that we inevitably seek as readers. Benjamin, in my view, is a master practitioner, along with Nietzsche, of defying his own textual authority. His tone, his style, his deliberate underminings of his own assertions, all lead the reader to be turned to her own resources. I do not pretend to share Benjamin's excellence at this task; nor was he himself always able to avoid a return to fetishism (this book will have a few examples of this in later chapters). Therefore there will be times when the tone of this book seems to militate for a truth, for a pure nonfetish, even as the words insist on denying this impulse. Speaking, as I will be doing, of fetishism automatically seems to imply an alternative that is free from such delusions. The text will always suggest a resolution into truth, but I ask the reader's help in collectively struggling against such a conclusion. If readers see truth in the text, it is probably my fault as an author that they have done so, but such a fault need not condemn us, reader and writer both, to the fetishism that results from such a conclusion. We must learn, as Benjamin instructs, not to say an absolute no to the fetish (just as we must learn not to say an absolute no to law), but rather to struggle with it, to acknowledge its power over us without succumbing to that power, to keep open a space for resistance to those forces that always compel us.

In this way, the term "antifetishist" is admittedly not quite accurate. Nor for that matter is "iconoclasm," since that term suggests an even greater denial or destruction of the fetish; even the terminology I am working with both advances and betrays the work this book attempts to do. I continue to use these terms, in part because of a lack of alternatives and in part because to do so preserves and reproduces the struggle over representation and truth that lie at the basis of Benjamin's political project. The "anti" in this case signifies, not a disengagement with the fetish, but its opposite: it stands for "wrestling," for working both with and against the fetish, for a protracted and ongoing subversion of the idols that form our reality.[39]

One final word about the turn to the Second Commandment that this book promotes: generally speaking, iconoclasm has been a force for conservativism, reaction, and a purely religious radicalism. Thus the Taliban's dynamiting of the giant sculptures of the Buddha in Bamiyan, Afghanistan, the persecution of Sufism and the shrines of its ancient saints throughout the Muslim world by fundamentalists (including most recently in Tombouctou and elsewhere in northern Mali), and the frenzied destruction of pictures, images, and even the forbidding of certain gestures during the height of the English Puritan reformation, are what we tend to think of when we think of iconoclasm and antifetishism.[40] Is it possible to think of a form of iconoclasm that serves a leftist political agenda? I will argue in these pages that such a view is not only possible, but necessary in our own time. I would ask that readers therefore be willing to suspend a great deal of baggage that comes along with thinking about religion—and specifically religious iconoclasm—as they consider this text. As I hope will become clear as this book progresses, the kinds of theology and iconoclasm I am promoting in these pages are not only unrelated to the iconoclastic movements we have seen in the past and the present, they are, in fact their direct, and utter, antithesis.

Similarly, although Benjamin explicitly draws upon the Western—and more specifically Jewish—tradition, evoking God and the Ten Commandments, messiahs, and law in this culturally specific way, I would like to think of Benjamin's contribution as not being entirely bound by that tradition. Rooted as he is in one tradition, Benjamin offers a way to engage with fetishism more generally. Insofar as the West has cast its shadow across the globe, the fetishism of the West has arguably become the fetishism of the whole planet; certainly the triumph of global capitalism has ensured that fetishism has engulfed many people, for the vast majority of whom the story of Adam and Eve has no meaning. In battling with this phenomenon, there are other approaches, other traditions, that could also be drawn upon as well, and not all of them need be religious. Perhaps then we can think of Benjamin as offering us one particular model from which we can abstract from the talk of God and Commandments to see the underlying methodology at play.[41]

This book is therefore not a work of political theology so much as a work that engages with a particular political theology in order to think further about representation and, more specifically, the representation of law. I will argue that Benjamin offers us another option besides the kind of Kantian/positivist return to traditional sources of legal authority, even in the guise of doing the opposite, as well as the general rejection of legal authority without much in the way of recourse, which is the (late) Derridean position. Benjamin, I argue, threads the needle between reality and fetish, between divine command and human ability, between justice and our absolute ignorance of divine law. In this way, his ideas about law and resistance remain timely and necessary and well worth revisiting.

With this overview and these caveats in mind, let us turn toward the heart of my argument: an explication of Benjamin's law as found in Benjamin's writings on the subject.

ONE

The One and Only Law

In terms of his contribution to legal theory, Benjamin leaves us in a strange position. On the one hand, in his "Critique of Violence," Benjamin sets out a very comprehensive overview of the law, ranging from natural to positive law. Here, he describes the parameters of law as we understand it, its basis for authority. On the other hand, via his notion of divine violence, also promoted in that essay, he offers a vision of a law-destroying deity that upends and subverts all human contrivances. If law is both the foundation of political authority and also, in its divine manifestation, the undoing of the same, what does this say about our actual practices? What kind of law are we permitted in the face of divine interference? Does law end up being completely meaningless in the face of a messianic force that seems purely destructive?[1]

In this chapter, I will argue that for Benjamin divine interference does not completely undermine law as a human practice; instead—as already suggested in the introduction—it leaves us with only one law, the Second Commandment against idolatry.[2] Insofar as the act of divine violence is itself an act explicitly directed against idolatry, it offers a celestial model for law that serves us on earth as well. At the outset, I should say that this argument is an *interpretation* of Benjamin. He does not come out and say that we must obey the Second Commandment and only this commandment—at least not directly. But I will argue that such a conclusion comes out of an engagement with his writing, especially in terms of his most extensive commentary on law, his well-known essay "Critique of Violence."

To obey one single law may seem to diminish law to a mere pith, a singularity that cannot address the complexity of human life and experience.

In fact, however, I will argue that from a Benjaminian perspective, this one law is the only law that we need. This law protects us from the ossification of law as a whole. It prevents law from being "bastardized" by myth (to use Benjamin's own term).[3] With it we are given just what is required for law to function as a way to safeguard and guide the human polity and no more. Indeed, as I will go on to argue, for Benjamin, by extension, all other laws must not only be superfluous but actually distort and interfere with this one, uniquely antifetishistic law.

The Origin of Law

In "On Language as Such and the Language of Man," an essay that he wrote in 1916 but which was not published in his lifetime, Benjamin sets out an origin story for law. Typical of his theologically inflected political theory, for Benjamin the origin of law has a supernatural basis; it comes, as already suggested in the introduction, with the Fall of humanity from paradise.[4] More specifically, for Benjamin, the law comes out of a change in language, at least as far as human beings are concerned, that was precipitated by the Fall.

Benjamin tells us that in paradise there was already language. When God created the world, it was done through words ("Let there be").[5] Benjamin says further,

> Language is therefore both creative and the finished creation; it is word and name. In God, name is creative because it is word, and God's word is cognizant because it is name. "And he saw that it was good"—that is, he cognized it through name. The absolute relation of name to knowledge exists only in God; only there is name, because it is inwardly identical with the creative word, the pure medium of knowledge.[6]

For Benjamin, human beings have a specific and unique position in terms of God's unmediated connection to created nature: "of all beings, man is the only one who names his own kind, as he is the only one whom God did not name."[7] Given his ability to name (including naming Eve), Adam also gives a spoken name to the things of the world, a name that corresponded perfectly and unmediatedly to the true (but mute) name that God had already given them.[8] In this way, Benjamin tells us that the "name-language of man and the nameless language of things [are] related in God."[9]

With the coming of the Fall, this harmony between human and divine (and material) language changes. Benjamin tells us that

> the knowledge to which the snake seduces, that of good and evil, is nameless. It is vain in the deepest sense. . . . Knowledge of good and evil abandons name; it is a knowledge from outside, the uncreated imitation of the creative word.[10]

In this way, by aligning ourselves with such a false imitation of truth (as initiated by the knowledge of good and evil), human beings abandon their connection to the "mute language" of things. Instead, an "other muteness" becomes manifest in the material world, a silence that reflects human abandonment.[11] As a result of this change, nature displays a "deep sadness" at the loss of human naming.[12] Objects become our tools as far as we are concerned; the world of simulacra and the phantasmagoria is born (the "uncreated imitation of the creative word"). As a result of such an imitation, human beings "f[a]ll into the abyss of the mediateness of all communication, of the word as means, of the empty word, into the abyss of prattle."[13] In other words, human beings become idolators one and all.

It is at this point that the law comes into force. Benjamin tells us: "In the Fall, since the eternal purity of names was violated, the sterner purity of the judging word arose."[14] Judgment is God's response to our idolatry. Benjamin also says of this:

> This judging word expels the first human beings from Paradise; they themselves have aroused it in accordance with the immutable law by which this judging word punishes—and expects—its own awakening as the sole and deepest guilt.[15]

Here, judgment itself becomes part of language but in a new guise, one that produces in its wake the guilty subjects that we all are (that is, the complicit, idolatrous beings that constitute the postlapsarian individual).

Although this may be considered the "origin of law," we see that for Benjamin, in some sense this origin was already predetermined, part of the architecture of paradise. In thinking about the Tree of Knowledge and the role that it plays in fomenting idolatry (as well as the judgment that results from Adam's disobedience), Benjamin tells us:

> The Tree of Knowledge stood in the garden of God not in order to dispense information on good and evil, but as emblem of judgment

over the questioner. This immense irony marks the mythic origin of law.[16]

This is, perhaps, the critical point to grasp in terms of Benjamin's notion of the sources of law. The Tree of Knowledge is, in effect, a tree of judgment. The knowledge of this tree is not new to the occupants of paradise and hence is not in and of itself the point of the tree's presence in the garden. Earlier in the essay, Benjamin tells us:

> Even the existence of the Tree of Knowledge cannot conceal the fact that the language of Paradise was fully cognizant. Its apples were supposed to impart knowledge of good and evil. But on the seventh day, God had already cognized with the words of creation. And God saw that it was good.[17]

Thus the concept of good (and perhaps by extension, evil) is already present in the garden. The tree's presence attests to a different calculation, one based not on good and evil (which Benjamin calls "nameless" concepts) but on law.[18] But it isn't until the actual expulsion from paradise that law comes into its own. This, in two critical senses: first, we see the creation of law as mythic. This is the law produced by the subjects of judgment born from our encounter with the Tree of Knowledge. This is the form of law that attempts to assuage its guilt by recourse to truths from which it is henceforth permanently banished (hence a "mythic" origin). Second, the law simultaneously becomes in effect divine law, God's commandments, which remain valid even in the face of human disobedience. Although in some sense God's law has always been present (just as the Tree of Knowledge has always stood as a tree of judgment), from the human perspective, it takes on a new valence as the source of judgment, as what is now withheld from us as a result of the Fall. These two forms—or perhaps appearances—of law delineate the context in which a consideration of how to obey the Second Commandment must operate.

Divine versus Mythic Violence

In order to connect Benjamin's theological understanding of the origin of law with questions of actual human practices, it is necessary to turn from an engagement with "On Language as Such and the Language of Man" to two writings of Benjamin's that directly pertain to the question of law and our relationship to it. These essays are his very well known "Critique of Violence" along with a corresponding (and less well known) essay fragment, "The Right to Use Force," which offers useful commentary and elaboration on the better-known essay. These essays were written very closely together in time (they were written in 1921 and 1920 respectively, although only the "Critique" was published in Benjamin's lifetime).

In the "Critique," Benjamin runs through many distinctions in law, including between the aforementioned natural and positive law and between lawmaking and law-preserving violence. The key distinction in this essay, however, as I and many others read it, is that between divine and mythic violence.

As is often the case with one of Benjamin's essays, as you move along through the work, the ground that the reader has assumed at the beginning becomes upended and subverted by later iterations in the text. Not unlike the usurpation of law that Benjamin attributes to divine violence in the essay, we as readers are left similarly upended, without recourse to those easier answers and assurances that the essay seemed to supply us with at the beginning.

The introduction of the distinction between mythic and divine violence, which comes about two-thirds of the way into the essay, calls into question much of the careful work that Benjamin had painstakingly laid out (and without evident foreshadowing) in the earlier portions of the essay. The iterations of law that he has cataloged are revealed to be instances of mythic law, that is, law that is idolatrous, a false, human-derived stand-in for divine law.

Benjamin introduces the distinction between mythic and divine violence by asking, "What kinds of violence exist other than all those envisaged by legal theory[?]"[19] In other words, what force or power of authority exists beyond the confines of the human imagination? He asks this because, as he sees it, there is a chronic "insolubility of all legal problems."[20] For Benjamin, despite the various distinctions that we make within contemporary practices of law, no iteration of it can serve as its own ground or foundation; no law that human beings derive on their own can ever actually produce a true form of justice.[21] Benjamin tells us that "it is never reason that decides on the justification of means and the justness of ends: fate-imposed violence decides on the former, and God on the latter."[22] Here we see that the law—such as we know it—is produced randomly, without recourse to any actually true principles. In this way, the law takes on the character of fate; a random destiny that we cannot resist.

For Benjamin, as we have already seen, there *is* a true and perfect law—God's divine law—but as postlapsarian subjects we are fated to never know it even as we remain subject to its judgment. In introducing the distinction between mythic violence and divine violence, Benjamin is distinguishing between the truth of law as we imagine it (i.e., as a myth, a human projection onto God), and what it actually is (as divine, something that lies only in the mind of God).[23]

Benjamin furnishes an archetypical example of mythic violence by considering the punishment of Niobe. In the Greek myth that bears her name, Niobe bragged that while she had fourteen children, Leto, the mother of Apollo and Artemis, only had two. In vengeance, Apollo and Artemis slew her children one by one (in some renditions, they leave one child of each gender alive to achieve parity). Niobe was then turned into a weeping rock, forever mourning the loss of her children. After connecting this kind of mythic violence directly to lawmaking violence, Benjamin notes:

> The function of violence in lawmaking is twofold, in the sense that lawmaking pursues as its end, with violence as the means, *what* is to be established as law, but at the moment of instatement does not dismiss violence; rather, at this very moment of lawmaking, it specifically establishes as law not an end unalloyed by violence but one necessarily and intimately bound to it, under the title of power.[24]

In other words, such an action does not eliminate violence in its manifestation but rather preserves it in the heart of the legal process. Niobe, Benjamin notes, is not killed but lives on, "more guilty than before through the death of the children."[25] As opposed to divine violence, which is based on the principle of justice and which (therefore) definitively settles matters—hence eliminating the need for more violence or new law—for Benjamin, mythic violence is endless, unresolvable. He tells us that "power [is] the principle of all mythic lawmaking."[26] Mythic law is, in the end, only force or violence (as is often noted by translators, the German term that Benjamin employs, *Gewalt*, applies to both); it has no other basis for existing than simple self-assertion.

Mythic violence is thus very much a product of the human world; it seems to come out of nowhere and has no source besides humanity's own conception. It is emblematic of the "prattle" that constitutes myth more generally. The law that is produced therefore remains in an ambivalent limbo, always vulnerable to change and exposure (Benjamin speaks of the "mythic ambiguity" of law).[27] Such ambivalence, as we have already seen, becomes disguised as fate, as undeniable destiny, in order to avoid exposing the vulnerability of law. Thus for Benjamin, "Violence . . . bursts upon Niobe from the uncertain, ambiguous sphere of fate."[28] Without the authority and finality of an act truly marked by justice (i.e., an act of divine violence), law—the product of mythic violence—is always grasping for as well as presuming a truth that it does not possess (hence it is idolatrous).

Benjamin writes further of this:

> Far from inaugurating a purer sphere, the mythic manifestation of immediate violence shows itself fundamentally identical with all legal violence, and turns suspicion concerning the latter into certainty of the perniciousness of its historical function, the destruction of which thus becomes obligatory.[29]

Benjamin responds to this fundamental ambiguity in law with a call to destroy the law. Or rather, it is not that he calls for its destruction, but notes that it is always in the process of being destroyed. For Benjamin divine violence, a force that comes from outside of the human realm (and, which, as it turns out, is not really a form of violence at all) is the answer to the problem of mythic law. Benjamin famously tells us that "just as in all spheres God opposes myth, mythic violence is confronted by the divine."[30]

Benjamin contrasts the story of Niobe to the story of Korah as an example of divine violence, a force that definitively answers the question of justice and which leaves no ambiguity in its wake.[31] In this story, Korah led a group of Levite priests and other followers in a rebellion against God's authority as instantiated by Moses and Aaron. While Niobe was left alive as a testament to a power that has to reveal itself over and over in order to exist (insofar as its basis for authority is tenuous and unresolved), Korah's punishment is decisive and leaves no sign: Korah and his followers are simply swallowed up by the earth, decisively settling the question of their idolatrous (i.e., mythic) challenge to God's authority.

Benjamin says of this (in another passage of the "Critique" that is very well known):

> God's judgment strikes privileged Levites, strikes them without warning, without threat, and does not stop short of annihilation. But in annihilating it also expiates, and a profound connection between the lack of bloodshed and the expiatory character of this violence is unmistakable.[32]

Here, there is there no sign (no blood) but there *is* an end to punishment. Niobe's punishment cannot end because a source for the authority of law that it produces would end along with it. Korah's punishment brings with it its own expiation; not only is the sin forgiven, it is erased, removed from the world entirely as if it did not exist. Benjamin writes:

> The dissolution of legal violence stems . . . from the guilt of more natural life, which consigns the living, innocent and unhappy, to a retribution that "expiates" the guilt of mere life—and doubtless also purifies the guilty, not of guilt, however, but of law.[33]

Divine violence thus cleanses the subject of law as a human contrivance, even as divine authority (or law) remains intact (a point I'll argue further in the conclusion). What is left in the wake of Korah's idolatry is a space that has been freed both from sin and from (mythic) law.

Here then is the crucial difference between mythic and divine violence. Mythic violence requires the sign or idol to perpetuate itself whereas divine violence brings nothing new into the world. Instead it merely removes its own idolatry, leaving a blank aporia in its place. Korah's idolatry was undone in a single moment, and in the space that he once occupied, we find a chance for a new beginning (including a new beginning for what human law is or could be).

Such acts of divine violence, Benjamin goes on to tell us, are "defined, therefore, not by miracles directly performed by God but by the expiating moment in them that strikes without bloodshed, and, finally, by the absence of all lawmaking."[34] The annihilation that divine violence instigates, Benjamin is careful to point out, is not purely and totally destructive. It is annihilating "but it is so only relatively, with regards to goods, right, life and suchlike, never absolutely, with regard to the soul of the living."[35] The destructive power of divine violence is not meted against human beings per se (although of course Korah was a human victim of it) but rather toward the idolatry that we foment.[36] As Benjamin tells us:

> Mythic violence is bloody power over mere life for its own sake; divine violence is pure power over all life for the sake of the living. The first demands sacrifice; the second accepts it.[37]

We see here the effects of a law that has its origins in the Fall. Divine violence is part of the judgment that comes along with our guilt—even as it serves as a possible answer to, or expiation of, that guilt.

The Right to Use Force

The arguments that we find in the "Critique" are both reinforced and expanded upon by Benjamin's earlier essay, "The Right to Use Force."[38] Part of this essay echoes the same language we find in the "Critique." In "The Right to Use Force," Benjamin contrasts "the violent rhythm of impatience in which the law exists and has its temporal order" with "the good (?) rhythm of expectation in which messianic events unfold" (question mark in original).[39] He goes on to write that although we think that "in a constitutional state, the struggle for existence becomes a struggle for law," in fact the reverse is the case insofar as "law's concern with justice is only apparent, whereas in truth the law is concerned with self-preservation."[40] Once again we see that (mythic) law is not concerned with preserving human life but rather with preserving its own existence over and above the human life it is charged with protecting.

The one principal way in which "The Right to Use Force" differs from or expands upon the "Critique" comes when Benjamin considers our options as legal subjects. One option, which he entitles "ethical anarchism," denies that either the state or the individual has any right to violence at all. In this vision it appears that we must turn our back on the law (as we know it) entirely, eschewing all forms of mythic violence, all lawmaking, as a solution to the perils that face human beings.[41]

Benjamin tells us that such a response is "fraught with contradictions as a political plan" and further that it is "invalid."[42] Yet he does not condemn this position entirely. He tells us that such a stance can "elevate the morality of the individual or the community to the greatest heights in situations where they are suffering because God does not appear to have commanded them to offer violent resistance."[43] Benjamin offers a concrete example of this approach to law:

> When communities of Galician Jews let themselves be cut down in their synagogues without any attempt to defend themselves, this has nothing to do with "ethical anarchism" as a political program; instead the mere resolve "not to resist evil" emerges into the sacred light of day as a form of moral action.[44]

Here we see an example of the possibility of how to live (or die, in this case) without recourse to mythic law. Without presuming that they could know anything about God's will, these communities of Galician Jews simply suffered the law of others without responding with any kind of corresponding violence—or law—of their own.

Yet if this is touted as an option for legal subjects—however partial Benjamin's support seems to be—this example seems like a formula for perfect passivity. Rather than being a meaningful, political response to the arbitrariness and ultimate instability of law, the notion of refusing to respond to force in any way suggests a recipe for total defeat and the death of political community (in this case, quite literally).

Benjamin himself, as we have seen, comments that this example does not offer a "political program." He is not presenting this example, therefore, as a model for resistance to a system of law that is not just. Yet this example suggests the possibility of resistance in ways that might not normally be recognized as such. The story of the Galician Jews at the very least suggests the possibility of refusing the law even in the direst of circumstances; it offers that we always have the choice not to engage in mythic law, that we are not in fact truly "fated" to suffer it.

And this refusal of mythic law can actually take a more positive form for Benjamin as well, one that affirms our ability to make many and varied choices in the face of law. Benjamin concludes "The Right to Use Force" by arguing that "a truly *subjective* decision [in terms of the response to force] is probably conceivable only in the light of specific goals and wishes."[45] In other words, in the face of mythic law (and without access to true law), Benjamin won't call for a systematic formula for how to measure our actions; he does not seek to replace one conception of law with another. What he leaves us with instead is a very different way to think about the law, a subjective, local, and temporary response.

Wrestling with the Law

Here, I return to my argument that for Benjamin, we do not need to give up on law entirely despite the fact that we receive it only in a "bastardized" form.[46] Similarly, in the face of a deity that tells us nothing and serves only to destroy those myths we develop in the absence of clear divine guidance, we do not need to give up on the possibility of justice either. Recall that for Benjamin there *is* a law, a perfect and true one, and there *is* justice, but we will never know it. Thus, our duty is to both accept the bindingness and judgment of the law and come to terms with the fact that we don't have access to what it demands of us.

Such a state of affairs leads to a peculiar attitude vis-à-vis actual laws, including laws that have been handed down to us from the divine. In the "Critique," Benjamin speaks, for example, of how we must approach the divine commandment: "Thou shalt not Kill." He writes of this that

> neither the divine judgment nor the grounds for this judgment can be known in advance. Those who base a condemnation of all violent killing of one person by another on the commandment are therefore mistaken. It exists not as a criterion of judgment, but as a guideline for the actions of persons or communities who have to wrestle with it in solitude and, in exceptional cases, to take on themselves the responsibility of ignoring it.[47]

Actually the original German here is even stronger in terms of what it advocates than the English translation that I have used; in German, Benjamin uses the phrase "und in ungeheuren Fällen die Verantwortung von ihm abzusehen auf sich zu nehmen haben," in which "abzusehen" does not mean ignore so much as to look away from (literally), or, more forcefully, abandon.[48] Here we see quite clearly that we cannot receive this commandment as a knowable, actionable policy (i.e., as an objective truth), one that dictates our behavior in all cases. Divine law is, by definition unknowable to us. Whereas mythic violence "will be recognizable as such," in part because it is of human derivation, divine violence, with its expiatory power, "is invisible to men."[49] We must therefore in a sense "abandon" various laws in their particular manifestations, just as moments of divine violence "cleanse" us—if only partially and temporarily—of mythic law.

Yet to abandon laws does not mean to abandon law itself, taken in its most absolute sense as divine law. Despite the invisibility of such law, we remain ethically "on the hook" (as Alenka Zupančič tells us too) for what law demands of us.[50] For Benjamin, were we not responsible at all, we could conclude that "what pleases is permitted."[51] However, this is not the case. He writes that such a conception "excludes reflection on the moral and historical spheres, and thereby on any meaning in action, and beyond this on any meaning in reality itself, which cannot be constituted if 'action' is removed from its sphere."[52] To avoid either giving up on moral and ethical claims altogether on the one hand, and merely reduplicating the fetishism of law—the basis of mythic violence—on the other, we must struggle against the ossification of all law by treating it "not as a criterion of judgment [since that province belongs to God alone] but as a guideline for action."

For Benjamin, as noted, in making such decisions, we must "wrestle in solitude," either as a community or as an individual. The Galician Jews made one such decision. In the "Critique," Benjamin notes that Jews more generally "expressly reject . . . the condemnation of killing in self-defense," thereby modifying the Sixth Commandment (by not taking it literally).[53]

As we have also seen, for Benjamin we can only make truly "*subjective* decision[s] . . . in the light of specific goals and wishes." If divine violence clears the earth—at least temporarily, at least in one place or another—of the fetishism of law that we have received and created, Benjamin is telling us that the rest is entirely and absolutely up to us.

The Only Law: The Second Commandment

Such a proposition may appear at first glance to be truly amoral and quite awful insofar as it suggests that different people and communities can and will make different decisions about law and force for different reasons. Why is this not just a recipe for relativism, and a horrible, endless relativism at that?

My first response to such a concern (somewhat repeating an argument I made in the introduction) is that we already do live in a world marked by endless relativism; by turning arbitrary decisions into "laws" (for Benjamin, "all mythic, lawmaking violence . . . is pernicious"), we ensure that randomness is enshrined in the heart of our political community, enforced by the sovereign entity.[54] At the same time, I don't think that the response to the falsities of law that Benjamin describes in the two essays under consideration is actually either random or relative. Instead, I would argue that there is a method at play in Benjamin's treatment that serves as a critical guide for us (the same method I describe in *Textual Conspiracies*), the method of antifetishism. It is true that this method will not always produce the same results. Contrary to our behavior with proscriptive (mythic) laws, when we seek out antifetishistic forms of law, we will not make the same decision in the same context over and over again. Nonetheless this other rendition of law still offers a coherence and ethical substance to our approach to law that does not merely constitute a surrender to purely negative or nihilistic forces. On the contrary, such an approach actually permits human decision in a way that is usually completely overridden by fetishism.

It is this "positive" aspect of Benjamin's approach to law (at the risk of using such a loaded term in an entirely different context—more on that in chapter 4) that, in my view, suggests we can speak of a kind of legalism in Benjaminian theory despite the appearance that he is opposed to law in all of its guises. In this instance, I would argue, as already suggested, that the law that Benjamin would have us follow (and the only law he would have us follow) is not the Sixth Commandment, but the Second.

Although Benjamin does not refer to it all the time or in all of his work, the commandment against idolatry, I would suggest, is one of the key elements that unite his work. We see his concern for this commandment in virtually every aspect of his political and legal theory. We see it in his rejection of commodity fetishism, in his theological rendering of the Fall of Adam and humanity's removal from paradise (in many ways for Benjamin these two events are deeply connected). We see it in his admiring claim about Franz Kafka, "No other writer has obeyed the commandment 'Thou shalt not make unto thee a graven image' so faithfully."[55] Finally, we see the central role that idolatry plays for Benjamin in fomenting the phantasmagoria. For all of these reasons, in his view, our contestation of and struggle with idolatry, whether in its theological, political, or aesthetic guises, must be absolute. Although he doesn't always specify what kind of law he is referring to (mythic or divine), I would argue that the only way to understand how Benjamin can insist that human beings hold onto law, even as they reject virtually every manifestation of law, is through the operation of the Second Commandment.

Benjamin's concern with the Second Commandment—both directly and indirectly—reflects his background in Judaism, but in his hands, I would argue, the commandment takes on a very different valence. In this case, the Second Commandment requires not only that we do not engage in idolatry but also that we actively struggle with all manifestations of the truth (for they must be idols) even if that truth takes on the form of God or the divine itself (because any idea that we have of God or God's truth must, by definition, be an idol).

In this sense, we emulate God's own acts of divine violence to overturn and subvert those myths that present themselves to us in God's name. We do this without the sure knowledge that what we are doing is just, but Benjamin's method of combating idolatry offers us a way, as already mentioned, to link our individual and collective acts of resistance into some kind of cohesive and enduring form of politics, that is to say, it does amount to a binding law, only one that takes on a radically different form than we generally associate with law.

Agamben and Law

In making this claim that Benjamin does not forsake law, I seem to be going against one of Benjamin's most prominent and celebrated—if controversial—readers, Giorgio Agamben. In his own reading of Benjamin's "Critique," Agamben appears to argue that Benjamin ultimately seeks to break with law in a definitive way. In *State of Exception*, Agamben claims that the "Critique" is a direct response to Schmitt's arguments that the subject cannot and must not escape the law. Agamben writes that, for Benjamin,

> Every fiction of a nexus between violence and law disappears here: there is nothing but a zone of anomie, in which a violence without any juridical form acts. The attempt of state power to annex anomie through the state of exception [Schmitt's attempt on behalf of the state, that is] is unmasked for Benjamin for what it is: a *ficto iuris* par excellence, which claims to maintain the law in its very suspension as force-of-law [with the word "law" crossed out in the original]. What now takes its place are civil war and revolutionary violence, that is, a human action that has shed [*deposto*] every relation to law.[56]

Many scholars read this as a pure rejection of law, a turn toward "life" or the instability that law forever puts off. Simon Critchley for one (whose arguments will be revisited in the Conclusion) makes this claim about Agamben's reading of Benjamin.[57]

Yet there is some ambiguity in Agamben's treatment of law that suggests that my position and his might not be as far apart as initially seems. For one thing, Agamben never makes it clear whether by "law" he is referring to mythic, human law or divine law. Agamben's lack of precision on this question muddles his argument a bit. Clearly, Benjamin *does* reject law when it is taken in its human, mythic sense, but this, as I have argued, does not mean that Benjamin opposes law per se.

Agamben seems to leave room for this possibility himself toward the end of his chapter "Gigantomachy Concerning a Void," still in *State of Exception*. There he focuses, not on Benjamin's connection to Schmitt, but to Kafka, who, when read in constellation with Benjamin, often serves as a muse that brings out Benjamin's best and clearest articulations of his thought. In thinking about this connection (and referencing some of the very language that Critchley, among others, draws upon to argue that Agamben rejects law entirely), Agamben writes:

> It is from this perspective that we must read Benjamin's statement in the letter to Scholem on August 11, 1934, that "the Scripture without its key is not Scripture but life" . . . as well as the one found in the essay on Kafka, according to which "[t]he law which is studied but no longer practiced is the gate to justice" . . . The Scripture (the

Torah) without its key is the cipher of the law in the state of exception, which is in force but is not applied or is applied without being
in force (and which Scholem, not at all suspecting that he shares this
thesis with Schmitt, believes is still law). According to Benjamin, this
law—or rather this force of LAW—is no longer law but life, "lived as
it is lived" in Kafka's novel [*The Castle*] "in the village at the foot of
the hill on which the castle is built." . . . Kafka's most proper gesture
consists not (as Scholem believes) in having maintained a law that
no longer has any meaning but having shown that it ceases to be law
and blurs at all points with life.[58]

Here, the connection to Kafka's *The Castle* is telling; that novel (described
in much greater detail in *Textual Conspiracies*) depicts a life being lived in
a village around the circumference of a phantasm (the phantasm is the
castle itself with all its imagined lords and majesty). The denizens of the
castle are never seen, or at least hardly ever, and yet the desire for them,
the hints of their existence, animates and manages the life of the villag-
ers. To allude to a life lived "in the village at the foot of the hill on which
the castle is built" is to refer to life as it is going on *even in the presence
of (mythic) law*. In this instance, Agamben seems to be connecting such
a life to a life that exists beyond or instead of law and, to be fair, if one
stuck purely to this passage, one would probably be right in concluding
that for Agamben the law is purely and only mythic and must be done
away with.

But Agamben goes on to consider what this "life" is, what its relationship to law remains even after a break with law as we know it. He speaks of
"the unmasking of mythico-juridical violence effected by pure violence,"
that is, mythic violence or law, as it is effected by the presence of divine
violence.[59] Agamben goes on to argue that

> there is, therefore, still a possible figure of law after its nexus with
> violence and power has been deposed, but it is a law that no longer
> has force or application, like the one in which the "new attorney,"
> leafing through "our old books," buries himself in study, or like the
> one that Foucault may have had in mind when he spoke of a "new
> law" that has been freed from all discipline and all relation to sov-
> ereignty.[60]

Thus, it is possible for law to survive its encounter with divine violence.
What results would not look like law as we know it:

The decisive point here is that the law—no longer practiced but studied—is not justice, but only the gate that leads to it. What opens a passage towards justice is not the erasure of law but its deactivation and inactivity [*inoperosità*]—that is, another use of the law . . . Kafka's characters [in *the Castle*]—and this is why they interest us—have to do with this spectral figure of the law in the state of exception; they seek, each one following his or her own strategy, to "study" and deactivate it, to "play" with [the law].[61]

Thus, for all the appearance that Agamben seeks to do away with law entirely, I would argue that instead he simply seeks to do away with mythic law (as does Benjamin himself). Agamben's failure to make this distinction clear makes it possible for other scholars (like Critchley) to read him as arguing against law entirely.[62] But when we insert this distinction into Agamben's work, we can see that there is a role for law after all, a deactivated, inactive (inoperable might have been a better translation) form of law.

But, it might be fair to ask, isn't a deactivated law not a law at all? Doesn't this suggest a law that is effectively useless, dead and gone? Such a question is posed from the perspective of a subject of mythic law, one who expects law to have a kind of substance, a promise of truth and justice that is the hallmark of mythic law's idolatrous structure. If we give up on that (false) promise, we see that a law that is denuded of its content, a law that is exposed as an idol, substanceless and deflated or deactivated, does not cease to be, in some sense, a law. When we think of human law as a remnant, a reminder of the connection it once had to true law, we see that it is, in fact, *only* as a deactivated, deflated law, a sign that has been stripped of its (idolatrous) significance, that law can be valid, that it can avoid idolatry. Such law is the product of its encounter with the Second Commandment, a law that unmakes (but does not eliminate) other laws.

In this way, the one tether that we keep with law (that is, with divine, rather than mythic law) is the Second Commandment. Even as the rest of law shrinks to a remnant, a ruin of what it was, the one aspect of law that remains robust, heartily "law-like" and absolute (in an argument that I will return to in the conclusion) is the law against idolatry.

The Second Commandment and the General Strike

To get a clearer sense of what form a life lived according to the Second Commandment actually would take, we need to look at a further example that Benjamin provides in the "Critique," namely that of the revolutionary general strike. By examining a concrete instance of what obeying one single law at the expense of all others (or at least in a way that reduces all others to a deflated remnant) might look like, we get a better idea of the political and legal upshot of such a radically divergent practice (in chapter 5, I will look at a different example, the case of the Haitian Revolution).

In looking at this example we can ask ourselves if a "law" of this type actually serves us in ways that we would desire. Would it continue to provide some of the functions of law that we have come to expect from it, such as protection and order? Would it accord with the desires and programs of the "Left"?[63] I will return more explicitly to these questions in the conclusion, but hopefully the following discussion will give a preliminary sense of how to think about the politics and practice of the Second Commandment.

The first thing to note is that Benjamin's discussion of the general strike has its roots in his own lived experience. The "Critique" was written in the aftermath of the failed German Spartacist Revolution and the mass general strike in early 1919. This experience helps to anchor the discussion of the general strike in the "Critique"; although not mentioned by name in that essay, actual political practices are being referenced by the theoretical discussion of this essay (I will revisit this connection in chapter 5 when I connect the Spartacist uprising to the slave revolt in Haiti as two distinct occurrences linked by their common enactment of the Second Commandment).[64]

Benjamin begins his discussion of the general strike by noting that (not unlike the example of Galician Jews) it appears to be a "nonaction" and hence not a real threat to the state. That is, it is seen as something that leaves the state its monopoly on "action" and hence violence, as the terms are generally understood.[65] In fact, for Benjamin the general strike *is* nonviolent insofar as it does not partake of the usual phantasms with which violence—that is to say, all forms of lawmaking and mythology—is engaged.[66]

Distinguishing between the political strike and the general strike (or rather engaging with Sorel's distinction between them), Benjamin argues that while the former is merely a change of accommodation with the state (and hence, remaining within law), the latter is outside of (mythic) law and violence altogether. He writes:

Whereas the first [political] form of interruption of work is violent, since it causes only an external modification of labor conditions, the second, as a pure means, is nonviolent. For it takes place not in readiness to resume work following external concessions and this or that modification to working conditions, but in the determination to resume only a wholly transformed work, no longer enforced by the state, an upheaval that this kind of strike not so much causes as consummates.[67]

For Benjamin to speak of the general strike as "pure means" suggests turning away from or abandoning ends (which are the province of God alone), just as we sometimes have to abandon (most of) God's commandments. When we abandon these ends and the mythic laws that promised them, the means that we were engaged in to serve those ends are left bereft of their original idolatrous purpose; they become "pure means," entirely subjective, and, as such, unrelated to the violence and force that marks our mythic practices.[68] Unexpectedly (because we were devoted to these ends and the instrumentalism that they instilled in us), we become unmoored from phantasm. What we have in our hand (i.e., "pure means") is not what we wished for; what we are busily doing (striking in this case) is not what we thought we were doing.[69] Here, what was once the means for further idolatry now becomes the basis of its undoing or subverting.

In looking at the general strike as consisting of "pure means," Benjamin is also—and relatedly—recommending that in turning away from the "objective" or the true, we are turning toward the subjective and the local, toward the "truly *subjective* decision[s]" that we must engage with in the face of divine laws that we cannot know. Here Benjamin is once again encouraging us to embrace the subjective as our only possible response to the unknowability of law. This accords with something that Benjamin argues in the *Origin of German Tragic Drama*: "Subjectivity, like an angel falling into the depths, is brought back by allegories, and is held fast in heaven."[70] We see here, as in the case of the general strike (and the example of the Galician Jews as well), that subjectivity, although itself a product of the Fall, is our path back toward truth, not insofar as it shows us truth, but insofar as it suggests and dramatizes our failure to know truth. To embrace our subjectivity as such is to acknowledge our failure to know the law (or our failure to know anything at all, a realization that is facilitated by a turn to subjectivity in Benjamin's schema). In that knowledge, we are freed, however temporarily or partially, from the idolatry we constantly foment and subscribe to; it becomes "useless" for our violent (and false) ends, pure means.[71] At the same time, the aporia of law is kept open, unknown and unknowable. In this way, too, what appears to be totally passive, inert, and a "non-action" can have a radical and subversive effect in the world. Here failure itself becomes the chief weapon, the strongest asset that we can possess, as befits our engagement with the Second Commandment.

This failure is at the heart of what distinguishes the revolutionary general strike, in Benjamin's view, from other (compromised) forms of political action. In further considering the difference between a political and a general strike, Benjamin writes that "the first of these undertakings [i.e., the political strike] is lawmaking, but the second [the general strike] anarchistic."[72] In this way we see that anarchism (which links us back to the previous discussion of "ethical anarchism" as well) can offer a way for human beings to act that is not itself lawmaking, not mythic, perhaps not even violent at all.[73] To engage in anarchism means, in effect, to turn our failure to obey the law into a weapon that annihilates mythic iterations of law (without producing some new law, new truth, or new idols in its wake). Anarchism in this way emerges as that political creed which follows only one law: the Second Commandment.

As already mentioned, in this way, too, we see how it is possible for human beings to act in the world in ways that are not inherently and automatically idolatrous. The general strike is coordinated with and enabled by an act of divine violence (once again without becoming one and the same, which would mean to reduce the general strike, and our anarchist tendencies more broadly, to another form of idolatry). The discussion of divine violence follows almost immediately after Benjamin's discussion of the general strike in the "Critique." While partial or political strikes are essentially acts of extortion, for Benjamin, seeking to intimidate the state into sharing its goods with one class or another, the general strike is, like God's elimination of Korah, both the annihilation and the expiation of the crime of state capitalism. There is no deal to be cut or compromise to be reached but simply a great sweeping undermining of the lawmaking violence that the workers oppose. This also accords with Benjamin's view that the coming of the Messiah and the act of human revolution are simultaneous, overlapping (but *not* identical) moments.

The fact that it is possible for human beings to engage in nonviolent and law-subverting behavior means that we are not condemned either to idolatry or to (true) passivity. As already suggested, when we think of the model of the Galician Jews and the general strike as being in the same mode, we can see that our own definitions of what constitutes a passive or active response is itself largely determined by our context. Both of these examples show that it is possible to not participate in law, as we understand it. At the same time, such nonparticipation does not constitute a total abandonment of law either. We see in these examples a sense that obeying just one law does not constitute capitulating to a free-for-all, or giving up on law entirely; there is a consistency, even a substance, to this engagement with the Second Commandment, a "law-like" remnant that survives the law's exposure and undoing as idolatry. These examples suggest it is possible for human beings, and not just God, to undermine mythic law and leave nothing in its wake.

Anarchism and Community

Or rather, something *is* left in the wake of acts of divine violence and of the human response (let's call the latter acts of anarchism), something besides the ruins and remnants of law that has been exposed as mythic and arbitrary. What is left is simply the human communities that already existed, those that may have been formed through mythic violence but which have an existence that is distinct from—which is to say not entirely or only produced by—that mythology. In both *Textual Conspiracies* and *Divine Violence*, I described such communities as being, like Kafka's Castle, formed around a hollow center: the center itself is the phantasm. These communities are built in expectation of delivery and truth by that phantasm, by mythic violence, but in actuality they have built themselves. The removal or interference with the central phantasm does not annihilate the idolatrous communities that surround them but rather leaves such communities to their own devices, allowing them to realize the extent to which they have always been self-forming, self-actualizing even while under the thrall of the phantasm.

This view harkens to what I was earlier calling (however problematically) Benjamin's "positive" legal theory, those aspects that are not entirely bound up with the pure, destructive force that comes from acts of divine violence, as well as corresponding human acts of "nonviolence" (i.e., the revolutionary general strike). What is "positive" here is something that has always existed but not, until now, been recognized. It is the nonphantasmic, ordinary, local, and subjective acts that are recuperated by an engagement with the Second Commandment. Such a view also recalls Benjamin's claim, already noted, that "mythic violence is bloody power over mere life for its own sake; divine violence is a pure power over all life for the sake of the living."[74] It is the living, the human beings who are not totalized by their own idolatry, that remain left over in the space where idolatry and mythic law have been overcome.

Benjamin offers a bit more insight on this community and the nature of its political practices in "The Right to Use Force":

The term "anarchism" may very well be used to describe a theory that denies a moral right not to force as such but to every human institution, community, or individuality that either claims a monopoly over it or in any way claims that right for itself from any point of view, even if only a general principle, instead of respecting it in specific cases as a gift bestowed by a divine power, as *absolute power*.[75]

Here we see more clearly that force (or *Gewalt*) is not legitimate as a thing that is owned (or thought to be owned) by an individual or a community. To engage in this kind of violence is to remain bound by mythic law or violence. The wielder(s) of such violence remain instrumentalist, using what might be called "impure" means devoted to some idolatrous end. Other human beings are merely means to an end as well (or as a result); those who engage in violence seek to extort or carve out a place at the table for a particular constituency at the expense of everyone else (as the example of the political strike suggests). Finally, and perhaps most critically, such an action presumes a power or authority that belongs to God alone. When we give up on ends, we abandon, not instrumentalism per se—since we remain availed of "pure means"—but an ends-oriented instrumentalism, a means that is captured by, and intended for, idolatry.

A violence or force that is recognized as "a gift bestowed by a divine power, an *absolute power*," on the other hand, becomes something altogether different, perhaps not a force or violence at all. This divine and absolute power is not ours, but when we act in accordance with it, that is to say when we cooperate with its interference and the idolatrous projections we associate with it, then a different political relationship—one that Benjamin here gives the label of anarchism—becomes possible. As opposed to "general principles," of Kantian-style categorical imperatives, and to other systems of legal philosophy that seek to avoid the subjective, as we have already seen, Benjamin turns *toward* the subjective as a way to avoid the idols that pose as objective truth (a question to be revisited in chapter 3). He does this by allying the subject with the one objective truth that really is objective, the "*absolute power*" that has nothing to do with terrestrial affairs or human intentionality. Rather than look up, toward heaven, for divine truth (as Kant would suggest—or at least a particular reading of Kant), Benjamin looks down, into ourselves. But such a looking down is also in a sense looking toward God insofar as it is looking away from or abandoning (*abzusehen*) the idols that pass for God in our world.

It is thus in our existence as entirely subjective beings, in our material practices, and those side relationships that occur in the shadow of the laws that we make and hold to that we find anarchist practices we can recuperate or recognize. Such relationships are not innocent of law insofar as they have been formed in the expectation of true law and justice; they remain a product of the idolatry that we all obey whether we realize it or not. But the removal of law by acts of divine violence and revolutionary action allows these communities to emerge in the space emptied of mythic law's domination, in a terrain I'm tempted to call "postlegal," although a fidelity to Benjaminian conceptions of time discourages such easy and progress-oriented terms. Also, it is not the case that this community has no law at all, for as we have seen, it does have and obey law, but only one.

A Community without (Much) Law

By way of reaching toward a conclusion for this chapter, I will speculate further about following the Second Commandment in expressly political terms. Here I return to a question that I already began to raise at the end of the earlier section about law: What would a community do or look like if it obeyed only this one law? What would it be like in practice? Perhaps more accurately, what would a community look like where engagement with the Second Commandment was not just accidental or episodic but sustained and widespread, the actualized basis for the community in question?

In chapter 5, I will look at the case of the Haitian Revolution (as already noted) in order to give a sense of the concrete practices, of the history and possibility of this notion of community. In the conclusion, I will speculate further about the nature of and sources of authority for such a community. In the meantime, let me speculate a bit more about that community in the abstract.

In thinking about this community and its relationship to law and crime (or sin), we must be careful not fall back into the unredeemed aspects of the phantasmagoria. An idealist reading of Benjamin's law is perilously easy to make. One could argue, for example, that if a community obeyed only the Second Commandment, then, without idolatry, there would be no "crime." Insofar as God's punishment expiates sin, it seems that a community without (much) law would also be a community without (any) sin (a reflection, it would seem of Augustine's vision of the City of God in which even the desire to sin is finally removed from us).[76] Such a vision is tempting insofar as it seems to finally resolve the "problem" of law, but it is important to note that such an outcome is actually highly unlikely—even undesirable—in Benjamin's schema. For Benjamin, the lure of fetishism is strong, and we will never be free of it. Furthermore, we must suspect any permanent leftist paradise as just another reiteration of the promises of future salvation that are the hallmark of the phantasmagoria. For Benjamin, we will never again live in a paradise where we have no crime or sin to worry about. The very notion of obeying one law that fights against idolatry suggests that idolatry itself will be a factor in our existence for as long as human beings exist.

It might help to think further about Benjamin's vision of lawfulness by returning once again to the idea, treated in the introduction, of "a slight adjustment." This idea can be referenced in terms of a story that Agamben cites from Benjamin (among others):

> There is a well-known parable about the Kingdom of the Messiah that Walter Benjamin (who heard it from Gershom Scholem) recounted one evening to Ernst Bloch . . . "A rabbi, a real cabalist, once said that in order to establish the reign of peace it is not necessary to destroy everything nor to begin a completely new world. It is sufficient to displace this cup or this bush or this stone just a little, and thus everything." . . . Benjamin's version of the story goes like this: "The *Hassidim* tell a story about the world to come that says everything there will be just as it is here. Just as our room is now, so it will be in the world to come; where our baby sleeps now, there too it will sleep in the other world. And the clothes we wear in this world, those too we will wear there. Everything will be as it is now, just a little different."[77]

In this way we can see once again that the world that Benjamin seeks is in most ways identical to the world that we already live in. As previously noted, for Benjamin it is useful once again to think of two perspectives, that of God and that of human beings. Although Benjamin references the divine perspective, his work is oriented toward the human experience. Accordingly, instead of offering us a full guide to moral, ethical, and legal behavior (such as we already have now in myriad—and mythical—forms), Benjamin's version of law forces us to face a world without such firm (and fetishistic) guidance. As we have already seen, we would be forced to "wrestle in solitude" (both individually and collectively) with our own judgments as well as with what appears to us as divinely sanctioned judgments that we must follow. The distance between law and politics, firmly separated under conditions of phantasmagoria, would largely vanish if we followed only one law; all of our legal decisions would perforce be political ones (and, by the same token, all of our political decisions would also be legal ones). Only one law would remain separate and distinct from our political practices: the Second Commandment itself.

Thus, Benjamin's understanding of law does not deliver us to a happy paradise where we know what to do and ethics are easy to apply. We would still have all the problems and impulses (and clothes and babies) that we do now, but what we would also have—what would be different—would be the ability to avoid being completely determined by phantasms. In fact, we always have had this ability—for Benjamin the material world we no longer name (but seek to represent) is in a constant state of rebellion against our fetishism of it. This rebellion includes the signs and symbols by which we seek to control and master representation. It even includes our own bodies, perhaps even our selves on some level. As I argued at great lengths in *Textual Conspiracies* (this was the central theme of that book), we must ally ourselves—or conspire with—this rebellion. In legal terms, a greater, more regular engagement with the Second Commandment would help us evade phantasm in a more widespread and systematic manner, bringing us more firmly into such an alliance or conspiracy.

Such an action does not give us any assurance that what we would do under such circumstances would be good or just; true justice, for Benjamin, is the province of God alone. But it would mean that we could have the chance to gesture at justice, to decide collectively what justice would mean for us. Furthermore, we would engage in such questions without the certainty of delusion, without the phantasms of law and sovereignty that override and render obscure the daily acts of antifetishism, subversion, and resistance that already mark our life in the world. We would have options besides mythic laws and its resultant and inevitable (fated) violence.

Rumors and Folly

If we return to Benjamin's conviction about Franz Kafka, that "no other writer has obeyed the commandment 'Thou shalt not make unto thee a graven image' so faithfully," we can see what it means to live a life—even a life in the midst of the phantasmagoria—that obeys the one and only law. As already noted, Benjamin admires the way that Kafka follows this law by allowing himself to fail. Benjamin writes about Kafka in a letter to Gershom Scholem:

To do justice to the figure of Kafka in its purity, and in its peculiar beauty, one should never lose sight of one thing: it is the figure of a failure. The circumstances of this failure are manifold. Perhaps one might say that once he was sure of ultimate failure, then everything on the way to it succeeded for him as if in a dream. Nothing is more remarkable than the fervor with which Kafka insists on his failure.[78]

Whereas failure is normally (that is to say, phantasmically) seen as something to avoid at all costs, for Benjamin, by failing to successfully produce the kinds of answers that he sought, Kafka thwarted the fetishism that he himself subscribed to.[79] We see here how Kafka himself achieves a form of what Benjamin would call "pure means" in his writing. Benjamin notes that once Kafka was assured of failure, that is to say, once he knew for sure that his idolatrous ends were thwarted (and so he was safely obeying the Second Commandment), "everything on the way to [failure] succeeded for him as if in a dream." His own idolatry, his own instrumentalism, becomes transformed, becomes something other than it was originally meant to be. It is for this reason that Kafka "insists on his failure"; it is his way of being loyal to the commandment against idolatry.

In his comments on Kafka, Benjamin also writes:

> In Kafka, there is no longer any talk of wisdom. Only the products of its decomposition are left. There are two of these. First is rumor of the true things (a kind of whispered theological newspaper about the disreputable and the obsolete). The other produce of this diathesis is folly, which, though it has entirely squandered the content of wisdom, retains the unruffled complaisance that rumor utterly lacks.[80]

What is left in the wake of his failure is, as Benjamin tells us, rumor and folly. Rumor is a "whispered theological newspaper," a remnant or vague memory of the lost fount of wisdom that was once Adam's (one is reminded here too of Derrida's "immense rumor" about the subversive possibility inherent in Western political thought).[81] As for folly, it too plays its unexpected but vital part. Folly, he tells us, "has entirely squandered the content of wisdom," but it serves nonetheless as a source of "unruffled complaisance," a basis to reorient our actions toward what they have always striven for on some level but never received from phantasms.

Benjamin concludes this passage by arguing:

> Of this much, Kafka was sure: first, that to help, one must be a fool; and, second, that only a fool's help is real help. The only uncertainty

is whether such help can still work for human beings. Perhaps it works only for angels . . . and they could do without it anyway. So, as Kafka, says, there is an infinite amount of hope—only not for us. This statement truly contains Kafka's hope. It is the source of his radiant serenity.[82]

We see here that once again, Benjamin is employing a double perspective. There is hope, as we have already seen, but "not for us." Hope is only for "the angels . . . and they could do without it anyway." Human beings, such as we are, seem beyond the scope of hope.

Yet, as I also described at greater length in *Textual Conspiracies,* when we once again take on the perspective of the divine as pertaining, not to the phantasmic world that we think we occupy, but the material world that is actual, we can see things differently. In this perspective, neither the idea of failure itself nor the idea of a "hope [that is] not for us" dooms us to passivity and gloom, but rather both serve as a reminder that the world that we are looking for is, in fact, already here. From the perspective of the phantasmagoria, Kafka is a failure, guided only by rumor and folly. But from the perspective of the actual world, Kafka is uniquely successful at subverting the phantasms we all subscribe to (Kafka very much included). From the perspective of the phantasmagoria, there is "no hope" for us, but as soon as we begin to engage with the Second Commandment, as Kafka does, we begin to discern the kind of hope that offered him "radiant serenity," a path of "pure means." In the same way that divine violence somehow connects both the dramatic actions of God burying a group of idolators in the ground and quieter moments of resistance and subversion on each of our parts, we see here too that we always have the power to follow the Second Commandment; such a power could be read as the necessary corollary to the ongoing fact of divine violence. The hope that comes with following this one law is the same hope that enabled the Galician Jews to go to their deaths without a struggle rather than break the one commandment that must never be abandoned. This is the hope of the general strike, the desire that it will be carried out without merely replacing one false regime with another. Such a hope is not for "us," that is, not for those who remain ensconced in idolatry, but any of us could, with a switch of perspective—a switch also in our understanding of the applications of law, how it is actualized and produced—partake in it at any time. In other words, we only need to make a "slight adjustment." To make such a change, we must be willing to fail (in the Benjaminian sense), willing to defy the definitions of success and power that are the hallmark of our ensconcement in the phantasmagoria.

With this understanding in mind, let us turn our attention in the next chapter to the ethical dimensions of such a vision of law, comparing Badiou's and Benjamin's approaches to this question. What is our ethical duty in the face of a notion of law that is almost entirely (but crucially not actually entirely) shown to be false and idolatrous? What political possibilities flow from this duty? To whom are we responsible and why?

TWO

The Law of the Break with Law

Badiou and Legal Ethics

In this chapter, I begin a comparison of Benjamin's legal theory to three central figures in political and legal theory: Alain Badiou, Immanuel Kant, and H. L. A. Hart, beginning with Badiou. I begin with him because of the three thinkers, Badiou is, as I see, the closest to Benjamin. All three thinkers appear to be, in their own very different ways, radical iconoclasts. My argument throughout will be that Benjamin is more radical still (as we move those three chapters, the distance from Benjamin grows accordingly). I say this not to denigrate these other thinkers: the goal of each chapter is to put these thinkers into conversation (or, perhaps more accurately, into constellation) with Benjamin as well as with one another. But in order to do so, I must first show how their own seeming iconoclasm does not come to the level of Benjamin's own. What I try to do in each of the following three chapters is to amplify each thinker's iconoclasm along Benjaminian lines. By doing so, I seek to bring these thinkers into a deeper engagement with Benjamin himself, to show that what remains in their work after their iconoclasm has been enhanced is of great service to a Benjaminian legal and political project.

In order to engage in a conversation with Badiou, I must introduce terms that on some level for Benjamin are anathema: namely the concepts of the universal and the truth. These terms form integral parts of Badiou's ethical vocabulary and are hence vital for understanding Badiou's larger project. It's not that Benjamin doesn't engage with this terminology (especially in terms of truth) but rather that, as already noted, he banishes these terms from the human world, thereby dictating that any manifestations of them in the world are surely idolatrous. Alain Badiou, on the other hand, is not at all hesitant to engage with this vocabulary in an earthly setting. But his understanding of universality and truth are, to be sure, nothing like what is usually meant by such terms. Badiou's universal is a radically negative endeavor; his truth serves mainly to unmake and to unform and, in this way, he definitely approaches Benjamin himself. Yet ultimately, I will argue that, at least when he is read on his own terms, Badiou's own approach to theology and ethics muddies his iconoclasm. By insisting that universality and truth only appear in the human realm, Badiou forces us to choose between true and false appearances—precisely the dilemma that Benjamin's strict avoidance of these terms, when applied to an earthly setting, saves us from. Because Badiou's approach to theology doesn't allow him to guard the distinction between false and true forms of the universal as diligently as Benjamin, what we get in the end is a lesser, more vulnerable form of iconoclasm. Later in the chapter, I will make a somewhat similar argument about Žižek and his own approach to the universal, arguing that Benjamin (despite Žižek's critique of what he calls "Jewish iconoclasm") once again practices a stricter, and more effective, form of antifetishism.

A similar—and related—dilemma arrives, I argue, in Benjamin's and Badiou's respective approaches to law. Both thinkers' work points to having only one law (in Badiou's case directly, in Benjamin's case, as I have argued, by strong implication) but the law they pick is different. Whereas a Benjaminian reading turns us toward the Second Commandment, Badiou's one law is the command to "love thy neighbor." In the concept of *agape*, Badiou sees a way to remain "faithful to the event," that is, to adhere to a form of law that negates all other (false and nefarious) laws and hence serves as a carrier for the universal potential that we always bear with us. Badiou's choice of one singular law reflects, once again, his worldly orientation, his requirement that any law deal purely and only with existing, and human, relationships. Benjamin's law, as we have seen, treats far more with abstract and otherworldly concepts. Yet, by turning to love, Badiou has brought in a great deal of all too earthly baggage; the concept of love carries with it many of the hierarchies, transcendental dreams, and other problems that Badiou is formally against. Once again, Benjamin offers us a purer, less compromised form of iconoclasm in the vehicle of a law that does nothing but fight fetishism

I should reiterate here that my engagement with Badiou is not one of rejection but rather an attempt to think about Badiou in relationship to Benjamin, to read them in constellation. I see Benjamin's notion of law as a "friendly" (but critical) amendment to Badiou's project, one that potentially immunizes Badiou from something he himself has been unable (at least as I see it) to completely resolve. In this spirit, I will end the chapter by focusing on what Badiou has to offer a Benjaminian legal theory, what happens, that is, when we read him through a Benjaminian lens. Whereas Badiou's negativity is of a fiery, transformative sort, Benjamin's negative (as we will see in the following chapters as well) is far less dramatic. It is, once again, simply the failure of truth to appear. When such a negative is applied to Badiou, we can reread his legal and ethical theory as contributing a great deal to a Benjaminian project. Through his notion of being "faithful to the event," we can see a way for the subject of the Second Commandment to engage in practices that are formed out of their relationship to that law. Through his idea of a nonliteral law or the "law of the break with law," we can see what happens to law more generally when it encounters, and passes through, the medium of the Second Commandment.[1]

Badiouian Ethics: The Universal and the Event

To begin this endeavor, let me leave behind Benjamin for the moment and look at Badiou's understanding of ethics more closely and, in particular, his notion of the event and its relationship to both true and false universals.[2] For Badiou, the vast bulk of Western ethics and religion has led to nothing but nihilism and the worship (and promulgation) of death. Contemporary doctrines of ethics, largely derived from Kant and a few other sources (Christian ones very much included) tend to look to general principles and always seek to avoid particularity as being somehow contaminating of universality. For Badiou, such a move is nihilistic because the universal that we submit ourselves to (Kant's universal, that is) is, in fact, a capitulation to a false "simulacra" in lieu of the truth (something that will be explained further). Western philosophy's hostility to particularity is a symptom of this falseness; for Badiou the universal can only be manifested in particularities even though it is itself "indifferent" to particularity as such.

For Badiou, the false universal promoted by Western thought breeds passivity and a deep limitation to human capacity. Such passivity allows the state and other actors who benefit from this scheme of ethics—and the concomitant various political systems that they produce—an enormous amount of power. We are taught to value human life above all and hence—in our fearfulness and grasping over this one life that we have—we become susceptible to what Badiou calls the "'Western' mastery of death," the systems of sovereignty and governance that determine and control our lives down to the most intimate level.[3] Paradoxically, by subscribing to a false universal, we become the very particularities (the mortal, fearful, divided entities) that Kantian ethics—among others—formally scorns.[4]

Badiou opposes this death-based ethical system to one based on the event, a shattering moment (his examples include the Chinese Cultural Revolution, the Paris Commune, France in May 1968, and, most importantly perhaps, Christ's Resurrection) that unmakes all previous "facts," which are themselves, for Badiou, merely reactionary parts of a history that reinforces their own self-declared inevitability. An event, he tells us, is a moment of "maximal" existence, that is, a maximal potential for change and possibility that forcefully enters into a world in which such possibility is—until that moment—completely absent.[5] Out of the event comes truth, a universality that is the same for all (akin to Marx's idea that the revolution of the proletariat is universal in the sense that it ends all forms of oppression once and for all).[6] Badiou writes of this truth producing nature of the event:

> Precisely because a truth, in its invention, is the only thing that is *for all*, so it can actually be achieved only *against* dominant opinions, since these always work for the benefit of some rather than all.[7]

In the aftermath of the event, we as subjects have the potential to be "faithful to the event." Badiou writes of this possibility:

> to be faithful to an event is to move within the situation that this event has supplemented, by *thinking*. . . the situation "according to" the event. And this, of course—since the event was excluded by all the regular laws of the situation—compels the subject to *invent* a new way of being and acting in the situation.[8]

For Badiou, prior to the event, we may not even be subjects at all (although Badiou recognizes that you can be formed by events that temporally precede you). He tells us: "The subject, therefore, in no way pre-exists the process. He is absolutely non-existent in the situation 'before' the event."[9] The event forces us to choose between the demand (placed by Western ethics) to remain as you are, "a perseverence in being," or to become "faithful to the event," to accept the radical disruption of the event and thereby "persevere in the interruption."[10]

In so doing, the subject is not erased but instead made into the "Immortal" that she is.[11] That is to say the subject who is faithful to the event partakes, at last, in the true universal, in the kinds of atemporal possibilities that Kantian philosophy promises but never delivers. Badiou writes of this that

> this [subject] is simultaneously *himself*, nothing other than himself, a multiple singularity recognizable among all others, and *in excess of himself*, because the uncertain course . . . of fidelity *passes through him*, transfixes his singular body and inscribes him, from within time, in an instant of eternity.[12]

Critically this subject does not abandon what Badiou calls an "animal body." Badiou does not share Kant's disdain for this body (or, rather, he does, but he won't abandon it the way Kant does). This is because unlike Kant, Badiou's universal is always situated somewhere, and that somewhere (in this case the subject's own individuality and body) is once again the only way that the universal can be known and experienced at all.

If this sounds very much like the Christian doctrine of agape, in which we are meant to be emptied of ourselves and serve as vehicles for God's love, which fills and unites each of us, it is no accident that Badiou turns so heavily to Saint Paul. He sees Paul as a key source of thinking about this universal that always looks like a particular.[13] It is, for Badiou, the agape-like excess that marks this individual as being "Immortal." Badiou finds this tendency to be perfectly encapsulated by the event of Christ's Resurrection (even as he suggests the possibility of this moment as being itself part of the "fable" of Christianity more generally).

In his book entitled *Saint Paul*, Badiou writes: "The eventful figure of the Resurrection exceeds its real, contingent site which is the community of believers such as it exists at the moment."[14] Here, once again, we see the universal occurring only in its particular site(s). Our immortality—that is to say the way that we are not merely beings determined for death (and often by the hands of the state or some other authority)—is reflected in, and a response to the denial of death that is implicit in, the ideas of Christ's Resurrection.

For all of this, it would be hardly fair to characterize Badiou as simply serving as a modern-day Luther. His Paul is quite different from any standard Christian reflection on the subject. Whereas a thinker like Luther seeks to annihilate all differences between human beings, to empty ourselves as a vessel for God's love (an idea I will revisit in the conclusion), for Badiou, even in the face of the event, *"there are differences."*[15] Although this love, the agape that is eternal, unites us in some sense, it does not and should not erase our particularity, or rather it should avoid being identified with any one particularity (and hence, betraying itself as a universal). It must be, Badiou tells us *"an indifference that tolerates differences."*[16] In this way, ethics for him is both singular and plural, specific and universal at the same time.

The Problem of Evil

In his book entitled *Ethics: An Essay on the Understanding of Evil*, Badiou concerns himself with the ways in which the appearance of truth and the event has a dark corollary in terms of the production of evil (and this is where he begins to really approach Benjamin, whom I will get back to shortly). For Badiou, there are three problems with thinking about the event (and hence what might be called "good" albeit with certain qualifications that will be demonstrated shortly). The three dangers are that of simulacra, that of betrayal, and that of absolutization of power.

The danger of simulacra is to see the event not as bringing in a void but rather bringing in some kind of substance into the world. In this case,

> The "event" is supposed to bring into being, and name, not the void of the earlier situation, but its plenitude—not the universality of that which is sustained, precisely, by no particular characteristic . . . but the absolute particularity of a community, itself rooted in its characteristics of its soil, its blood, and its race.[17]

The prime example Badiou offers of this evil is Nazism, but he also sees it in his own contemporary France in terms of the question (which he finds absurd and, indeed, evil) of "Who is French?" He contrasts this question to Paul's own approach, who writes famously, "There is neither Jew nor Greek, there is neither slave nor free, there is neither male nor female."[18]

Against the notion of the simulacra and its faux content, Badiou writes:

> What allows a genuine event to be at the origin of a truth—which is the only thing that can be for all, and be eternally—is precisely the fact that it relates to the particularity of a situation only from the bias of its void.[19]

When the void is denied, we get instead a "full" parody of truth—the simulacra, the markings of a false universal that substitute for the true universal.

Betrayal, the next source of evil, comes from a refusal to be faithful to the event (to the real event, that is). Betrayal is in fact the opposite of this fidelity. It involves not only renouncing the truth but insisting that the becoming-subject, the "Immortal that I am," never existed. It is to scurry back to the nihilism of Western ethics (and hence to death, to true, and fatal, particularity).

Finally, the absolutization of the truth is simply the idea that the truth gives you a "total power." The temptation of such a power turns truth into a dogma, another generalizable situation irrespective of particularity, thereby inviting in the wrong, false universal. Badiou tells us that

> the Good is Good only to the extent that it does not aspire to render the world good. Its sole being lies in the situated advent . . . of a singular truth. So it must be that the power of a truth is also a kind of powerlessness.[20]

When we absolutize truth, we override what Badiou calls its "unnameable" aspect, that part of the truth and the eternal which we cannot have access to. To avoid this, we must avoid a sense of power over the world that any engagement in truth gives us and seek instead a kind of "powerlessness" (which is not by any means the same as passivity).

Fighting the False Universal

What all of this amounts to, more or less, is an argument that evil is a form of idolatry (although Badiou doesn't really use this language). The simulacra that we turn to to replace the truth are not unrelated to the true and the good (hence, Badiou's insistence that "it is from our positive capability for Good . . . that we are to identify Evil—not visa versa").[21] Achieving the ethical is, for Badiou, a very delicate, complicated matter. As we have seen, truth can be mimicked by simulacra. But this isn't just mimicry insofar as the relationship to false truth is actually built upon our relationship to actual truth (hence Badiou's priority of good over evil). Just as crucially, even if we know the truth, it can evade us, as the suggestion of the temporal power it seems to put in our hands can readily turn it into more simulacra. When we understand the universal as being a void, something that disrupts us and exceeds us, we remain in the ethical domain. Yet, as with Benjamin, such a stance is a hair's breadth from its opposite for Badiou (or, if not opposite, its evil counterpart); the universal and its false variant are distinguished from truth only by the extent to which we allow the event to shatter rather than form us, to accept the negative and subtractive qualities of the event as the basis for any relationship to truth and universality.

Thus in some ways it becomes very hard to spot and root out the false universal for Badiou. It appears so much more substantial and more fulfilling, by definition, than an actually ethical position. Badiou appreciates Paul as a model for how to respond to the event (in this case, Christ's Resurrection) without succumbing to such temptations. Badiou praises Paul for basically ignoring the facts of the life of Jesus. Such details are the "substance," the infilling—that serves as an unmaker of the truth that the Christ event (the Resurrection) conveys. For Badiou, the apostles and the Gospels (all of which were written after Paul's epistles) in some sense constitute betrayals of the event and hence of the universal that was promised in Paul's version of Christianity. While Paul scrupulously engaged with all communities, turning his back neither on Jews nor on gentiles (and hence practicing a kind of literal universalism), Badiou accuses the writers of the Gospels of currying favor with the Romans. He writes that between Paul's life and the writing of the Gospels, the Jewish uprising was crushed and the temple of Solomon was destroyed. By portraying the Jews as complicit with or guilty of Jesus' death—as Paul never did (indeed, he always proudly considered himself an Israelite)—the Gospels not only codified centuries of Christian anti-Semitism but also departicularized the universal by turning their back on the original site in which Christianity occurred (i.e., among the Jews). Here, the nimble and delicate treatment of universality that Badiou appreciates in Paul quickly deteriorates into its opposite. The false universal—that is, a particularity in the guise of universality as opposed to a universality in the guise of a particularity—rather than being undermined and subverted by the event of Christ's Resurrection becomes instead another iteration of falseness, a new part of the simulacra of illicit power and determinacy.

Badiou's advice, which we see both in his favorable—indeed hagiographic—treatment of Paul and in his *Ethics*, is

> Do all that you can to persevere in that which exceeds your perseverance. Persevere in your interruption. Seize in your being that which has seized and broken you.[22]

In other words, the truth-seeking subject must take her own disruption as the basis for who she is and what she will do. Elaborating on this further, Badiou tells us:

> "Never forget what you have encountered." But we can only say this if we understand that not-forgetting is not a memory. . . . Not-

forgetting consists in thinking and practising the arrangement of my multiple-being according to the Immortal it holds and which the piercing through . . . of an encounter has composed as subject.[23]

Paul, for Badiou, epitomizes this spirit; he serves as an exemplar of how to be "faithful to the event" and the truths that it makes available to the subject. By refusing to get into questions of which community made the most faithful Christians and by leaving most of the details of Christ's life and mission unexplained—even refused—Paul focused on what was most crucial: the event itself. Without allowing a particularity to contaminate the event (even as he remained open to all particularities), Paul models how to remain faithful to what is eternal and true in the face of a world marked by death and evil. Badiou argues that claims that Paul is in fact the epitome of dogmatism and Christian orthodoxy come from reading Paul through the lens of what came next: the Gospels and popes and schisms that have made contemporary Christianity a far cry from the true universal message it began as.

"Jewish Iconoclasm"

It might seem perverse or strange to link Badiou's praise for a central Christian figure like Paul with someone like Walter Benjamin, who was not only ethnically Jewish—like Paul—but theologically Jewish (albeit in a highly unorthodox fashion), especially given the fact that Badiou expressly parts company with Jewish notions of the other (especially with Levinas) and similar bases of a Jewish ethics (although as we have already seen, Badiou approvingly notes the fact that Paul never turned his back on his own Jewish origins). Nevertheless, I find that on the surface of things (and not only the surface—the degrees of similarity go quite deep, although not all the way down) that Badiou and Benjamin are remarkably similar.

For Benjamin, as for Badiou, evil is created by trying to fill the world with truths that are either no longer are available to us (for Benjamin) or that have been betrayed (Badiou). Both thinkers, in other words, struggle against all forms of idolatry. The main difference between them, as already noted, is that for all his engagement with theological language, Badiou distances himself, ultimately, from theology. At the very beginning of his engagement with Paul and his consideration of the Resurrection, Badiou tells us that the "what we are dealing with here is precisely a fable."[24] For Benjamin, on the other hand, theology is fully embraced as the solution to the pseudosecular idolatry both authors struggle with.

As already noted, for Benjamin, idolatry has fundamentally theological roots beginning with the Fall. As we saw, in "On Language as Such and on the Language of Man," Benjamin tells us that knowledge (at least human knowledge), as opposed to truth, has a unique character insofar as "knowledge of good and evil abandons name; it is a knowledge from outside, the uncreated imitation of the creative word."[25] This "uncreated imitation of the creative word," then, is the equivalent of Badiou's simulacra. It imitates and grasps at truth, seeking to reproduce it in an earthly setting in a way that promises domination and control (but actually offers nothing of the kind). This is another version of a false universal. Here we find a pseudo-truth that is not independent of truth but—as with Badiou—is a kind of pale or failed copy (one that does not recognize itself as such).

Benjamin and Badiou also share a concern that the promise of truth and knowledge constantly tempt us toward a vision of absolute power. Insofar as knowledge demands a kind of truth of its own, we turn to myth as a basis for the way we order our lives. In this way, our fetishism takes on explicitly political and legal forms through the practices of mythic violence producing, once again, a phantasmagoria (in Benjamin's terms) or a false universal (in Badiou's terms).

So far then Badiou and Benjamin seem to be in strong agreement. Nor does the Jewish Benjamin ignore Christian figures either. Although Paul is not as interesting to Benjamin as he is to Badiou, Benjamin does consider the life of Jesus himself (a question I will return to again later in this chapter). In the *Origin of German Tragic Drama*, Benjamin considers Jesus both as symbol and as allegory. As symbol, he tells us that Jesus is the false universal, the idol incarnate. He is the manifestation of (what passes for) truth on earth, and in his name the entire apparatus of control and power, the entire mechanism of the phantasmagoria, operates. To think, on the other hand, of Jesus as an allegorical figure—as he is portrayed however accidentally and incompetently by the German Baroque dramatists Benjamin studies in that book—is to challenge and call into question this portrayal, as well as the "truth" that such a portrayal conveys.

Benjamin argues that the Baroque dramatists achieve this subversion of the symbolic Jesus by turning the (false) "universal" Jesus into a particular Jesus. Benjamin tells us that the German Baroque dramatists give "examples of birth, marriage, and funeral poems, of eulogies and victory congratulations, songs on the birth and death of Christ, on his spiritual marriage with the soul, on his glory and his victory."[26] As Benjamin puts it further, it "is an unsurpassably spectacular gesture to place even Christ in the realm of the provisional, the everyday, the unreliable"[27] Furthermore, by this move

> the symbolic becomes distorted into the allegorical. The eternal is separated from the events of the story of salvation, and what is left is a living image open to all kinds of revision by the interpretive artist.[28]

Such a move seems to be the exact opposite of what Badiou appreciates in Paul. Recall that it is by *avoiding* the details of Jesus's life that Paul succeeds, in Badiou's view, in escaping the lures of the false universal otherwise inherent in the person of Jesus Christ. But for Benjamin, by focusing indeed on the banal and ordinary existence of Jesus, the dramatists succeed (not in any intentional way, however) in calling into question Jesus's power as a symbol, helping it to fail as such. Here the emphasis is different (perhaps explaining the diametrically opposed paths the two thinkers take): for Badiou, the emphasis is on the particular as a vehicle for the true universal; for Benjamin, the particular is the site in which the universal can legibly be seen to fail to appear (once again offering a different kind of failure). Yet both thinkers agree that the local and temporal is the only possible site for ethics. And both thinkers share a desire to see the shattering of the false universal that surrounds the figure of Jesus.

Theology and Truth

For all their similarity, as already indicated, ultimately I don't think Badiou's approach to the universal is as successful as Benjamin's. Even though they are "fellow travellers," there is a way in which Badiou's universal is closer to the false universal—or at least more difficult to pry apart from it—than Benjamin's. As already suggested, I think this difference can be explained in part because Badiou is somewhat coy about his own engagement with theology and therefore does not address some of the theological implications of his work head-on. The other—and related—reason, as also previously suggested, is that in his choice of Paul as the figure he lauds as exemplifying the correct approach to the universal, Badiou has picked the wrong law as a vehicle for that universal. Let me address these two concerns in turn, beginning with the question of theology.

In *Saint Paul*, as already noted, Badiou begins by distancing himself from Paul's religiosity as "a fable." In another principal work, *Ethics*, we do not have even this disavowal. In that book, we seem to be reading an entirely secular document, even as he uses terms, as we have already seen, like "the Immortal that I am" and "eternity" and "truth." These are words that we are not used to seeing coming from radical French philosophers. Badiou is not afraid of such terms to be sure, but he may not always be able to control the implications of such terminology. Or rather, because he does not face religion head-on (as Benjamin does) he is somewhat disabled from addressing those creeping tendencies that he is otherwise so very alert to and suspicious of.

Evoking ideas of truth and universality is, as Badiou ably demonstrates, a dangerous game, but he seems to think that he can safely engage with such usage because he is inoculated precisely by his disavowal of religion. He can laud Paul as being more of a communist hero than a Christian one by calling Paul's creed—and even the event that it is based upon—a fable.

For Badiou, one of the dangers of a formal turn to religion is that such a move obscures the negative implications of whatever doctrine is being promoted. He makes this point most clearly when he discusses Levinas in the *Ethics*. He looks at Levinas's (Jewish) notion that for an ethical stance, we must turn, not just to the other, but the absolutely other. Badou points out that for Levinas, if we remain only with the other as such, we do not transcend our own categories and thus we are returned to a kind of false universal. For Levinas, the absolutely other is required so that the other is not merely "another me," that is, a projection of our own desires and needs onto the other as a way of servicing and rationalizing those desire. Badiou says of this:

> Lévinas's enterprise serves to remind us, with extraordinary insis-
> tence, that every effort to turn ethics into the principle of thought
> and action is essentially religious . . . distanced from its Greek
> usage . . . and taken in general, ethics is a category of pious dis-
> course.[29]

Badiou warns us that when we strip away this religious veneer we get "a dog's dinner. . . . We are left a pious discourse without piety."[30]

One question we might pose to Badiou at this point is why we get a "dog's dinner" when we strip away the religiosity from Levinas but not when we do the same thing to Paul. Badiou's answer would no doubt be that Levinas doesn't really offer us much in the way of a true ethical code; his religiousness allows him to get away with a code of ethics that doesn't actually work, except as a form of piety. His is not a truly universal approach to ethics (in Badiou's view), unlike Paul's ethical code. Still, it is worth noting that Badiou doesn't see the possibility of a similar danger in his own work—that is, that his own unacknowledged or semiacknowledged turn to religion might not itself rely on that religiosity for his ethical system to appear to function (or at least to have its dysfunction remain hidden from view).[31]

Badiou's ambivalent relationship to religion can perhaps be seen most clearly in the way that he deals with the actual event that motivates Paul, the Resurrection itself. After telling us that "what we are dealing with here is precisely a fable," Badiou goes on to say:

> and singularly so in the case of Paul, who for crucial reasons reduces Christianity to a single statement: Jesus is resurrected. Yet this is precisely a fabulous element . . . since all the rest, birth, teachings, death, *might* after all be upheld.[32]

Thus, whereas the other facts of Jesus' life may actually have happened ("might . . . be upheld") the Resurrection is the one thing that surely did not (is a fable). Badiou complicates this claim a bit when he goes on to write:

> A "fable" is that part of a narrative that, so far as we are concerned, fails to touch on any Real, unless it be by virtue of that invisible and indirectly accessible residue sticking to every obvious imaginary. In this regard, it is to its element of fabulation . . . alone that Paul reduces the Christian narrative, with the strength of one who knows that in holding fast to this point as real, one is unburdened of all the imaginary that surrounds it. If it is possible for us to speak of belief from the outset . . . let us say that so far as we are concerned it is rigorously impossible to believe in the resurrection of the crucified.[33]

What this amounts to saying is that for Badiou, the very fabulous nature of the idea of resurrection (i.e., the fact that it didn't actually happen) is a kind of weapon against all the "facts" and opinions that constitute the world of the simulacra. It is precisely the impossibility, the nonhappening of the Resurrection, that unmakes all the false associations ("all the imaginary") that otherwise surround it.

Indeed, in admiring the way that Paul "splendidly ignores" Jesus' teaching and his miracles, Badiou goes on to say that "the rest [besides the Resurrection], all the rest, is of no real importance. Let us go further: the rest (what Jesus said and did) *is not what is real in conviction, but obstructs or even falsifies it.*"[34]

Here we see an ontological reversal of sorts: what (possibly) really happened is "not real," and this irreality is in turn "falsified" by the fable of the Resurrection, helping us to hold onto the void-like qualities of truth that are required for a subscription to the true universal.

But such a move leads to an important question. If the example of Paul being faithful to an event that didn't actually occur is meant to be indicative of our relationship to the event more generally, what does it mean or do to other events that are based on things that actually did happen? Badiou himself would hardly call into question the veracity of the events that he elsewhere discusses, the leftist revolutions and upheavals of the past two hundred years. But if the actuality of one of these events can be in question, even if obliquely, how do we draw a line between the truth of the event and the simulacra of evil more generally? If a fable can be the basis for truth, can a nonfable serve as one as well? Badiou focuses on the void-like nature of our relationship to truth, its powerlessness and its ambiguity, but at some point ambiguity can also become confusion and a lack of clarity about what constitutes truth and what constitutes simulacra.

Benjamin himself has no such trouble with the question of truth. For him truth is, and has always been, unchanging. It is we human beings who have changed. In choosing knowledge (at least human knowledge) over truth, we have abandoned our connection with reality, replacing it with a pseudoreality suggested through or grasped at by our acts of representation.

Benjamin is just as comfortable as Badiou using the term truth (this is something that unites and distinguishes them from many other thinkers in the radical tradition). Yet Benjamin means something very different than Badiou by this term. For Benjamin, once again, truth is absolutely unknowable. Our task is not to seek out truth, not to give ourselves over to it (as we must for Badiou) even as a pure negative, but once again to reveal the failure of truth, its absence in the process of representation (the exposure of such a failure is probably the closest to truth we can come for Benjamin).

For Benjamin, we have an important ally in this process, namely God. Benjamin's (rough) equivalent to Badiou's notion of the event is his concept of "divine violence." Like the event, there is a negative quality to this violence. Yet there is a crucial difference: rather than create new truths in its wake (as is the case for Badiou and the event), divine violence unmakes the idols we have raised in God's stead. As we have seen in the previous chapter, the example that Benjamin furnishes of divine violence in the "Critique of Violence" is the story of Korah. Nothing is left in the wake of such an "event" (if we may borrow Badiou's term). The human witnesses to this moment are left without any new certainties (no truths) but, at the same time, they are perhaps a bit freer from untruth. They are left in a sense radically alone; the Messiah has come and gone and hasn't given them anything, but rather has taken something away from them.

As we have seen, both Badiou and Benjamin are attentive to an inherently negative or subtractive quality to truth. Yet for Badiou, truth is tangible, articulable (either as the fable "Christ was resurrected" or in terms of ideas about the working class and its power that emerge from the events Badiou looks at in a book like *The Communist Hypothesis*). While Badiou tells us that the truth must have a certain powerlessness to avoid becoming a part of evil, for Benjamin there is no danger of this because truth is not so much powerless as nonexistent, as far as we are concerned. Thus the negative quality of truth is far stronger for Benjamin than it is for Badiou. For Benjamin, truth is not merely void-*like*, it is void full stop (at least as far as humans are concerned).

In this case, I would argue that it is not just the presence of a directly acknowledged theology that serves Benjamin better than Badiou but the fact that, having so directly acknowledged this theology, Benjamin can then go about seeing that it does not betray his cause. Because of his connection to theology, Benjamin can relegate truth to another world—to the realm of God—and, in this way, prevent us from having any temptation to see truth where it isn't; Benjamin can use the "fire" of his own antifetishistic theology to fight the "fire" of the false truths presented by the phantasmagoria. In this sense, while we may still be idolators, the resistance to idolatry is enabled by the fact that we are never forced to choose between truth and simulacra. For Benjamin, there is nothing but simulacra (representation) in the world; we can assume that *all* of our assertions, all of our principles, are merely knowledge and not truth.

For his own part, as already suggested at the beginning of this chapter, Badiou cannot banish truth altogether from the world because he only sees one world. There is nowhere else to "put" truth for him. As such, the truth remains in the human realm alongside the simulacra, and thus we have the danger that real truth might slide into the false.

The perhaps surprising upshot of all of this is that it is ultimately Benjamin who is the more secular thinker of the two, this despite his more open use of theology. Insofar as Badiou grapples with the legacy of theology but does not ultimately vanquish the false universal that such theology can produce, he remains mired, to some extent, in a theological quandary about the nature of truth as such. In Benjamin, we are absolved of that quandary to a large extent (although we are never free from the threat of phantasm in his view either). Furthermore, in the aftermath of the unmaking of false truths (akin to the undoing of Korah and his followers) that Benjamin sees as occurring at all times and in all places, we are left radically alone, on our own. Whereas Badiou's universal has both a negative and a "positive" face (the positive face being the appearance of truth—however shattering and negative it may be—and the fidelity to the event that he demands), Benjamin's universal is entirely and only negative, as far as we are concerned.

Which Law?

There is another, previously mentioned, important way that these thinkers differ, namely in terms of the one law that they choose to keep (or, in the case of Benjamin, the one law I see his theory as asking us to keep), after casting out all the rest. As noted, Badiou, in turning to Paul, duplicates his message that the only law that matters (akin to the only event connected to Jesus that is relevant) is that of love; this is the positive upshot of "being faithful to the event" of Christ's Resurrection. Badiou cites Paul's famous statement that

> the commandments, "You shall not commit adultery, You shall not kill. You shall not steal. You shall not covet," and any other commandment, are summed up in this sentence, "You shall love your neighbor as yourself." Love does no harm to a neighbor; therefore love is the fulfilling of the law.[35]

Understanding the commandment to love thy neighbor as the only law that we must follow is, in many ways, consistent with Badiou's position about universality more generally. Badiou spends a chapter of his book on Paul considering how the latter rejects Jewish law seemingly in its entirety even as he acknowledges that the law is "holy."[36] In the chapter that immediately follows, however, he redeems law from this abyss by turning to love. He tell us that love "names a nonliteral law, one that gives to the faithful subject his consistency, and effectuates the postevental truth in the world."[37] Treating love as the only law we need to follow preserves the law, connecting us to the immortal and universal in the process. As Badiou puts it:

> For the Christian subject, love underwrites the return of a law that, although nonliteral, nonetheless functions as principle and consis-

tency for the subjective energy initiated by the declaration of faith. For the new man love is the fulfillment of the break that he accomplishes with the law; it is the law of the break with law, law of the truth of law.[38]

Love understood as a break with law does seem to accord somewhat with Benjamin's own notion of divine violence as a break with idolatry (indeed, I will return to these passages in the conclusion of this chapter to reconsider them from a Benjaminian perspective). And yet, by choosing love as the one law we must follow, Badiou risks once again bringing in some of the very problems—the simulacra, betrayals, and temptations toward power that he seeks to redress—in his concept of truth and law in the first place.

For one thing, as previously noted, the idea of love is not innocent of exactly the kinds of hierarchies and particularities disguising themselves as universalities that Badiou himself is so opposed to. There is a long history to the usage of love as a political and philosophical construct that suggests a much less void-like, or negative, aspect than Badiou would like to suggest. He tells us that "Paul gives the name 'love,' *agapē*—translated for a long time as 'charity,' a term that no longer means much to us."[39] Agape, the Greek form of *caritas* (the Latin term), is seen as the highest manifestation of love building on (in Greek), first, *eros*, the base love, expressed as erotic desire and then moving up to *philia*, the love of one's fellow citizens (as we see in Aristotle's concept of *philia politike*) or friendship. Agape is the highest love, the love of God that we can reflect but not serve as an origin for.[40] While this notion of a universal and higher form of love may to some extent reflect Badiou's own desired goals, the history of this concept is marked by a great tension between an agape that erases and replaces our particularity (such as is proposed by Luther) and one that works in synchronicity with our *eros* (such as is advanced by Saint Augustine).[41] Thus the question of what we are "filling" ourselves with when we turn to love, whether it is purely void or whether it has a content—or a particularity—of its own (all crucial questions for Badiou, as we have seen), cannot be so easily overlooked. Agape doesn't exist in a vacuum—it is built on the shoulders of the lower forms of love, and in this way it is bound up with the very world of simulacra, of hierarchies and (bad) particularities that Badiou would have it avoid.

More to the point perhaps, for Badiou, without a direct relationship to theology, the critical question of the nature of agape is left largely unresolved; what is a love that we receive from a deity who may not even exist? It's true that putting God's existence into question allows for the same void-like quality that we saw in Badiou's discussion of Christ's Resurrection as fable; the nonexistence of God would ensure that no truths that were associated with such a God's love could become idols or simulacra. But once again there is a crucial difference between being void-*like* and being void. A law based on the love of a God that might not or does not exist cannot banish the kinds of terrestrial associations that the practice of such love has had throughout its history; once again, with no recourse besides the world, Badiou has nowhere to go to enlist or draw upon a purely empty agape, one that transcends rather than partakes in the problematical associations that such a concept has always brought along with it. Rather than making agape a force of pure unmaking for the self who receives it, for Badiou it risks smuggling within itself a great deal of terrestrial (and mythic) baggage.

For Benjamin, once again, we are faced with a much purer, more absolutely negative form of universal in the form of a law based on the Second Commandment. As we have already seen, for Benjamin, to say that we must "wrestle with [the law] in solitude," to see such a law as a "guideline" rather than an absolute rule (all things that Badiou would approve of, no doubt and which are consistent with his own ethical stance), does not suggest the usurpation of law but rather its purification, its reduction to a pith.

The Second Commandment is almost purely negative in that it, not unlike the notion of divine violence, produces no new truths but only removes false ones. This commandment, then, is in the service of the true universal or, perhaps we might say more accurately, it is wholly against the false. It is an entirely negative and subtractive commandment that, however has a very positive effect on those who obey it insofar as they are released, at least to a large extent, from the certainty of idolatry and hence are left, once again, radically on their own.

Accordingly, I would argue that Benjamin's turn to an explicitly anti-idolatrous law—as opposed to Badiou's turn to love—is much more in keeping with the goal both authors share of combating falseness and evil. Benjamin embraces, with a thoroughness that we rarely see with other thinkers, the void itself, the absolute lack of truth that we have in our world. To some extent, Benjamin is able to embrace the void with such fearlessness *because* he is theological; that is, understanding that God and the truth exist, only not in a way we can ever discern, Benjamin can safely leave them out of the world that we live in least they become confused for their copies and simulacra. Put a bit more cynically, you could say that Benjamin protects us from the universal and even from truth (because they will always take on false guises in this world) by locking them away safely in paradise. By telling us that there is a truth and there is a God and a universal, but that we will never have access to these things, Benjamin allows us a world that remains undetermined, available for politics.

Žižek and "Jewish Iconoclasm"

Much of the previous discussion of Badiou and iconoclasm can be extended—albeit in different ways—to the work of Slavoj Žižek. Žižek engages with the question of iconoclasm when he describes Judaism as a religion wherein

> God remains the transcendent irrepresentable Other, i.e., as Hegel was right to emphasize, Judaism is the religion of the Sublime: it tries to render the suprasensible dimension not through the over-whelming excess of the sensible . . . but in a purely negative way, by renouncing images altogether.[42]

In his considerations, Žižek offers that Christianity in facts improves on Judaism's pure negativism without abandoning the fundamental iconoclasm that is central to both faiths:

> Christianity . . . renounces this God of Beyond, this Real behind the curtain of phenomena; it acknowledges that there is NOTHING beyond the appearance—nothing BUT the imperceptible X that changes Christ, this ordinary man, into God. . . . It is only here that the iconoclasm is truly brought to its conclusion: what is effectively "beyond the image" is that X that makes the man Christ God. In this precise sense, Christianity inverses the Jewish sublimation into a radical desublimation: not desublimation in the sense of the simple reduction of God to man, but desublimation in the sense of the descendence of the sublime Beyond to the everyday level.[43]

We need not accept Žižek's claims about Christianity (which are obviously not uncontroversial) to take his description of iconoclasm seriously. In effect he is saying that it is only Christianity that offers the correct formulation for combating idolatry. Christianity avoids the Jewish "nothing," the representation of unrepresentability, and instead offers an approach to God whereby the divine only exists in an earthly manifestation, a particularity that stands for—or produces—the universal.

Here, Žižek approaches very close to Badiou's ideas on the subject and, like Badiou, he reads the manifestation of this kind of terrestrial sacredness through the notion of love. Žižek writes:

> Love is to be opposed here to desire: desire is always caught in the logic of "this is not that," it thrives in the gap that forever separates the *obtained* satisfaction from the *sought-for* satisfaction, while love FULLY ACCEPTS that "this IS that" . . . IS the Thing I unconditionally love; that Christ, this wretched man, IS the living God. Again, to avoid a fatal misunderstanding: the point is not that we should "renounce transcendence" and fully accept the limited human person as our love object, since "that is all there is": transcendence is not abolished, but rendered ACCESSIBLE—it shines through in this very clumsy and miserable being that I love.[44]

Love, in this sense, is, for Žižek, how we experience the divine. It represents an acceptance that the divine only exists as far as we are concerned in its earthly manifestations (and here I would simply repeat my comments about Badiou that love brings with it a lot of baggage—baggage of the idolatrous sort).

Just as with Badiou, Žižek sees that transcendence is therefore "accessible." Indeed, one could argue we see an extension of the fulfillment inherent in Badiou's reading of Saint Paul. Without focusing on the Resurrection quite as much as Badiou does, nonetheless for Žižek the divine quality of Jesus (the "X") ensures that a particular quality of truth is possible in the world:

> Christ is thus not "man PLUS God": what becomes visible in him is simply the divine dimension in man "as such." So—far from being the Highest in man, the purely spiritual dimension towards which all humans strive, the "divinity" is rather a kind of obstacle, of a "bone in the throat"—it is something, that unfathomable X, on account of which man cannot ever fully become MAN, self-identical. The point is not that, due to the limitation of his mortal sinful nature, man cannot ever become fully divine, but that, *due to the divine spark in him, man cannot ever fully become man.*[45]

Here, the promise of the Resurrection, the promise to create truths that disturb and expose simulacra, is extended to become the possibility by which all other material objects and, most importantly, all human beings, are not fated to be simulacra. If "man" were ever to become "MAN," in

Žižek's terms, it would mean that each of us became only what we (mythically) determine ourselves to be; there would be no position from which to resist being so determined and, as a result, we would risk total ossification as subjects. The divine X that Žižek sees as extending analogically from Christ to the rest of us prevents this from occurring. It is the "bone in the throat," the one flaw in the illusion of material perfection that saves us from falling into a complete idolatry.

Here, Žižek makes Christianity sound like the perfect vehicle for Benjamin's own project. Explicitly parting ways with Judaism, Žižek portrays Christianity, and in particular, the example of Jesus, as a vehicle to resist idolatry or simulacra, to preserve the kind of unbalanced and tenuous, ultimately empty, sorts of "truths" that these philosophers prefer.[46]

For Žižek, Jewish iconoclasm is not only incomplete but it also fails to recognize the way that Judaism itself has "FULLY 'anthropomorphized'" God in a way previous, pagan religions did not.[47] Žižek goes on to say that

> the Jewish God experiences full wrath, revengefulness, jealousy, etc., as every human being. . . . THIS is why one is prohibited to make images of him: not because an image would "humanize" the purely spiritual Entity, but because it would render it all too faithfully, as the ultimate Neighbor-Thing.[48]

In this way, Judaism requires iconoclasm to countermand its own tendency to idolatry (an idolatry that is more extreme, more anthropomorphizing than with any other religion, he implies). Christianity completes this iconoclasm by rendering the mystery of God itself into something almost perfectly human and, in this way, reduces the mysterious anthropomorphized God into just another human being (almost):

> Christianity only goes to the end in this direction by asserting not only the likeness of God, and man, but their direct *identity* in the figure of Christ: "no wonder man looks like God, since a man (Christ) IS God." . . . [I]nstead of prohibiting the image of God, why not, precisely, allow it and thus render him as JUST ANOTHER HUMAN BEING, as a miserable man indiscernible from other humans with regard to his intrinsic properties?[49]

In this way, for Žižek, the fact that Christianity does portray God (in the form of Christ) does not make it less iconoclastic than Judaism (which strictly forbids any image of God whatsoever). Žižek's argument is that exactly by using this image, Christianity *avoids* idolatry by rendering the image into a means by which God's mystery is rendered human, not an "other" at all (and hence safe to represent). By bringing godhood into humanity, by rendering it barely anything, just an "X" (first in Jesus and then, by extension to everyone else) the very problem of idolatry seems resolved, perhaps even impossible.

Benjamin's Jesus (Revisited)

This is an interesting argument and is, at least on the surface, quite similar to Benjamin's own description of how rendering Jesus Christ human undermines the idolatry that his image otherwise foments. As already noted, in his *Origin of German Tragic Drama*, Benjamin describes how the Baroque dramatists produced a very human Christ rather than rendering Christ into an idolatous absolute symbol (and, in this way, they failed to represent—or perhaps more accurately, represented the failure of the divinity that they sought to convey in their plays). Repeating an already cited passage where he is speaking specifically of the playwright Sigmund von Birken, Benjamin tells us that he

> gives "as examples of birth, marriage, and funeral poems, of eulogies and victory congratulations, songs on the birth and death of Christ, on his spiritual marriage with the soul, on his glory and his victory." The mystical instant [*Nu*] becomes the "now" [*Jetzt*] of contemporary actuality, the symbolic becomes distorted into the allegorical. The eternal is separated from the events of the story of salvation, and what is left is a living image open to all kinds of revision by the interpretative artist.[50]

Here we can already begin to see a difference in what Benjamin and Žižek are proposing. For Benjamin "the eternal is separated from the events of the story," and the mystical becomes the "now . . . of contemporary actuality." Thus, rather than show God in the man, as Žižek argues, von Birken has shown the man in the man. There is no ambiguity here as there is with Žižek; there is no meeting of the human and the divine (not even a little bit of the divine). This is the denuding of the spiritual altogether, leaving the divine a perfect and total aporia. This is in fact almost the opposite of what Žižek is looking for (with Badiou, perhaps, somewhere in between these positions); here, we have, not the troubling of the human by the divine, but its complete absence in the human, announcing once again—if only by negative impression—a realm of divine truth that is markedly and legibly unavailable in the world.

In his treatment of the image of Christ, then, Benjamin has done something markedly—and critically—different than Žižek. Whereas Žižek pronounced the image of Christ innocuous, safe because it was not "other" to us (hence fulfilling the potential problem raised by Judaism whereby God may be too similar for comfort), for Benjamin the idolatrous potential of the image remains highly dangerous. Benjamin uses the idol of Christ as a weapon against itself; recall that he tells us that "it is an unsurpassably spectacular gesture to place even Christ in the realm of the provisional."[51] It will also be recalled that he labels this treatment of Christ as allegorical, as opposed to symbolic. In other words, by turning this most idolatrous of all images into a weapon against idolatry (by rendering it terrestrial, denuding it of its sacred meaning and, in the process, gesturing toward a divine that is not representable at all), Benjamin has done maximal damage to the idol. By excluding God from the depiction of Christ, the German Baroque dramatists allowed (however inadvertently) God to remain God.

Žižek, it could be argued, has done just the opposite: by declaring the image of Christ to be nonidolatrous, not other, he has allowed the divine spark, the X, to be present and unquestioned in each human being. Rather than serving to unmake false truths and simulacra, this move potentially preserves them. Rather than removing the divine to a realm that is out of reach, Žižek effectively makes every person, possibly every object in the world, potentially divine (and hence, an idol), even if the "divinity" in this case takes on a distinctly terrestrial form (as X). Žižek's evocation of love only reinforces this danger by ensuring that each individual will welcome and internalize this sort of mass divinization of human actors.

Here again we come to a problem that we faced with Badiou as well; in such a state of affairs, it becomes incumbent on us to discern what is true and what is false. Insofar as he scrupulously avoids the language of truth and falsity, Žižek may not have exactly the same problem as Badiou does in this regard (although his Lacanian category of the Real may be quite similar to Badiou's notion of truth). Yet, at the same time, Žižek muddies the waters between the divine and the secular in a way that is possibly worse, more intractable, than with Badiou.

In the very idea of an "accessible transcendence," a divine X that lies in each of us—or, more accurately, that disturbs the possibility of our own wholeness—we see evidence of why Žižek (or Badiou's) version of iconoclasm is perhaps not as pure of what it struggles against as he (they) might think. In his own relationship to the notion of divinity on earth, Benjamin offers us not even an X. Rather than rely on a sense of incompletion that adheres in this world (Žižek's response), Benjamin, as we have seen, banishes the divine utterly (so if there is an X, it exists in an entirely different—and utterly inaccessible—realm). I suppose Žižek would argue, yes but if you get rid of the X in this world, what is to stop you from becoming "MAN," that is, what stops you from becoming a pure idol? The answer, as I've tried to argue throughout this book, is the Second Commandment. Rather than looking to the divine spark or flaw that saves us from our own idolatry, we must think of the divine as being indeed "wholly other." Only this otherness is not to be accessed, addressed, or otherwise engaged with (this distinguishes Benjamin from someone like Levinas, who would never say that we should, at times, abandon our notion of God). Instead, for Benjamin, we must cleave to the one law that unmakes idols (even the idol of our self) and, in this way, continue to avoid being "MAN" (to remain in a Žižekian lexicon).

Although in saying this it might sound like I am therefore coming down on the side of "Jewish iconoclasm" after all, in comparing Žižek and Benjamin (and Badiou for that matter as well) in terms of their respective notions of idolatry, I would prefer not to get into a "Judaism versus Christianity" debate. As we have seen, Benjamin's version of Judaism and Badiou and Žižek's respective versions of Christianity are so unlike the ordinary practices of those religions that the use of such labels is deeply suspect or at least highly problematical. Furthermore, these thinkers themselves do not pose this division as an opposition; Žižek himself states that one should adopt aspects of both Judaism and Christianity and, as we saw, Benjamin invokes Christ as a kind of anti-symbolic figure as part of his own struggle with idolatry. Instead of thinking about "Jewish" versus "Christian" iconoclasm, I would simply argue that Benjamin's own form of iconoclasm offers more of a safeguard against idolatry than either Badiou's or Žižek's versions do. For Benjamin, there is, once again, no ambiguity about what is divine and what is not. He shows us a model for how to *not* represent the divine, to gesture at it through a wholly or purely negative device. Although he appears to simply be stripping Christ of all divine aspects, Benjamin is taking Jesus's divine nature more seriously than it seems; he is dynamically engaging with the image of Christ as a way to thwart, disrupt, and subvert the idolatry that surrounds that image. Christ's divinity then can be said to exist as a site that is occluded—perhaps one could speak of an act of de-representation—in order to produce a notion of the divine that cancels out its own idolatry, leaving us, once again, only with "the human" (i.e., with no "X" at all).

The Law of the Break with Law:
Reading Benjamin and Badiou in Constellation

As a way to conclude this chapter, I want to return to a point that I made earlier in this chapter. I see Benjamin as offering a "friendly amendment" to Badiou's (and, for that matter, Žižek's) project. In making the criticism of Badiou that I have, I do not want to suggest that I think that Badiou is somehow a poor thinker or that his work has nothing to say to us. I think that in fact Benjamin and Badiou have a great deal to say to one another and thereby to us, their readers (and I think the same of Žižek). Let me first summarize what Benjamin can offer Badiou in terms of his own iconoclastic project before turning to what Badiou can, in turn, offer to Benjamin.

For Badiou, Benjamin offers, as I've already suggested, a better way to combat the idolatry that both thinkers see as inherent to the world that we live in. It is particularly in terms of his particular theology and the resultant law against idolatry that Benjamin offers Badiou the most direct way to combat the turn to evil. It's true that Badiou has a theology of his own, but it is one that is based in a highly secular (and, indeed, antitheological) perspective. Yet, I would argue that, as already stated, it is ultimately Benjamin and not Badiou who offers us a true secularism. As I have been claiming, Benjamin offers us a theological fire by which to confront and counteract the pseudotheological fires that mark our own time.

Benjamin's "theology," as I have shown, is nothing like the kinds of theologies we generally see; it is a more purely negative (but not nihilistic) way of approaching questions of universality and, as such, it tends to undo or unmake even itself. As I have been suggesting throughout this chapter, while the idea of universalism in Benjamin's theory (i.e., the idea of God's truth) remains crucial, by removing it from the human realm, Benjamin effectively does away with the concept itself, as far as we are concerned. In this way Benjamin allows us access to a politics in which the local, the particular, and the temporary are all that we can engage with, all that exist. This is the key, as we have seen, to Badiou's ethics as well, but such a stance is stymied by Badiou's insistence on bringing the universal back into the picture, albeit in a largely (but crucially not entirely) negative form. It may be that Badiou would never accept even such a radically denuded form of theology as we find with Benjamin (i.e., one where the universal can never appear in the world, nor the truth that bears it), but he pays a high price for clinging to a secularism that isn't quite what it seems to be.

As for what Benjamin stands to learn from Badiou, in a general sense, I think the latter offers what Benjamin never quite does—a fully thought-out politics. Badiou offers a relationship to action and its consequences and a way to realize something that Benjamin hints at but never fully articulates, namely a way to think about how our encounter with the negative effects and organizes us, recuperating our own possibilities in the process. With Badiou, we have more than hints and suggestions; we have a sense of an entire way of life, an ethical code stemming from our engagement in antifetishism. It is for this reason that I turn to Badiou, and not Benjamin himself, in chapter 5 to discuss how to think about the Haitian Revolution in a way that recognizes the effect such a moment had on subsequent history and on the human subjects who engaged in that event.

If their respective techniques of antifetishism are what distinguish them, then by reading Badiou through a Benjaminian lens, or substituting a Benjaminian negative for a Badiouian one, many of the insights that Badiou offers about his own form of ethics become available for a Benjaminian project as well. In particular, as noted previously, I'd like to focus on two Badiouian concepts that are helpful for Benjamin: the notion of being "faithful to the event" and the notion of what happens to law, and the subjects of law, when it becomes reduced to one single law.

In terms of the idea of being "faithful to the event," if we replace Badiou's choice of event—such as the Resurrection—with the Second Commandment, we can think of practicing a different kind of faith (a faithless faith). To think of being "faithful to the event" of the Second Commandment—an event that occurs not once but all the time and in all places—means to allow ourselves to continually be unmade by our struggle against fetishism. It means to accept the way that divine violence is constantly unmaking the idols we promote, showing us a way that we too can take up that resistance (just as the material objects of the world similarly resist our representations of them). This substitution also suggests that, rather than engage in a periodical encounter that we must hold faith with ever after, we may continually and always be unmade and reformed through this ongoing and permanent encounter.

I think too the quality of this faith would be altered by a turn to a more properly Benjaminian negative. Insofar as the faith in question stems from our realization of the failure of the divine to appear in any tangible or apparent form—for Benjamin we only know the divine through its endless disruption of, and resistance to, our own fetishism of it—we cannot speak of faith even in as delimited and generally negative way as we see with Badiou. Instead, using a phrase from Benjamin that I discuss at some length at the conclusion of *Textual Conspiracies*, I would speak here of taking a "faithless . . . leap," that is, a leap away from the false faith that normally animates us.[52]

And perhaps we don't need to move so far away from Badiou himself in the process. In the passage from *The Origin of German Tragic Drama* that this phrase comes from, Benjamin addresses the question of the way that allegory addresses phantasm, specifically in terms of how allegory resuscitates resurrection and, in particular the Resurrection of Jesus. So perhaps we don't have to substitute for Badiou's emphasis on the Resurrection so much as rethink or reread it along Benjaminian lines. Speaking once again of how the same phenomenon can both be the announcement of the ultimate and mythic symbol and, at the same time, serve as an allegory that unmakes that symbol, Benjamin writes (in a passage that is worth citing at some length):

> The bleak confusion of Golgotha . . . in [its] transitoriness, is not signified or allegorically represented, so much as, in its own significance, displayed as allegory. As the allegory of the resurrection. Ultimately in the death-signs of the baroque the direction of allegorical reflection is reversed: on the second part of its wide arc it returns, to redeem . . . Allegory, of course, loses everything that was most peculiar to it: the secret, privileged knowledge, the arbitrary rule in the realm of dead objects, the supposed infinity of a world without hope. All this vanishes with this *one* about-turn, in which the immersion of allegory has to clear away the final phantasmagoria of the objective and, left entirely to its own devices, rediscovers itself, not playfully in the earthly world of things, but seriously under the eyes of heaven . . . [T]hese allegories fill out and deny the void in which they are represented, just as, ultimately, the intention does not faithfully rest in the contemplation of bones but faithlessly leaps toward the idea of resurrection.[53]

There is a lot in this passage that bears analysis. We see that allegorizing, that is, engaging in the Second Commandment, turns "the bleak confusion of Golgotha" into something else. This something else is not "allegorically represented" (that is, subsumed back into the world of false representation) but simply "displayed as allegory." This does not mean that allegory is hereby offered as truth but rather simply as the subversion of or resistance to the fetish. As such, allegory loses "everything that was peculiar to it": it is taken from the world of dead things and arbitrary rule—that is, the world of the phantasmagoria, which is "cleared"—and becomes subject to a different calculus, that which is deemed "under the eyes of heaven." Finally allegory, in this sense, "denies" the void, that is to say, it denies the void that poses as truth. As a result of this, (human) intention "faithlessly leaps" toward this idea of resurrection.

What has been resurrected here, then, is not the symbol, the triumph of falseness over reality, but the allegory itself; it has been taken from the world of false appearances and reborn as a weapon that resists and unravels those appearances. The "faithless" leap that Benjamin evokes here is a leap away from falseness. It is not a leap toward a promised truth because that would mean simply reiterating what is being leapt away from (hence, it is faithless). To "persevere" in the face of this event, to be faithful to *this* resurrection, one that is neither a symbol or a fable but is only the renunciation of the promises of this world, is to sustain this practice, this unmaking and undoing; it is to cease the "contemplation of bones" and take up the "faithless . . . leap" itself as our central political and legal project.[54]

Thus, if we can amplify or alter the quality of the negative in Badiou, if we can make it less of a present negative and more of a failure to appear—as we find with Benjamin—we also redeem or alter the particular as such, that is to say the particular being that we are. We see, once again, a version of Benjamin's notion of "pure means" being enacted in this rereading of Badiou. In this case, the particular, once a platform in which the universal can appear (in all its negativity), becomes instead a place where the failure of the universal to appear becomes apparent to us. In the way that Badiou normally thinks about it, the particular is something of an instrument, a necessary means to an end (the universal). But if those ends have been removed once and for all (removed as a possibility, even as a hope), the means become bereft of this purpose; they become something other than they were. They still serve as a site for the negative revelation of the universal, but now that revelation has the quality of telling us that, effectively *there is no universal*, and so the means become in a sense, their own end, a dead end perhaps, wherein we are forced onto our own devices. The particular becomes less a site in which we must pick between false and true universals and more a site where we realize that we are well and truly on our own. After passing through the "acid bath" of the Second Commandment, our relationship to law in general is marked not so much by obedience as by responsibility. Badiou calls this relationship being "faithful," and so it is. But it is a peculiar sort of faith. It's the faithless faith that remains after the fetishes of law and mythic violence are reduced and exposed, the faith of the legal subject who sees law as a set of failed signs, now reduced and denuded to "pure means." What is critical, however, what I would seek to retain from Badiou, is the notion that such a practice, whether we call it of faith or faithlessness, itself becomes a way of life, a code of conduct that we can carry forth in our worldly activities. In this way, Badiou reminds us that an engagement with the negative can have very "positive" results (in a way that I will explore further in chapter 4).

Relatedly, and just as critically, Badiou shows us something important about how the Second Commandment might operate, how this one law can unmake all other laws. He does this in his consideration of what love does to law in his treatise on Saint Paul. As previously noted, two already cited passages in *Saint Paul* are particularly helpful in this regard. Recall, first of all, that Badiou tells us: "Under the condition of faith, of a declared conviction, love names a nonliteral law, one that gives to the faithful subject his consistency and effectuates the postevental truth in the world."[55]

Shortly afterward, in the same chapter, Badiou tells us (here, I am adding a bit more to the passage than what I cited earlier):

It is from this point of view that, for the Christian subject, love underwrites the return of a law that, although nonliteral, nonetheless functions as principle and consistency for the subjective energy initiated by the declaration of faith. For the new man, love is fulfillment of the break that he accomplishes with the law; it is law of the break with law, law of the truth of law. Conceived in this way, the law of love can even be supported by recollecting the content of the old law (Paul never misses an opportunity for an extension of political alliances), a content that, through love, is reduced to a single maxim that must not be carved into stone, on pain of relapsing into death, because it is entirely subordinated to the subjectivization by faith.[56]

Taking these two passages together, we see a helpful guide for our own exploration of the Second Commandment and its effects on the subject. Here, if we once again substitute the Second Commandment for what Badiou looks to—in this case the command to "love thy neighbor"—we can come to a better understanding of what this alteration of law does for us, recuperating many of Badiou's most critical insights in the process. The Second Commandment too can be considered "nonliteral" in the sense that it functions differently than other laws; it serves, not to manifest law (literally) but rather to unmake and challenge other iterations of law. To put this in a Benjaminian vernacular, I would say this law is "allegorical" rather than nonliteral. But critically, for Badiou, such a law, rather than being wholly destructive, actually "gives the faithful subject his consistency" and "effectuates the postevental truth in the world." In this way, the Second Commandment is the source of the very order and consistency that we might otherwise see it as undermining and erasing. What it erases is not consistency but rather the false pose of consistency inherent in mythic law; indeed, as I will argue further, the Second Commandment is what makes (actual) consistency possible in the first place.

Similarly, and perhaps most critically, when Badiou tells us that the law is the "law of the break with law, law of the truth of law," he is indicating the way that the Second Commandment remains a law even as it is a law that unmakes and exposes other laws. Here, saying that this law is the "truth of law" can be read in the Benjaminian sense as meaning: the truth is that there is no truth to law. And too, Badiou tells us (in the section I added to the earlier quote) that such a move does not entirely erase our relationship to the very laws that this law unmakes: "The law of [the Second Commandment, if I may be permitted this textual insertion] can even be supported by recollecting the content of the old law." Here we see that the old law does not disappear but becomes something else. It becomes reduced to "a single maxim that must not be carved into stone," that is, it becomes reduced almost to a pith, in such a way that it must not itself become another idol or dogma, a carving in stone (in chapter 5, I'll give a specific example of how the law can become a single maxim).

These passages then give us a strong indication of what the law becomes when it encounters the Second Commandment; it shows how law is not annihilated but radically altered and is always "entirely subordinated to the subjectivization by faith." In other words, the Second Commandment changes other laws so that they remain subject (along with the human practitioners of such laws) to the "faith" (or, better yet, faithlessness) that the commandment produces and makes possible. I will return to these insights periodically throughout this book in order to maintain the constellation between Benjamin and Badiou as well as the other thinkers that I treat here).

Reading Badiou and Benjamin together in constellation—and perhaps even Žižek too—makes all of them stronger and more effective thinkers. Thinking of each of them as advocating for an engagement with the Second Commandment fulfills, I think, the iconoclasm that each of them calls for.[57] Reading them in constellation does not give us the "truth" or the "universal" that Badiou calls for, but it surely does upend the false contenders for those titles that always threaten the pure negativity that Badiou seeks as much as anyone. And Badiou in particular, as I have argued above, offers us several critical ways to think about what law is and what it can be, when he is read through a Benjaminian lens.

In the following chapter, I will turn from a consideration of Badiou, universality, and ethics to a discussion of Kant, law, and the sublime. In this case too, I will seek to show how the iconoclasm that Kant promises and looks to is not ultimately delivered by his own version of law (nor by the operation of the sublime). Yet reading a different Kant, a Kant that lies in constellation with Benjamin, offers us a greater elaboration and appreciation of what a politics based on obeying only one law would look like (and, in the process, further helps to enrich our understanding of what a Benjaminian practice of politics, law—and ethics—would look like).

THREE

Raving with Reason

Kant and the Moral Law

The Sublime Passage and Kant's Retreat from Iconoclasm

In her analysis of Kant's treatment of Judaism, and in particular, Jewish iconoclasm, Susan Meld Shell notes a transformation (and in a very short period of time) between Kant's writing of the *Critique of Judgment* (1790) and his *Religion within the Limits of Reason Alone* (1792) (Henceforth *Religion*).[1] In the *Critique of Judgment*, Kant famously states (in a passage that I will return to at several points in this chapter): "Perhaps the most sublime passage in the Jewish Law is the commandment: Thou shalt not make unto thee any graven image."[2] According to Shell, in the two years that transpired between these writings, Kant moves from praising Judaism as being superior even to Christianity in forbidding any attempt to imagine the supersensual realm, to criticizing Judaism for just the opposite reason. She writes:

> In sum, the *Critique of Judgment* seems to lift Judaism, at least in its "ancient," radically iconoclastic form, above Christianity as historically practiced. This elevation, as we shall see, contrasts sharply with Kant's treatment of Judaism only two years later, when he presents it as unique among historic faiths in having no moral content at all. In Kant's later work, Judaism's radical rejection of all sensual mediation of the transcendent becomes a fatal defect rather than a strength.[3]

Shell argues that part of the reason for this change is a response to the reactionary politics (and theology) of Friedrich Wilhelm II. In such an atmosphere, Kant's seeming downplaying of religion—and especially of the Christian religion—became politically untenable. More pointedly, Shell argues that Kant came to despair of seeking change "from below" and began to look to the church and the state for solutions. Accordingly, Kant dropped his insistence that the concept of the moral law alone was enough grounds for the subject to contemplate the supersensual realm. Instead, he began to embrace a more sensuous (and indeed, idolatrous) view based, at least to some extent, on existing Christian practices. For Shell:

> Kant grants in *Religion* that the spiritual message of Christianity—pure moral religion—must first be sensualized, especially for purposes of popular education. Christianity is superior to all other known historical faiths in maximizing the effect of such sensualization at minimum spiritual cost. The key to Christianity's superiority, for Kant, lies not only in the moral teaching of the Gospels (which on a strict Kantian understanding must be accessible at all times and places); it lies even more in the figure of Jesus himself as an "ideal" that makes concrete the idea of moral holiness.[4]

For the purposes of this discussion, we can say that, in moving between these two books, Kant has gone from a stricter iconoclasm to a reluctant (and as we will see, only partial) turn back toward idolatry. His sense that Christianity is a relatively "safe" religion to engage with allows Kant, it seems, to risk the sensualization that he sees as coming inevitably with any move away from a pure engagement with moral law.

Shell tells us that for Kant, Christianity makes a far better vehicle for an iconoclastic project than Judaism. She notes that even Kant's initial praise for Jewish iconoclasm is tempered and partial. Shell writes that Kant's comments about the Second Commandment in the *Critique of Judgment* do not amount to a claim on Kant's part that Judaic law is the key for moving toward moral law. Even in that text, Shell argues, Kant's praise for Jewish iconoclasm is undermined by a conviction that Judaism is not truly a moral religion:

> Adapting Spinoza's views as to the wholly political character of biblical legislation, Kant concluded that the "ethical" aspect of Judaism had also vanished with the destruction of the temple. As with Hobbes, the Jewish state is the prototype of a "merely" juridical

condition, without ethical content or motivation. The Jewish notion that one can obey the law without improving morally makes it a "pure" cult, without intrinsic moral content. The sublimity of Judaism in its ethical period consisted wholly in its iconoclasm rather than in any alleged moral universalism.[5]

Yet, if we are to take the value of Kant's iconoclasm seriously—if, that is, we want to read him in constellation with Benjamin—we need to rethink the disconnect Shell perceives (or at least attributes to Kant) between the sublimity of Jewish iconoclasm on the one hand and the promulgation of the moral law on the other. In Shell's rendering of Kant, it seems that Jewish iconoclasm is only appreciated as an aesthetic approach to the moral law rather than any actual engagement with it. Yet, from a Benjaminian perspective, the question of iconoclasm is not a purely aesthetic issue. As we have seen in the previous chapters, the relationship between iconoclasm and law is fundamental, and thus we need to take Kant's appreciation for the Second Commandment seriously precisely as a way to think further about moral law itself.

In this chapter, therefore, I intend to read Kant in constellation (or perhaps in conspiracy) with Benjamin. As in the previous chapter on Badiou, I seek to align these two very disparate thinkers for the purposes of mutual illumination.[6] In thinking about this alignment, we initially see a great number of both similarities and differences. Both thinkers embrace iconoclasm even as they are interested in questions of truth (as is the case with Badiou as well). Both engage in thinking about a realm that is unavailable to us as human beings. For Kant this realm is the noumenal, a notion of pure, moral law that we can only intuit. For Benjamin, this realm is heaven, the realm of God and divine law. And, for both thinkers, the world that we live in is a distortion, one that forever threatens to separate us from truth and law. Yet it is here that the differences between these thinkers announce themselves. For Kant, the distorting world is the material world itself. For Benjamin, it is the distortion of representation that leads us to the falseness that he calls the phantasmagoria. For Kant, the only way to anticipate the noumenal is via a rejection of the empirical world that surrounds us (and of which our own bodies are a part). For Benjamin, it is quite the opposite; it is only by aligning ourselves with the material world, with the way that the objects of the world defy the representations that we project onto them, that we can escape the distortions of the phantasmagoria; only thus can we escape the ways in which our own intentions (our "minds") are utterly formed and compromised by fetishism.

These thinkers also differ in terms of their respective understandings of the accessibility of the supersensual realm. For Kant, we can engage in acts of discernment via the operation of the categorical imperative that allows us to anticipate the moral law even as we have no real access to it. For Benjamin, any assumption on our part of what the law might be is invariably an idol, a false projection.

Despite these deep differences, I will try to reconcile these thinkers by taking Kant very seriously in his invocation of the Second Commandment and, in doing so, bring that consideration front and center in his treatment of law more generally. This chapter seeks to answer a single question: What happens to Kant when we put the Second Commandment over and above all other questions of law? As we will see, to do so transposes Kant; it brings out a radical potential in him that has been spotted by thinkers ranging from Lyotard to Lacan to Zupančič.[7] Perhaps we can say that to read Kant along Benjaminian lines serves to recuperate Kant even from his own compromises with idolatry (or at least his retreat from iconoclasm), to subject him once again to a purifying "acid bath" of Benjaminian iconoclasm and see what emerges.[8]

In engaging with these questions, I will be focusing primarily on the two aforementioned texts, Kant's *Religion* and his *Critique of Judgment*. The (slightly) later *Religion* will be the primary focus of this discussion because it deals with the compromises Shell suggests that Kant makes vis-à-vis idolatry. Yet, ultimately, I will argue that this spirit of compromise is evident even in the *Critique of Judgment*. Reading the two texts side by side allows us to see Kant's compromises more clearly: by spotting the more highly visible forms of compromise in *Religion*, we can also see the same, albeit more subtle, phenomenon in the *Critique of Judgment* (and, in particular, in his concept of the sublime). Toward the end of this chapter, I will begin reading Kant through a Benjaminian lens; that is, I will be amplifying Kant's iconoclasm in order to bring him into constellation with Benjamin. To some extent, I will be doing this by applying to Kant his own suggestions in *Religion* for how to read Scripture, that is, his argument that one should not read Scripture literally and that, furthermore, one can and should "force" the text in certain directions.

The crux of my argument will be that, when read via Benjamin, Kant's apparent move to compromise his iconoclasm in *Religion* is, however paradoxically, also a move *toward* Benjamin. This can be explained by the fact that in approaching the sensual realm as he does, Kant is also moving toward a relationship with objects that aligns him to some extent with Benjamin's own project. From a Kantian perspective, the move in *Reli-*

gion is a shift away from iconoclasm, yet from a Benjaminian perspective it also abandons an imagined relationship with the noumenal (one that I will argue produces nothing but idolatry). In this way, such an attitude possibly allows Kant a new relationship with the material world. Thus by shifting perspectives from a Kantian to a Benjaminian view (i.e., by reading them in constellation, with Benjamin as the brighter star) we can rearticulate what Kant is doing in ways that enhance his own iconoclasm. Ultimately, I seek to bring about this alignment in order to help us think more about Benjamin's own approach to law, especially in terms of Kant's critical distinction between statutory laws and true, moral (i.e., nonstatutory) laws. To help in my reinterpretation of Kant, I will enlist a reading of him by Peter Fenves that suggests that Kant may be more aligned with Benjamin than we ordinarily think and that, in a sense, seeing him through a Benjaminian lens is reading him in accordance with his own resistance to some of the implications of his texts (as Fenves suggests).

The Kantian Turn to Religion: A Sensible Move

Let me begin this inquiry, then, by engaging in a deeper examination of the question of Kant's seeming turn away from a more pure iconoclasm as demonstrated in *Religion*. We can see Kant's embracing of ordinary religion, however partial, in this passage:

> The concept of a divine will, determined according to pure moral laws alone, allows us to think of only *one* religion which is purely moral, as it did of only *one* God. But if we admit statutory laws of such a will and make religion consist of our obedience to them, knowledge of such laws is possible not through our own reason alone but only through revelation, which be it given publicly or to each individual in secret, would have to be an *historical* and not a *pure rational* faith in order to be propagated among men by tradition or writ. And even admitting divine statutory laws (laws which do not in themselves appear to us as obligatory but can be known as such only when taken as the revelation of God's will), pure *moral* legislation, through which the will of God is primordially engraved in our hearts, is not only the ineluctable condition of all true religion whatsoever but is also that which really constitutes such religion; statutory religion can merely comprise the means to its furtherance and spread.[9]

By "statutory law," Kant means something akin to positive law (the subject of the following chapter). This is a law that is merely asserted or posited as far as human beings are concerned. Such a law is in contrast to nonstatutory laws (to be discussed further at the end of this chapter), wherein their relationship to the moral law is evident and discernible by reason. Kant's distinction between *historical* and *pure rational* faith similarly involves the difference between a religion based on revelation—on events that were reported to be true (but whose actual truth cannot be known)—versus a religion based on truths that can be derived by reason alone. The former kinds of truths ultimately depend on taking someone's word for a thing's having happened. Thus even the advent of the Ten Commandments is, for Kant, a revealed, historical truth because the Israelites had to take Moses's word for what happened on Mount Sinai (and even if all the Israelites had seen God give Moses the laws, we, later readers of the Bible, would still have to take their account on faith). Although Kant would prefer that all human beings look to themselves for truths, he allows that even a "statutory religion"—a religion that is based on revelation rather than reason— can "comprise [albeit "merely"] the means to [true religion's] furtherance and spread."

For Kant, temporally speaking, statutory religion is generally prior to true religion:

> In men's striving towards an ethical commonwealth, ecclesiastical faith [another term Kant uses for statutory religion] thus naturally precedes pure religious faith; *temples* (buildings consecrated to the public worship of God) were before *churches* (meeting places for the instruction and quickening of moral dispositions), *priests* (consecrated stewards of pious rites) before *divines* (teachers of the purely moral religion); and for the most part they still are first in the rank and value ascribed to them by the great mass of people.[10]

Kant inserts a footnote in the first sentence right after he uses the word "precedes" to say that "morally, this order ought to be reversed."[11] Thus, in history, in the humanly derived and interpreted narration of the world, we understand revealed and statutory faith as prior, but in moral terms things are—and must be—the other way around.

The temporal primacy of revealed and historical religion is due to human weakness and our need for sensible evidence for our belief (despite the fact that for Kant, the sensible can never be proven):

Because of the natural need and desire of all men for something *sensibly tenable*, and for a confirmation of some sort from experience of the highest concepts and grounds of reason (a need which really must be taken into account when the universal *dissemination* of a faith is contemplated), some historical ecclesiastical faith or other, usually to be found at hand, must be utilized.[12]

Kant also tells us that "popular faith . . . cannot be neglected, because no doctrine based on reason alone seems to the people qualified to serve as an unchangeable norm. They demand divine revelation, and hence also an historical certification of its authority through the tracing back of its origin."[13] Recall Shell's claim that Kant turns to popular religion because of his disappointing realization that human beings need some sort of intermediary in order to make the reign of reason possible. The notion of the Kingdom of God is a path, for Kant, toward the possibility (at least as an ideal) of a Kingdom of Ends.[14]

Thus, although we begin with the sensible, as we have already seen, Kant's desire is that statutory religion serve as the basis or building block of true religion (the so-called revelations being themselves discarded in the process). Kant gives us some evidence about how this could work:

If such an empirical faith, which chance, it would seem, has tossed into our hands, is to be united with the basis of a moral faith (be the first an end or merely a means), an exposition of the revelation which has come into our possession is required, that is, a thoroughgoing interpretation of it in a sense agreeing with the universal practical rules of a religion of pure reason.[15]

Thus a given religion, insofar as it conforms to the moral laws that are the basis of true religion, can advance the human being on a moral journey because "the final purpose even of reading these holy scriptures, or of investigating their content, is to make men better."[16] Kant tells us that the historical element of this religion is "indifferent"; it is not the content of religion but its form that makes it an appropriate basis for producing moral virtue.[17]

As we have already seen, for Kant, of all the worldly religions, Christianity is best suited for this purpose. In practice, as also noted, this means he asserts Christianity at the expense of Judaism. Kant repeatedly argues against the idea that Judaism constitutes the foundation for Christianity.[18]

Kant asserts (as Shell notes) that Judaism is a moribund, merely statutory, religion, whereas Christianity has within it the possibility of moving away from the religion per se and toward the moral law it suggests in us. He tells us further:

> The proof that Judaism has not allowed its organization to become religious is clear. *First*, all its commands are of the kind which a political organization can insist upon and lay down as coercive laws, since they relate merely to external acts; and although the Ten Commandments are, to the eye of reason, valid as ethical commands even had they not been given publicly, yet in that legislation they are not so prescribed as to induce obedience by laying requirements upon the *moral disposition* (Christianity later placed its main emphasis here).[19]

In a direct refutation of his appreciation for the Jewish Second Commandment written two years earlier, Kant writes in *Religion* that "we should not rate too highly the fact that this people [i.e., the Jews] set up, as universal Ruler of the world, a one and only God who could be represented through no visible image."[20] More generally, Kant announces a definitive break (if that is what this is) with Judaism: "A kingdom of God is represented not according to a particular covenant (i.e. not Messianic) [as with Judaism] but *moral* (knowable through unassisted reason). The former . . . had to draw its proofs from history."[21]

Even so, for Kant, Christianity is itself highly problematic from the perspective of moral truth. He tells us that "the Christian faith as a *learned* faith, relies upon history and so far as erudition (objectively) constitutes its foundation, it is not in itself a *free faith*. . . or one which is deduced from insight into adequate theoretical proofs."[22] In *Religion*, Kant struggles mightily against the idea, for example, that good works and public displays of devotion will please God and lead to salvation. For Kant, when what is "revealed . . . is to precede religion" (with "precede" here having the moral rather than historical sense), what results is a *"pseudo-service,"* that is, an apparent duty to God that is actually nothing of the kind.[23]

Kant summarizes the danger of this kind of idolatry:

> Anthropomorphism, scarcely to be avoided by men in the theoretical representation of God and His being, but yet harmless enough (so long as it does not influence concepts of duty) is highly dangerous in connection with our practical relation to His will, and even

for our morality; for here *we create a God for ourselves*, and we create Him in the form in which we believe we shall be able most easily to win Him over to our advantage and ourselves escape from the wearisome uninterrupted effort of working upon the innermost part of our moral disposition.[24]

Kant explicitly uses the language of fetishism and idolatry quite often, especially toward the end of *Religion* as he contends with the dangers of revealed faith (he speaks, for example of a "fetish faith").[25] Not unlike Badiou, Kant appreciates a Christianity that is almost devoid of content. Yet, at the same time, he writes off what for Badiou is the central event (even if he sees it as "only" a fable) of the faith: the Crucifixion and Resurrection of Christ. Speaking of these occurrences, Kant writes that they "took place before the eyes only of his intimates [and therefore] cannot be used in the interest of religion within the limits of reason alone without doing violence to their historical valuation."[26] He adds that "this . . . added sequel [i.e., the Resurrection] is, indeed, very well suited to man's mode of sensuous representation but . . . is most burdensome to reason in its faith regarding the future."[27] Yet more dangerous, for Kant there is a possibility that in reading about the "body" of Christ, a sense of material embodiment more generally will affect the reader. Still discussing the case of Christ's Crucifixion, Kant writes:

> Taken literally [the Crucifixion] involves a concept *i.e.*, of the materiality of all worldly beings. . . . This concept involves both the *materialism of personality* in men (psychological materialism), which asserts that a personality can exist only as always conditioned by the same *body*, as well as the *materialism of necessary existence in a world*, a world which, according to the principle, must be *spatial* (cosmological materialism).[28]

In this way, to focus too much on the reality of an event, a thing or a text, leads us away from the moral possibilities inherent in our reading of the phenomena. It draws us into a limiting (and idolatrous) conception of truth as requiring both a bodily and a spatial existence (and here, Kant seems to anticipate Badiou's own arguments about the reality of the Resurrection minus the latter's appreciation for the radical potential of its nonoccurrence). Here we can see how the dogmas of Christianity can come to compete with, and even replace, the kinds of moral contemplations that Kant desires for Christianity to instill in us.

Reading with Kant: The Sublime Analogy

The question to ask at this point is what can be done about this situation: What does Kant counsel his readers to do about the constant (and, seemingly, unavoidable) threat of idolatry given the necessity (or Kant's perceived necessity) of engaging with statutory religion? We get a better sense of Kant's strategy when he suggests that when it comes to representation, we must subject our reading to a criterion that measures the degree of its success in evoking the moral law. In this way, we can (if not safely, than at least in a way that minimizes our danger of corruption) engage even with apparent idolatry as long as we have some means to ascertain our true purpose and the degree to which it is being realized (or not). In a footnote that he appends to an already cited passage wherein we run a danger of creating our own God, Kant adds:

> Though it does indeed sound dangerous, it is in no way reprehensible to say that every man *creates a God* for himself, nay, must make himself such a God according to moral concepts . . . in order to honor in Him *the One who created him.* For in whatever manner a being has been made known to him by another and described as God, yea, even if such a being had appeared to him (if this is possible), he must first of all compare this representation with his ideal in order to judge whether he is entitled to regard it and to honor it as a divinity. Hence there can be no religion springing from revelation alone, i.e. without *first* positing that concept, in its purity, as a touchstone. Without this all reverence for God would be *idolatry.*[29]

We see here that for Kant *even if* the revelation or physical manifestation of truth is in fact true, we must suspend that assumption and check the empirical phenomenon against our own interior moral processes. For Kant (in a way that is very consistent with his philosophy—and by extension, his theology—more generally), to take the physical world at face value is to engage in idolatry, a false mode of representation that renders a "pseudo-service" to God. We must, in effect, suspend the question of whether what we are reading is true or false as such and look instead to the effect that such a reading has on our relationship to moral law.

Throughout *Religion*, Kant both describes and models a method of reading wherein the representation is not taken literally but rather as a suggestion, one that might lead the reader to the apperception, if only by negative example, of moral law (although the experience of the moral law can have "positive" aspects as well). Discussing this specifically in the language of reading, Kant writes:

> Frequently [a moral] interpretation may, in the light of the text (of the revelation), appear forced—it may often really be forced; and yet if the text can possibly support it, it must be preferred to a literal interpretation which either contains nothing at all [helpful] to morality or else actually works counter to moral incentives.[30]

Kant furnishes an example of this kind of reading in a footnote to this passage where he considers a biblical selection from Psalm 59:11–16 that seems to be "a *prayer* for *revenge*," one that is justified and sanctified by God.[31] Kant asks "whether morality should be expounded according to the Bible or whether the Bible should not rather be expounded according to morality."[32] He speculates that the enemies that are referred to in that and related passages might be "spiritual enemies" and says that if "this cannot be managed, I shall rather have it that this passage is not to be understood in a moral sense at all but only as applying to the relation in which the Jews conceived themselves to stand to God as their political regent."[33] In other words, when reading Scripture, we are entitled, even required, to read against the text, to rearticulate those parts of the text that lead us toward the moral law. If we cannot sustain such a reading, we are entitled to jettison that piece of text as having no validity at all (from a moral perspective).

A perhaps even clearer example of Kant's method of reading can be seen in another footnote where Kant considers the question of gravity. Although he argues that the causes of gravity remain a mystery, Kant tells us that gravity itself, its tangible reality,

> is no mystery but can be made public to all, for its *law* is adequately known. When Newton represents it as similar to divine omnipresence in the [world of] appearance . . . . this is not an attempt to explain it (for the existence of God in space involves a contradiction), but *a sublime analogy* which has regard solely to the union of corporeal beings with a world-whole, an incorporeal cause being here attributed to this union. The same result would follow upon an attempt to comprehend the self-sufficing principle of the union of rational beings in the world into an ethical state, and to explain this in terms of that principle. All we know is the duty which draws us toward such a union; the possibility of the achievement held in

view when we obey that duty lies wholly beyond the limits of our insight.[34]

In this concept of "a sublime analogy," we get a clearer sense of how Kant would have us read more generally. It is in the failure to perfectly grasp what the analogy is telling us (hence it is "sublime") that we come to avoid the trappings of phenomena, the world of bodies and space. The sublime, which I will discuss in more detail shortly, is that experience of representational failure which releases us from our captivity to materiality; such an experience tells us that we do not know and we do not understand even as the operation of law remains intact and requires our response. The sublime feeling, this legible failure of knowledge, is itself a signpost, for Kant, of a higher, supersensible truth of which we otherwise cannot be aware.

Forcing the Text

For Kant, then, reading in this way is a model for a larger training in how to use the empirical world as a springboard for contemplating the moral law without being compromised by material phenomena. As we have seen, a phenomenon can be judged, reread, and possibly discarded, depending on the degree to which it serves the moral law (or not).[35] Kant acknowledges, as we have seen too, that such a reading may be "forced," but this forcing is only indicative of the moral law operating through us. Kant's devotion to a text, then (or, by extension, to any phenomenon), is partial at best. Indeed, at one point he argues:

> A holy book arouses the greatest respect even among those (indeed, most of all among those) who do not read it, or at least those who can form no coherent religious concept there-from.[36]

Yet, despite such sentiments, it is not the case that Kant has no interest in or allegiance to these texts. He argues, for example, that without these texts, there would have been no possibility for (potentially) morality-producing faiths to maintain themselves. Somehow the (relative) constancy of the written word preserves a marker for the kinds of transcendent readings that Kant is calling for, a necessary basis to be overcome by a sublime reading (very much in keeping with his larger conception of the sublime).

Such markers can be used to oppose various antimoral uses of the text themselves (depending on who is doing the interpreting and what kind of position of power that person is in). Immediately following the sentence just cited, Kant writes:

> The most sophistical reasoning avails nothing in the face of the decisive assertion, which beats down every objection: *Thus it is written.* It is for this reason that the passages in [the Bible] which are to lay down an article of faith are called simply *texts.* The appointed expositors of such a scripture are themselves, by virtue of their occupation, like unto consecrated persons.[37]

Here, the physicality of the text can be used as a way to insist on *a* meaning, and the main concern then becomes how we read, what meaning we extract from the text (i.e., one that is idolatrous or not). With this permission to engage in exegesis that freely disassociates itself from the text—even as it bases itself entirely on the text's demand for meaning—Kant has put a weapon into the hands of his readers (a weapon to counter the myriad misreadings by which texts are normally determined). We could call this Kant's method of purposive misreading, or moral misreading (however paradoxical this may seem).

While this method of reading may seem antithetical to a philosopher who insists on ends versus means, on moral truth at all times, for Kant, this represents a kind of grand compromise:

> If this very faith . . . were to be regarded not merely as a representation of a practical idea but as a faith which is to describe what God is in Himself, it would be a mystery transcending all human concepts, and hence a mystery of revelation, unsuited to man's power of comprehension; in this account, therefore, we can declare it to be such. Faith in it, regarded as an extension of the theoretical knowledge of the divine nature, would be merely the acknowledgement of a symbol of ecclesiastical faith which is quite incomprehensible to men or which, if they think they can understand it, would be anthropomorphic, and therefore nothing whatever would be accomplished for moral betterment. Only that which, in a practical context, can be thoroughly understood and comprehended, but which, taken theologically . . . transcends all our concepts, is a mystery (in one respect) and can yet (in another) be revealed.[38]

Thus this form of failed or sublime representation is the only way for (most or perhaps all) human beings to be able to apprehend the divine.

Though it risks (and even flirts with) idolatry, the alternatives are either a wholly abstract incomprehensibility or a totally idolatrous misreading; either way, God—and through God, the moral law—would not be apprehended.

A fuller comparison between Kant and Benjamin's respective reading methods will be engaged with shortly. For now, let me simply denote that their formal reading models are diametrically opposed. Whereas Kant will force the text from an ideal perspective, overcoming the empirical text with the power of the moral law (even while basing such a reading on the physical fact of the text), for Benjamin, it is just the opposite; our moral (and hence, mythic) beliefs are overcome by forcing the text in the direction of the "mere" letters and figures. In so doing, the reader allows the resistance to idolatry inherent in letters and pages to subvert and prevent her own allegiance to those idols. In this way the reader surrenders some of what she thought was her agency over the text. Aligning herself with the text as such, she can perhaps read the text in a different, nonidolatrous way; it is not the text but the reader herself who is "forced" away from idolatry in Benjamin's case.

Despite the fact that Kant and Benjamin look in diametrically opposed directions for any sense (or perhaps, more accurately, absence) of truth, for both readers the point of reading and interpreting is the same: to experience the *failure* of representation. As I will argue, Benjamin's failure is more absolute, more irrevocable than Kant's (just as was the case with Badiou, and as will be the case with Hart) and so his iconoclasm is more definitive as well (perhaps explaining why with Benjamin, unlike Kant, there is no instance of compromising with idolatry; when Benjamin gets interested in idolatry it is always for the purpose of subverting it from within, not for using it as a springboard to something else). In order to get a better sense of the differences between these two styles of failure, we must first spend some time examining perhaps the greatest, best example of representational failure in Kant's work, namely his concept of the sublime in the *Critique of Judgment*.

The Sublime and the Second Commandment

As we have seen, in the *Critique of Judgment*, Kant famously states: "Perhaps the most sublime passage in the Jewish Law is the commandment: Thou shalt not make unto thee any graven image, or any likeness of anything that is in heaven or earth, or under the earth etc."[39] He goes on to write:

This commandment alone can explain the enthusiasm that the Jewish people in its civilized era felt for its religion when it compared itself with other peoples, or can explain the pride that Islam inspires.[40]

In addition, Kant further argues that the Second Commandment serves as the correct basis for, or a parallel to, the experience of the higher, moral law:

> The same holds also for our presentation of the moral law, and for the predisposition within us for morality. It is indeed a mistake to worry that depriving this presentation of whatever could commend it to the senses will result in its carrying with it no more than a cold and lifeless approval without any moving force or emotion. It is exactly the other way round. For once the senses no longer see anything before them, while yet the unmistakable and indelible idea of morality remains, one would sooner need to temper the momentum of an unbounded imagination so as to keep it from rising to the level of enthusiasm, than to seek to support these ideas with images and childish devices for fear that they would otherwise be powerless.[41]

This is the summit of Kant's iconoclasm. It would appear that here he argues against even the need for an empirical basis, the transcendence of which leads to an encounter (of sorts) with the moral law. But in fact, by his use of the term "sublime," we see that this is not quite the case. The sublime experience Kant looks for begins with an object or set of objects. Generally speaking, it could be a text, an image, a mountain range, an ocean, the stars at night, but in this instance—and very critically for our purposes—it is a law. Based on our apprehension of that object, the inability of the mind to grasp what it sees produces a pleasing sense of absence.[42] When Kant writes that "once the senses no longer see anything before them," he is alerting us to the temporal progression of the sublime. We see something and then we no longer do. That absence informs us of a greater absence still, that of the moral law itself. This is a more sophisticated version of the kinds of entanglements with Christian religion that are the subject of *Religion*. But the operation is essentially the same. The solution to the unfathomability of the moral law is to give us an experience of that unfathomability precisely by erasing or removing from our sight the tangible and the material; the representation of law becomes an absence.

Kant reinforces this view when he describes the sublime experience more generally. He tells us, for example, that whereas our admiration for beauty may constitute a positive pleasure, "the liking for the sublime contains not so much a positive pleasure as rather admiration and respect, and so should be called a negative pleasure."[43]

In describing the kinds of liking or pleasure that we receive from experiencing the sublime, Kant tells us that "this liking is by no means a liking for the object (since that may be formless), but rather a liking for the expansion of the imagination itself" (although to trigger our experience, the object must be somehow sublime in the first place so it is not irrelevant to the experience).[44] Kant goes on to say of this:

> [What happens is that] our imagination strives to progress toward infinity, while our reason demands absolute totality as the real idea, and so [the imagination,] our power of estimating the magnitude of things in the world of sense, is inadequate to that idea. Yet this inadequacy itself is the arousal in us of the feeling that we have within us a supersensible power. . . . [Thus, the sublime] *is what even to be able to think proves that the mind has a power surpassing any standard of sense.*[45]

For Kant, it is critical that this inadequacy remain on the level of an aesthetic experience. Only an aesthetic experience allows us to "perceive the inadequacy of the imagination."[46] Otherwise, we might imagine that we *are* seeing a bounded limitation (as in the case of the mathematical estimation of magnitude where "the imagination is equal to the task of providing, for any object, a measure that will suffice for this estimation, because the understanding's numerical concepts can be used in a progression").[47]

And yet, even as a purely aesthetic and emotional experience, the encounter with the sublime produces an engagement with reason. For Kant, the aesthetic experience of the sublime "refers the imagination to *reason* so that it will harmonize subjectively with reason's *ideas* (which ideas they are is indeterminate)."[48] In other words, in producing a sense of an inadequacy to judge, a sense of limitlessness, reason emerges to produce a kind of response after all in the form of the harmony we perceive between the abstract concepts of reason as ideas and our own subjective experience.[49]

For Kant a sublime experience has nothing to do with the object and everything to do with the mind. He tells us that through this encounter the mind "can come to feel its own sublimity, which lies in its vocation and elevates it even above nature."[50] Kant goes on to write that the sublime is "an object (of nature) *the presentation of which determines the mind to think of nature's inability to an exhibition of ideas.*"⁵¹ Thus, through our engagement with the sublime, we see how certain objects can undermine our habitual reliance on empirical things. It also produces a concomitant realization that the mind is capable of apprehending far more than the natural world within which it is suspended. Here the objects of the world—at least the sublime ones—help undo our reliance on the material, purportedly objective world.⁵²

Raving with Reason

For Kant, the effects of an encounter with the sublime are not limited to ideas about the mind and moral law; they have a theological implication as well. In an argument that will anticipate what he says in *Religion*, Kant tells us in the *Critique of Judgment* that in terms of our religious response to the sublime, whereas our experience of terrifying natural phenomena might—and usually does—reduce us to a state of groveling inadequacy, if the subject "is conscious that his attitude is sincere and pleasing to God . . . these effects of might serve to arouse in him the idea of God's sublimity, insofar as he recognizes in his own attitude a sublimity that conforms to God's will."⁵³

Thus the sublime can even lead us to an understanding about God. What is striking about this view is that, unlike in *Religion*, in the *Critique of Judgment*, such talk is not accompanied by a lengthy warning on the dangers of idolatry, at least not to the same extent. Immediately after discussing the sublimity of the Second Commandment, Kant tells us:

> This pure, elevating, and merely negative exhibition of morality involves no danger of *fanaticism*, which is the *delusion of wanting to see something beyond all bounds of sensibility*, i.e. of dreaming according to principles (raving with reason). The exhibition avoids fanaticism precisely because it is merely negative. For *the idea of freedom is inscrutable* and thereby precludes all positive exhibition whatever; but the moral law in itself can sufficiently and originally determine us, so that it does not even permit us to cast about for some additional determining basis.⁵⁴

Here the operation of the sublime itself seems to serve as a form of protection against the kinds of idolatry that Kant worries about in *Religion*. If we understand the sublime experience as a wholly negative event, there cannot be a "something" to see, no basis for a delusion, nothing to want. The sublime's mental subtraction of the object seems to save us, then, from treating that object as a fetish or idol.

At the same time, the very idea of "raving with reason," even if presented as a thing to avoid, suggests the potential dangers of such an approach. If reason itself does not guarantee a direct relationship to moral truth but can be contaminated by the empirical world it treats with (that is to say if it can be "raving"), then it seems that Kant's safeguard against idolatry, a reliance on pure negativity, is not as unproblematic as seems at first glance; perhaps the "delusion of wanting to see" is itself a reflection of the delusion that one is no longer "seeing" the object that begins the sublime experience in the first place, the sense of a pure negativity that is not, perhaps, quite so pure—or negative—after all.

The question to raise at this point is this: given that reason can still be subject to contamination (to "dreaming according to principles" or "raving with reason"), is it possible that Kant's depiction of the sublime is not as absolutely opposed to the positive and the idolatrous as Kant claims it to be?

My short answer to this question is yes. To make this answer clearer, let me turn to a comparison between Kant's and Benjamin's respective understandings of reading and engaging with representation. The potential dangers in Kant's method become much more evident when they are seen against the deeper negativity that Benjamin advocates in his own considerations.

Beyond Beauty

Benjamin's approach to reading as a mode of failure, that is, his own version of the sublime, can be seen in his notion of allegory, a subject already touched on in previous chapters. In his *Origin of German Tragic Drama*, Benjamin quite famously contrasts the allegorical and the symbolic. He tells us that "as a symbolic construct, the beautiful is supposed to merge with the divine in an unbroken whole."[55] Here the symbol promises access to the eternal. Yet Benjamin warns us, directly citing Kant in this case, that such a promise is not realized:

But once the ethical subject has become absorbed in the individual, then no rigorism—not even Kantian rigorism—can save it and preserve its masculine profile. Its heart is lost in the beautiful soul.[56]

In other words, the promise of a redemptive merger with the divine leads to the subject's unmaking (the loss of its "masculine profile"). Even a "Kantian rigorism" is not enough to keep such a merger from becoming something other than it is intended to be, not a glimpse of the divine but a muddle, a "heart . . . lost in the beautiful soul."

For Benjamin, the allegorical, by contrast, is "non-conceptual, profound, and bitter." It is serves as a counterweight to the symbolic.[57] Benjamin writes that allegory points not to perfection and truth but to death, rot, and corpses, to mundanely physical objects that exist (and decay and cease) in time, although, as we have already seen, not in an unredeemable manner. Speaking specifically of the kinds of allegorical images created by the dramatists of the Baroque plays that are the subject of the *Origin*, Benjamin tells us:

> The allegorical physiognomy of the nature-history, which is put on stage in the *Trauerspiel* [mourning plays] is present in reality in the form of the ruin. . . . And in this guise history does not assume the form of the process of an eternal life so much as that of irresistible decay. Allegory therefore declares itself to be beyond beauty. Allegories are, in the realm of thoughts, what ruins are in the realm of things. This explains the Baroque cult of the ruin.[58]

Here we see that the allegorical is the opposite of (or antidote to) the symbolic in some important senses. It is "beyond beauty" but not in the same way that the sublime is. In fact, Benjamin's "beyond" lies in a direction diametrically opposed to Kant's.[59] Whereas Kant's sublime lies beyond beauty in the sense of stretching toward the supersensible, Benjamin's beyond lies the other way, toward the ordinary and all too sensible. Such a beyond leads us to a world of failed representation, ruins, and mere objects that decay and pass into dust (as already discussed in previous chapters and in other volumes of this trilogy).

As noted, this turn toward decay and ruin is not for the sake of sheer nihilism. Benjamin tells us that

> if it is in death that the spirit becomes free, in a manner of spirits, it is not until then that the body comes properly into its own. For this much is self-evident: the allegorization of the physis can only be carried through in all its vigour in respect of the corpse. And the characters of the *Trauerspiel* die, because it is only thus, as corpses, that they can enter into the homeland of allegory. It is not for the sake of immortality that they meet their end but for the sake of the corpse.[60]

Here we begin to see a critical difference between Benjamin and Kant. Unlike the sublime experience, the allegorical does not reach for a glimpse of the eternal, even in an entirely negative fashion. Once again—as we saw in the previous chapter—it does quite the opposite; it seeks to eliminate the eternal entirely. It is only when the "spirit is freed from the body" that the body itself is free for its own sake. In other words, when the illusion of truth (the spirit) is eliminated, then, and only then, can we see a body for what it is. The corpse is the body without any projections. It is empty, an abandoned ruin; it is a failed sign of the beautiful being or soul it seeks to represent. Only as such does the body "come into its own." And it is only this site, denuded of any possibility of higher meaning (thus, once again, the very opposite of the symbol), that is safe, at least relatively, from various projections of the eternal, all of which are idolatrous.

Thus the sense of failure here is much keener with Benjamin than with Kant. It is not merely the failure of our ability to understand or grasp the supersensible that we get from allegory; it is a larger sense of failure, of the failure to be perfect, true, immortal, and the like, the failure *even to apprehend* anything more than what we have before us. The allegory shows us exactly what we are rather than all that we cannot be. In this way, Benjamin's concept of allegory returns us to ourselves (albeit an impoverished and diminished self vis-à-vis what the symbol promises).

At the same time, for all of this, the allegorical is not unrelated to the divine, as we have seen. Benjamin tells us that "a critical understanding of the *Trauerspiel*, in its extreme, allegorical form, is possible only from the higher domain of theology" (although he also tells us, contrary to Kant, that it is a "historical theology").[61] For Benjamin, allegory is a response to the fall of Adam (the larger theological implications of this event for Benjamin have already been discussed). Echoing his sentiments in "On Language as Such and on the Language of Man," in the *Origin of German Tragic Drama* Benjamin interprets the ruin of the world (that is, the reality of ruin that allegory embodies and exposes) as a state of silent mournfulness for all that has been lost:

> Because it is mute, fallen nature mourns. But the converse of this statement leads even deeper into the essence of nature: its mournfulness makes it become mute. In all mourning there is a tendency to silence, and this infinitely more than inability or reluctance to communicate. The mournful has the feeling that it is known comprehensively by the unknowable. To be named—even if the name-giver is god-like and saintly—perhaps always brings with it a presentiment of mourning. But how much more so not to be named, only to

be read, to be read uncertainly by the allegorist, and to have become highly significant thanks only to him.[62]

Here we see that the absence of truth that we also saw in Kant's sublime has a different quality for Benjamin. The lack that is to be perceived in the world is not merely nothingness, it is a silence. It reflects what we have lost, a mournful emptiness that reflects a state of truth that once existed but is no more.

This also gives us a bit more insight into the way Benjamin would have us "read" the world around us. The idea that as a corpse the body "comes into its own" does not in fact mean that the body is bereft of divine meaning, but rather that that meaning is now lost to us. This is not Kant's sublime where the truth twinkles alluringly just beyond our capacity to understand. This truth is entirely lost to us, or rather, we can see its effects, but those effects lie in indecipherable ruins, the stuff of allegory. Thus, for Benjamin, the allegorical simultaneously denudes the world of its "spirits" (its phantasms) even as it connects us to greater truth—albeit only in the form of mourning, bitterness, and guilt.[63]

Nonetheless, for Benjamin, to think of allegory only as a purely bleak and negative force is to miss its true power:

As those who lose their footing turn somersaults in their fall, so would the allegorical intention fall from emblem to emblem down into the dizziness of its bottomless depths, were it not that, even in the most extreme of them, it had so to turn about that all its darkness, vainglory, and godlessness seems to be nothing but self-delusion. For it is to misunderstand the allegorical entirely if we make a distinction between the store of images, in which this about-turn into salvation and redemption takes place, and that grim store which signifies death and damnation. For it is precisely visions of the frenzy of destruction, in which all earthly things collapse into a heap of ruins, which reveal the limits set upon allegorical contemplation, rather than its ideal quality.[64]

We see here that the exposure of allegory and all of its seeming negativity as being itself a kind of delusion serves to give allegory its truly subversive power. As a form of representation, allegory is as idolatrous as anything else, but it is a form of idolatry that subverts and disrupts other idols. In this way, it perhaps serves as the rhetorical analogue to what the Second Commandment does for law. Unlike other forms of representation, allegory resists its own "ideal quality"; it does not exempt even itself from its iconoclastic powers.

In this way, Benjamin's notion of allegory is protected from a dynamic we already saw occurring within Kant's notion of the sublime. As noted, Kant assumes that the negativity that comes from the sublime experience is sufficient to unmake idols, to give us a sense, if only by an entirely subtractive process, of the moral law. Yet Kant neglects[65] to protect against the idolatry fomented by the experience of the sublime itself. The sublime is, after all, also based on an object, via representation; it is an encounter with something "seen," even if that seeing is then erased by the experience of absence that follows this encounter. Let me repeat an already cited passage from *The Critique of Judgment* that speaks directly to this point:

> This pure, elevating, and merely negative exhibition of morality involves no danger of *fanaticism*, which is the *delusion of wanting to see something beyond all bounds of sensibility*, i.e. of dreaming according to principles (raving with reason). The exhibition avoids fanaticism precisely because it is merely negative. For *the idea of freedom is inscrutable* and thereby precludes all positive exhibition whatever; but the moral law in itself can sufficiently and originally determine us, so that it does not even permit us to cast about for some additional determining basis.[66]

Revisiting this from a Benjaminian perspective, we can say that Kant expresses here a faith—one that Benjamin does not share—that the very inscrutability of freedom and the moral law's purely negative character (as far as we are concerned) is enough to ensure that the subject who so engages with it is (therefore) free from delusion, free from anything "positive" or statutory. From a Benjaminian perspective, even this idea is itself potentially a delusion. And, unlike the delusions of allegory, such an idea has no mechanism to bring itself into question. Kant really does believe that by this exercise, we are in some sense freeing ourselves, at least potentially.

Along similar lines, Benjamin is not as quick as Kant is to accept that the failure of representation is a wholly empty, ultimately objectless, experience (and hence "safe" from idolatry). Let me recall a passage considered in the previous chapter where Benjamin tells us that

> allegories fill out and deny the void in which they are represented, just as, ultimately, the intention does not faithfully rest in the contemplation of bones, but faithlessly leaps forward to the idea of resurrection.[67]

We see here that Benjamin acknowledges and expects that there will always be a "positive" in the act of representation (this is exactly why he, unlike Kant, turns to the ordinary object and away from the supersensible in the first place). To deny this is to fall into the faith that a wholly negative experience is possible, with the concomitant belief that there is therefore no further danger of idolatry, that there is nothing we now need to protect ourselves us from. Benjamin's negativism is not of this sort; it is not a denial of objects but rather his alternative understanding of divinity that makes him the more iconoclastic theorist.

What Benjamin has to offer Kant, then, is, once again, this idea of a "faithless . . . leap." Rather than having faith in the possibility of a pure experience—even a purely negative one—of the moral law, we have instead with Benjamin the assumption that all ideas, all manner of speaking, all representation is a delusion. But this delusion can be "fill[ed] out and den[ied]" by the allegorical, by a process that never accepts the possibility of a pure and nondeluded experience. As we saw in the previous chapter, it is this "faithless" leap that Benjamin asks us to take, a leap toward and not away from the material world.[68]

Kant's Law

Having laid out some of the bases for Kant's complicated relationship to iconoclasm in general, I would like now to bring this question to bear more specifically on questions of law. In these last sections of this chapter, I will seek first to discuss how Kant's notion of law follows a pattern similar to his discussion of the sublime and then try to think in the final sections about what a Kantian law would look like that was more faithful to the iconoclasm he professes but doesn't quite attain (in my reading) in his admiration for the Second Commandment.

To begin to think about the question of the operations of Kant's law, we must turn back to *Religion*, for it is here, in the midst of compromises (compromises that, as we have seen, are also evident in the *Critique of Judgment*, albeit in more subtle forms), that we see the effect that Kant's only partial iconoclasm has on the law itself. In *Religion*, he echoes a sentiment that we see in many of his writings, that law is both something we give to ourselves and something we experience as external and, hence, binding:

> Equality arises from true freedom, yet without anarchy, because though each obeys the (non-statutory) law which he prescribes to

himself, he must at the same time regard this law as the will of a World-Ruler revealed to him through reason, a will which by invisible means unites all under one common government into one state.[69]

In some ways then, the moral law for Kant is experienced as a parallel to earthly law, earthly rulers and statutes. Yet this is only a way for subjects to understand that, although they prescribe this law to themselves (and hence remain free), this is not a law that they can follow or not follow as they chose. To think so would be "anarchy" (and, as I have already argued, the approach to law that Benjamin prescribes does indeed lead to anarchy, although not in the negative sense that Kant holds to here).

Kant's distinction here between statutory and nonstatutory law is vital. As noted, statutory law is like positive law, akin to what Benjamin calls "mythic" law, that is, a law that is purely an invention of human beings, although its origins are attributed to divine or natural, "objective" sources. Such law is empirical, historical, and/or revealed. Recall too that even divine commands can appear on earth in the form of statutory laws. If we return to his comments about Judaism and the Ten Commandments, Kant tells us that "they are directed to absolutely nothing but outer observance," that is, they are not directed toward moral law itself (which lies inward).[70] A nonstatutory law, on the other hand, is a law that isn't merely posited; it is a law that allows us our freedom because it is a law that, in effect, we give to ourselves.

Nothing but Laws

In thinking about the way that we can move from statutory to nonstatutory law, that is, from human law to moral law, Kant goes on to say:

> The basis for the transition [to a community run by moral, nonstatutory law] must lie in the principle that the pure religion of reason is a continually occurring divine (though not empirical) revelation for all men. Once this basis has been grasped with mature reflection, it is carried into effect, so far as this is destined to be a human task, through gradually advancing reform.[71]

Ultimately, Kant tells us, "The one true religion comprises nothing but laws, that is, those practical principles of whose unconditioned necessity we can become aware, and which we therefore recognize as revealed through pure reason (not empirically)."[72] This, then, is Kant's goal, the boiling away of historical, revealed statutory law and its replacement by "nothing but [moral] laws," a progression that duplicates the one between religion and moral law more generally.

In furthering the progression from earthly (statutory) to moral (non-statutory) law, Kant notes the key role of public recognition:

> Truth and goodness—and in the natural predisposition of every man there lies a basis of insight into these as well as a basis of heart-felt sympathy with them—do not fail to communicate themselves far and wide once they have become public, thanks to their natural affinity with the moral predisposition of rational beings generally. The obstacles, arising from political and civil causes, which may from time to time hinder their spread, serve rather to make all the closer the union of men's spirits with the good (which never leaves their thoughts after they have once cast their eyes upon it).[73]

Here, we see something of the same dynamic that we saw with the operation of the sublime, albeit in a new and explicitly political guise. Once again, Kant seeks to use the empirical as a basis for its own overcoming. We see in this passage that the contingencies and falsities of the actual practice of law serve, precisely by negative example (by acting as obstacles), to make the moral law more evident to us, especially (or perhaps only) in a public context. This is not unlike the operation of the sublime in that the failures of the law become apparent and hence highlight the contrast between such laws and the true, moral law that is, as Kant tells us, "primordially engraved in our hearts."[74]

In seeing the similarity between the operation of law and the sublime, we get a better sense of why Kant's goal of achieving "nothing but [moral] laws" may not be achievable even as an ideal or ultimate goal. Kant concedes at several points that the perverse nature of human beings threatens his operations, but here again the cause may in fact lie in the way he himself has conceived of the process. Here, as with our previous discussion of the sublime, the threat may come from the very methods that Kant engages with to advance his cause. In the case of law specifically, his idea that the pursuit of moral law must begin with a model of earthly rule (a "World-Ruler," as opposed to "anarchy") may hinder rather than aid Kant's icono-clastic project; the search for moral law begins with that most idolatrous of beings, the sovereign, the figure who is supposed to directly stand in for (and thereby replace) God.

In a footnote to the passage just cited about obstacles helping to advance

the move toward moral law, Kant describes a progression from the sensuous to the supersensuous in law that parallels what we have already seen in
terms of the operation of the sublime (and religion as well):

> To combine a unity of ecclesiastical belief with freedom in matters
> of faith is a problem towards whose solution the idea of the objec-
> tive unity of the religion of reason continually urges us, through
> the moral interest which we take in this religion; although, when
> we take human nature into account, there appears small hope of
> bringing this to pass in a visible church. It is an idea of reason which
> we cannot represent through any [sensuous] intuition adequate to
> it, but which, as a practical regulative principle, does have objective
> reality, enabling it to work toward this end, *i.e.*, the unity of the pure
> religion of reason. In this it is like the political idea of the rights
> of a state so far as these are meant to relate to an international law
> which is universal and *possessed of power*. Here experience bids us give
> over all hope. A propensity seems to have been implanted (perhaps
> designedly) in the human race causing every single state to strive
> if possible to subjugate every other state and to erect a universal
> monarchy.[75]

We see in this passage that the empirical practice of sovereignty seems
fated to thwart the transformation that Kant would have it perform (and
by Kant's own acknowledgment). The analogy he offers here is telling; the
attempt to create an actual practice of moral law is *like* the international
system, where the actors, rather than serving to join forces for the common good, turn on each other for their own self-aggrandizement (with
predictably woeful results for all). But here again, the problem may not
just be that human beings are prone to delusions but that Kant has made
such delusions a basis for their own overcoming. The negation that he
hopes will arise out of this process is—perhaps even more clearly than with
the example of the operation of the sublime—insufficient to overcome the
vehicle by which it is delivered. The model of a "World-Ruler" as a necessary (and temporary) corollary to the kinds of self-rule that Kant looks to
has no basis for overcoming itself; rather than delivering a purely negative
experience of law—one that in this case is public and powerful—we find
the positive and the representational serving to overwhelm and prevent
the transition to nonstatutory law. Here we see once again that not even
"Kantian rigor" is enough to overcome the dilemmas of engagement with
the empirical world that Kant faces. And here too, the solution lies not in

seeking the negative through the positive, looking for the divine/moral law itself, but turning, as Benjamin does, *away* ("abzusehen") from the divine. Only in that direction, it appears, can we have any sort of relationship with law (that is, law that is not a product of myth).

Reading Kant Again

As I have argued throughout this chapter, Kant's iconoclasm is enhanced through an engagement with Benjamin. Benjamin offers Kant a way to take his own appreciation for the Second Commandment and extend it, strengthening it against his own reluctant compromising in his search for a human relationship to moral law. Benjamin also offers a related way for Kant to apply his (i.e., Kant's) own notion of reading Scripture—a move away from literalness and toward a looser sense of representation we have seen him advocating in *Religion*—and applying that reading to his own writings (the *Critique of Judgment* and *Religion* very much included). Reading Kant in this Benjaminian light ensures a greater fidelity to iconoclasm on Kant's part, a departure from a more literal reading of a text that may otherwise condemn or compromise Kant's appreciation for the Second Commandment.

In this, the penultimate section of this chapter, I would like to reverse this relationship and see what Kant can do for Benjamin (and, by extension, for us as readers and responders to Benjamin), first by rereading Kant (in this section) and then (in the next and last section) looking at the political and legal upshot of such a rereading. If we read Kant through a Benjaminian lens, a very different reading of Kant emerges. I am particularly interested in such a reading in terms of looking at what, if anything, remains when Kant has been purified of his own faith in his ability to avoid "the positive" or the taint of representation altogether in his quest for the moral law, that is, when Kant himself takes—or is forced to take—a "faithless . . . leap."[76] What happens when we substitute the Second Commandment itself for the moral laws that Kant seeks on his own terms? What happens when we take seriously his claim that this commandment is the most "sublime law"?[77]

To read Kant in this way is to see what looks like a set of accidents or even mistakes, internal tensions within Kant's system, as being somehow deliberate, a strategy of resistance against the very moral laws he would otherwise foist on us. This is why I have argued that, although, at first glance, it would appear that by moving from the *Critique of Judgment* to

Religion, Kant is becoming more idolatrous, in fact, this move can be reread ("forced") via a Benjaminian interpretation, to be seen as a step *away* from idolatry. This is a step away from the apparent iconoclasm of the sublime, which is not quite what it seems (and therefore, perhaps, a more tempting, more dangerous form of idolatry in the sense that we do not see or read it as such), to a more direct engagement with those objects that potentially deliver us from the idolatry they otherwise (for both Kant and Benjamin) produce.

In this way, we can think of the objects Kant uses as a basis for transcendence as deliberately thwarting the encounter—no matter how negatively it is framed—with the moral law (which can only come to us as an idol). In *Textual Conspiracies*, as previously noted, I describe a situation in which the objects of the world are in a constant state of rebellion and conspiracy against the idolatry we project onto them.[78] I argue there that for Benjamin, we must seek to ally ourselves with this rebellion, to do an end run around our own complicity with the phantasmagoria by conspiring with the signs and objects that make it up. Applying this notion to the objects, figures, signs, and concepts that Kant engages with—the sublime mountains, oceans, starry nights, and laws (especially the Second Commandment), even the figure of a "World-Ruler" that Kant enlists as a basis for moving from statutory to nonstatutory law—they become legible to us as being in on this conspiracy. Reading these objects, signs, and figures as purposefully foiling our encounter with the moral law allows us to read Kant as being saved from his own potentially idolatrous ends (more on that in a moment), enacting in the process a different kind of law: the Second Commandment.

We can even think of Kant himself as being in on this conspiracy, thwarting his own goals in connivance with the material objects that realize the failure of the moral law to appear. In this reading, Kant's engagement with objects, his use of religion, his theory of the sublime, and his understanding of law can be read as seeking out a different kind of failure: not the pleasing failure to encounter the divine, but a failure to even have an inkling, whether of the negative or positive variety, of the truth. By colluding with the sublime objects against his own desire for transcendence, Kant in effect overcomes himself through and by his compromises with the material world (his alliance with material objects). In the resulting absolute failure of the moral law to appear (despite Kant's own strong intentions to the contrary), we have an aporia, a space for another kind of law and another kind of politics.

One author who offers a view of Kant that is compatible with this reading is Peter Fenves. In his recent *Late Kant: Towards Another Law of the Earth*, Fenves argues for a Kant who was always subverting his own obedience to the rational and moral order that he is known for. Although Fenves does not use the language of fetishism and iconoclasm in his study, his portrayal of Kant dovetails nicely with a conspiratorial, Benjaminian reading of Kant (and Fenves is a well-known author on Benjamin as well, so reading these authors in constellation through Fenves makes a lot of sense).[79] In his book, Fenves employs the figure of lateness in several senses. First, he notes that for all the stories about Kant being obsessively timely, he was very often late—sometimes extraordinarily late—for his own self-proclaimed deadlines. Thus, whereas Kant announced in a 1772 letter that he was going to publish his first Critique in three months time, Fenves notes that it actually came out nine years later.[80] Fenves also employs the figure of lateness to refer to Kant in his own latter days. He portrays an old man who suffered from "brain cramp" and "oppression in the head," and whose work at that age, work that grows bolder and more contradictory to his earlier writing, is often dismissed as the ramblings of a man well past his prime.[81] Taking these notions of lateness together, Fenves argues that throughout his life, but especially toward the end, Kant can be read as being in rebellion against his own strictures, against the intense devotion to reason, duty and the moral law that he so ardently pursues. For Fenves, one way this rebellion can be most clearly read as a conscious strategy comes in Kant's suggestions, sometimes overt, sometimes coy, that the human race as we know it is not the ultimate and best manifestation of subjects of the moral law, not the acme of perfection that we often hold ourselves to be. As Fenves puts it, for Kant

> the last residues of the ancient prejudice that the human species is the undisputed master of the earth are reduced. . . . [Kant] disputes the claim that the human species as a whole constitutes the permanent nobility of the earth, who . . . can claim the surface of the planet as its own.[82]

This helps to explain Kant's tendency to speak of humans and "other rational beings" throughout his texts. For Kant, future challengers to the hegemony of contemporary humans might take the form of other species already on earth, or indeed life on other planets. Here we find yet another form of "lateness": Kant is anticipating late arrivals in the world (or indeed beyond it) who are the true inheritors and intended targets of his moral philosophy. As such, human beings as we know them are taken down from their privileged perch in terms of anticipating a "Kingdom of Ends." Instead we are reduced to a state of what Fenves calls "radical mean-ness":[83]

> For late Kant . . . the mean-ness of human beings has nothing to do with an end that they themselves should aim to accomplish: human beings do not exist so that reason can be realized but for the sake of another "species (race)" of human being, whose entrance on earth is an entirely contingent matter. In the meantime—which, for all we know, lasts forever—the mean-ness of human beings is without a corresponding end.[84]

To this point, Fenves adds a footnote stating: "Kant is therefore closer to Walter Benjamin's concept of 'pure means' than to Fichte's proposal that human beings be understood as means through which reason actualizes itself."[85] Here Fenves puts his finger exactly on how Kant and Benjamin can be read in constellation. Benjamin not only describes but performs the concept of "pure means" in many of his essays, the "Critique" very much included. There, as already noted, he begins by allowing readers to think that they are reading a document that is beholden to the usual ends of law (as we normally understand such things). It is only two-thirds of the way through the essay that we are suddenly faced with his description of law as mythic violence. This upends all the assumptions we have been working toward. We are informed that there is an end to law but that only God knows what that end is. Thus we are left with "pure means"; the instrumental way we have been reading his text so far (reading it as a means to understanding the ends of law) become cut off from its own purpose; our reading and interpretation become mere (or "pure") means with no purpose, no teleology. The text then becomes available for another reading, one that is not predetermined by phantasm or by a sense of "fate."

In Fenves's view, Kant achieves the same thing in his decentering of the human race as we know it. Generally, Kant writes as if this race was to be the bearer of the moral law, the subject of ends, but then in a late move, he tells us that we aren't going to be those agents after all. Those agents are "late" and yet to come (and maybe never will arrive). In this way, the strange instrumentalism for the purpose of anti-instrumentalism that we see throughout Kant's work becomes unmoored from what we thought was its original purpose. The radical, Benjaminian (and also Nietzschean) Kant frees us from the awful and impossible burden of being subject to (idolatrous) ends, leaving us, as we find with Benjamin too, to our own devices. We become "pure means" without any ends (not any more, anyway). We can think, then, of *this* Kant as being, like Benjamin's description of Baude-laire, someone who "conspires with language."[86] This Kant allies himself with the signs and symbols that form our world, not with the purpose to "transcend" them but instead to expose the ways that such transcendence is not for us (just as Benjamin evokes Kafka's notion of a hope that is similarly "not for us").[87]

With such a reading of Kant, we can reconsider his work more gen-erally as being more in alliance (or conspiracy) with Benjamin. Although normally, as already suggested, Kant looks up to the heavens and Benjamin looks down to the ground, if we read Kant with a Benjaminian light (a dark light, to be sure, a light that obscures and subverts rather than clarifies and answers), we can read them as looking in fundamentally the same direc-tion. We can think of Kant's failures—and his lateness, to borrow from Fenves—as amounting to a strategy of resistance from within. We can—as already suggested—read Kant's turn toward the material and the histori-cal (in *Religion*, among other works) not as an attempt to allow the mass of humanity to have some inkling of the moral law, but rather as a move toward his material allies, toward the objects that he would otherwise treat as fetishes and traps.[88] What looks like a desperate gamble can be reconsid-ered as a way to thwart a goal (or an end) that is itself the real trap, a way to ensure that we will never be saddled with the kind of ends that Kant is usually understood as promoting.[89]

Finally, reading Kant in this conspiratorial way allows us to glean from him a hidden anarchism, the political and legal upshot of his self-subversion. It will be recalled that Kant tells us:

> Equality arises from true freedom, yet without anarchy, because though each obeys the (non-statutory) law which he prescribes to himself, he must at the same time regard this law as the will of a World-Ruler revealed to him through reason, a will which by invisi-ble means unites all under one common government into one state.[90]

A subversive reading of Kant then reads him as offering a freedom that comes "with" (or maybe through) anarchy. It eliminates one half of Kant's formulation: we continue to prescribe a law to ourselves, but we do so without the figure of the world-ruler (or we do so in a way in which this figure too, as we have already seen, subverts our desire to be commanded).[91] To remove this external source of law, even the idea of law as necessarily coming from outside of us, is to effectively undermine the last vestiges of Numa's trick. Without any kind of world-ruler—even as a pure figure that we impose on ourselves—we have no one to pass responsibility onto, we have no way to wash our hands of our decision, no phantasm to guide or control us. The anarchy that emerges is produced through the failure of such a figure, leaving us, as Benjamin tells us, "non-conceptual, profound and bitter."[92]

Kant and Law Revisited

If we see this potential of reading Kant according to a Benjaminan methodology—a "slight adjustment" or forcing of our engagement with the text—we can see that it would be a great mistake to dismiss Kant as insufficiently iconoclastic and leave it at that. Clearly, Kant's iconoclasm is as fervent as Benjamin's, perhaps even more so (we should always take seriously his stated enthusiasm for the Second Commandment). Reading him in constellation with Benjamin brings out, not just the iconoclastic desire (which is evident throughout Kant's writing), but a more iconoclastic outcome as well.

Such a reading of Kant tells us, as already noted, not only about Kant but about Benjamin as well, specifically in terms of his legal theory. There are several ways in which Kant's complex and sophisticated understandings of law (when subjected to a deeper engagement with the Second Commandment) can lend a coherence and structure to a Benjaminian practice. For one thing, while for Benjamin, we generally must "wrestle in solitude" with the law, adopting or abandoning it as we see necessary, for Kant the engagement with law must always occur in a public way; despite the fact that our intuition of the moral law is always an inner journey, he sees that we must undertake this endeavor together, in ways that guarantee that we are approaching these questions in an open and widely accessible way.

By insisting on this public element of law, Kant is helping to ensure that law remains a political force. This is a goal that is important to both Kant and Benjamin even as Benjamin dwells far less on this requirement (although he does offer that this "wrestling" can happen as either an individual or a collectivity). An anarchic form of law that avoids becoming just "what pleases" requires a public expression, a collective process, exactly because such pleasures are not always easy to distinguish from the law itself (as we saw in chapter 2). Too much "wrestling in solitude" might actually return us to the kind of inward solipsism that Kant himself advocates but which is anathema to the struggle with idolatry both thinkers engage in.

In *Religion*, Kant argues that when attempting to put the moral law into practice (or at least to engage in a political practice that relates to the search for the moral law), the creation of a public institution is essential. Speaking specifically of the practices of a church, Kant writes:

> For pure religious faith is concerned only with what constitutes the essence of reverence for God, namely, obedience, ensuing from the moral disposition to all duties as His commands; a church, on the other hand, as the union of many men with such dispositions into a moral commonwealth, requires a *public* covenant, a certain ecclesiastical form dependent upon the conditions of experience.[93]

By analogy, any political organization would need to be similarly public. It seems here as if publicness is, for Kant, a potential antidote or at least corrective for the kinds of delusions that are inevitable in a worldly organization (and Arendt would surely agree with this). By extension, we can say that publicness for Benjamin too could help to politicize what he is trying to do when he describes acts of collective iconoclastic behavior (such as his description in the "Right to Use Force" and the "Critique of Violence" of the actions of the Galician Jews as well as those who engage in the revolutionary general strike).

Similarly, Kant's distinction between statutory and nonstatutory law is an important aspect of supporting a Benjaminian legal practice. Statutory law is the hallmark of both mythic and historical law, as we have seen. The concept of nonstatutory law seems at first glance to be merely another iteration of the impossible negation that Kant strives for in his understanding of the moral law. But the very unavailability of this form of law helps to eliminate the residual sovereign subjectivity in each of us. Rather than being represented to us via the figure of a world ruler, this reading of Kant would make such a figure impossible exactly because of the distance moral law has from human practices. Even if we are rid of an actual world-ruler, the habit of obeying rules as a tangible fact in their own right is just as pernicious, just as much a source of lingering or resurgent idolatry, as the desire for rulers itself (it is a desire for the "rule of law"). The idea of obeying a law that cannot be reduced to some form of earthly power, read according to some calculus of violence, on the other hand, is a vital idea for the practice of law in an anarchist context; if we think of the subject and author of law as not being two separated—if simultaneous—ideas, as they usually are with Kant, and instead as being one and the same, we can see that the subject can engage with law (and not just by herself but in constellation with others) in order to (continually) form herself and themselves.[94]

Kant himself gives a sense of that continuity, it will be recalled, when he writes of nonstatutory law that the "the pure religion of reason is a continually occurring divine (though not empirical) revelation for all men." If we "forced" this sentence along more Benjaminian lines, the distrust of the empirical would be removed (as well as the use of "men" to mean people, although this probably would not have bothered Benjamin himself overmuch). We are left with a sense of the continual presence of the moral law, that is, in the sense, the continuing presence, and availability, of the Second Commandment.

At the same time, Kant acknowledges, in the same passage treated above, that public organizations may not be able to completely avoid—and maybe shouldn't avoid—statutory laws, at least in some form (consonant with what we saw in the last chapter in terms of Badiou's discussion of "old law"). He says that the public covenant or "ecclesiastical form" of the church in question, being "contingent and manifold[,] cannot be apprehended as duty without divine statutory laws."[95] Yet Kant goes on to write:

> But the determination of this form must not be regarded forthwith as the concern of the divine Lawgiver; rather we are justified in assuming that it is the divine will that we should ourselves carry into effect the rational idea of such a commonwealth.[96]

In this way, Kant insists that members of the Church risk being wrong and ceaselessly endeavor to manifest the moral law in a political, human context. Kant goes on to say that, given the difficulty of the task and the fact that this task of discerning divine truth is uniquely the task of the members of a church,

> we therefore have no reason straightway to take the laws constituting the basis and form of any church as divine *statutory* laws; rather it is presumptuous to declare them to be such . . . [I]t is a usurpation of higher authority to seek, under pretense of a divine commission, to lay a yoke upon the multitude by means of ecclesiastical dogmas.[97]

Here we see the essential nature of these ecclesiastical laws in play; they lie somewhere between statutory and nonstatutory in terms of their status. For Kant, it seems that this status shifts back and forth even during a given moment in time (the last few citations are all from one long paragraph in *Religion*). The negotiation between dogma and openness is part of how the laws operate without becoming either bogged down in orthodoxy or disappearing into an invisible abstraction.[98]

If we think of this view of ecclesiastical law as a model for a political polity—an analogy Kant himself makes very possible—we can see a more nuanced and complicated understanding of law in general. If we read Kant in a nonliteral (to cite Badiou yet again) or conspiratorial way, we can see a suggestion that laws may be engaged with and representations of the divine may be encountered, but they cannot be taken either as dogma (that is, false and idolatrous) or as truth (that is, correct). We must adopt a loose, nonliteral reading of law, something that lies somewhere between statutory and nonstatutory law. In other words, we should read law in general the way Kant tells us to read Scripture.

The upshot of this is that our anarchic community may have laws, but they wouldn't look like the kinds of laws we are used to. Such laws would be shifting, temporary, (recalling Benjamin) to be struggled with, perhaps at times abandoned. A devotion to the Second Commandment need not mean that we abandon the rest of law entirely but that, just as this constellation between Kant and Benjamin (and Badiou) suggests, we treat other forms of law as representations, that is, as failed forms and ruins. We cannot abandon the form of law altogether (Kant's willingness to hold onto the form of a church shows his devotion to the forms even though he realizes the peril this causes for his iconoclastic project). To give it up is to invite either the fallacy that we can "do what we please" or that we have moved beyond representation to truth (an ultimate idolatrous position).

Kant's notion of a law that hovers between statutory and nonstatutory serves us less as a contradiction than as a paradox that helps us think that we can hold onto law but recognize at the same time that it is itself only our (temporary) understanding, part of a shifting collective, public, and legal experience. When law has been exposed and possibly abandoned, when its status as an idol has been made clear to us and its authority has been stripped away, and when we recognize that its siren call to us is an invitation to resist rather than obey the phantasms it instills in us, then, and only then, might we recuperate the remnant, the ruin of law.[99] This, then, could be a conspiratorial version of Kant's insistence that law always be something that we give to ourselves (minus his own insistence that we yet follow it as if it were a universal and unimpeachable rule), part of how we "form," or perhaps now unform, ourselves in relation to law (how, to cite Badiou one final time, we can remain "faithful to the event"). Our relationship to such ruined forms of law would be, once again, one of pure means; rather than serving as our instrument, they would be our allies. In our shifting and inconstant relationship to these laws, we would learn to imitate, and benefit from, their own constant rebellion against the fetishism we would otherwise project onto them.

The one element of law that could not be treated in this shifting, loose way, that is, the one law that we would have to treat as absolutely nonstatutory, is the Second Commandment. This is the one law that cannot be compromised, cannot be wrestled with or abandoned ("abzusehen"). To follow this one law scrupulously is to permit a looser and more openly failed relationship to the rest of law as well. When we substitute the Second Commandment for Kant's general treatment of moral law (as we did in the previous chapter with Badiou as well), we can see more clearly that a radical Kant can be found by "forcing" the text in a Benjaminian direction. In this way the Second Commandment can be read as sublime after all. We can say this without fear of idolatry because the Second Commandment continually works—as other laws do not—against its own idolatry. It ensures that the experience of failure that it offers is truly that, a failure, not the peeking into the world of some higher moral law.[100] We might even be able to say that the Second Commandment is the only divine law we can apprehend, at least in a nonstatutory form; it ensures that we can never completely overwrite God and the world with our phantasmic projections. If the operation of such a law is sublime, it does not cease to be, at the same time, allegorical, hence saving us even from the phantasms it itself brings along with its operation.

In the next chapter, I will look at legal positivism, reading it as a descendant of Kantianism (despite the fact that Kant is far more often hailed as a figure of the "opposite" camp, natural law theory, as well as the fact that legal positivism is marked by an express disavowal of all moral theories, Kantianism very much included). As with Kantianism itself, the twentieth- (and twenty-first-) century variants of legal positivism display an apparent iconoclasm that is revealed to be less than promised. Yet here too, we can learn to read the legal positivists, and, in particular H. L. A. Hart, who will be the main focus of the chapter, through a Benjaminian lens and, in so doing, offer more in the way of understanding what a radical legal theory might offer this study of the Second Commandment.

FOUR

A "Useful Illusion"

H. L. A. Hart and Legal Positivism

"Kanticism" and Legal Positivism

The Kant I portrayed at the end of the last chapter, a radical Kant, often at odds with his own philosophy, is, to be sure, not consistent with the general reception of Kant in terms of either legal or ethical philosophy. Linda Ross Meyer describes the Kantian inheritance for legal scholarship in particular as an "incomplete and dogmatic understanding of Kantian philosophy, a kind of Kantian catechism, or 'kanticism.'"[1] Kanticism, she argues, offers a vision of law wherein "justice is usually understood as acting according to reason" and where that reason is the "glue" of community.[2]

Describing Kanticism further, Meyer writes:

> This ideal of justice as a system of rules is deeply embedded in our legal system. Reason is the touchstone for law. Irrational laws are unconstitutional; irrational people are not criminally responsible. Differences in treatment must be either explained as reasonable or eliminated. "Interest," "feeling" or "opinion" is not universal and therefore not a reason; selfish prudence is not a reason.[3]

As Meyer tells it, Kanticism is a retreat from both emotional and moral positions (at least of a certain sort). Under the spell of Kanticism, she tells us, the law rejects any social scientific calculus as well as utilitarianism

(Meyer rhetorically asks us, "Why should society not judge judges on how beneficial their rulings turn out to be for our collective social welfare?").[4] There is something delightfully counterintuitive about this understanding of law; when our legal reasoning perversely overrides what we strongly feel to be obvious and true, it makes the law seem impartial and objective, above the fray of transitory moral, emotional, and empirical convictions. In this way, Kanticism can be read as another version of the operation of the sublime, whereby through the process of subtraction (in this case the subtraction of our own intuitions, feelings, and other forms of nonlegal calculation) we are led to feel the workings of the law upon our limited, contingent selves.

Although it is a highly imperfect copy, Meyer implicates Kant strongly as the originator of Kanticism. Citing from Kant's *Groundwork of the Metaphysics of Morals*, she tells us that "for Kant, human will is only free of causal necessity if it is an exercise of reason, for reason follows its own principles of logic and consistency, and the claims of logic are not affected by the arbitrary power of nature's relations of cause and effect."[5] She tells us further that "the first statement of Kant's categorical imperative can be restated as 'always act in accordance with reason.' The good will, the ethical will, the free will, is, at the same time the reasonable, consistent, rule-bound will."[6] Accordingly, the results of what you do are less important than the good-will and reason that underlies them; judging an action by its consequences reintroduces the messy, contingent empirical world.

As previously noted, Meyer also reminds us that for Kant reason serves as the one and only appropriate social "glue" that holds our community together (anything else would be redolent of the contingency and baseness that always threatens to rip our community apart). Thus:

> Kant derives the second statement of the categorical imperative, which can be stated as "Treat reason, whether in yourself or others as an end in itself, and not a means only." Here, then, reason becomes not only the basis of freedom and responsibility, but the basis of community. I recognize the other as "like" me when the other is also a creature capable of reason (even if nonhuman).[7]

The final piece of Kantian thought that for Meyer that underlies Kanticism is the requirement of a universal applicability insofar as "reason demands that our law be universal. We cannot make unjustified exceptions for ourselves, our friends, our families. We cannot make exceptions for 'just this once.'"[8]

With its foundation in Kantian principles of reasonableness, publicness and generality, the Kanticist view is that law not only creates a political basis for our community but allows human beings to transcend their biases and corruptions and produce something akin to a "Kingdom of Ends," even as this remains only on the level of an ideal. Meyer quotes Kant from the *Groundwork* directly as saying:

> And it is just in this that the paradox lies; that the mere dignity of a man as a rational creature, without any other end or advantage to be attained thereby, in other words, respect for a mere idea, should yet serve as an inflexible precept of the will, and that it is precisely in this independence of the maxim on all such springs of action that its sublimity consists; and it is this that makes every reasonable subject worthy to be a legislative member in the kingdom of ends: for otherwise he would have to be conceived only as subject to the physical law of his wants.[9]

Here we return again to the concept that human beings can, via the operation of the sublime, imitate or approximate some version of the divine (or, if not the divine, then a pure, rational, and universal form of subjecthood that has nothing to do with earthly foibles).[10]

If Kanticism forms the general background of our legal philosophy these days, the foreground seems, if anything, even further removed from Kant. One of the key tenets of contemporary legal theory (and the main focus of this chapter) is legal positivism, the inheritor and chief articulator of the idea of "positive law." Here thinkers ranging from H. L. A. Hart (the main figure I will be discussing) to Joseph Raz deliberately distance themselves either explicitly or implicitly from all moral philosophy, including Kantianism, which, as we have seen, is generally hostile to statutory law and therefore, presumably, to legal positivism as well. Despite this critical difference, I will argue that legal positivism remains indebted to Kant in part because as Kantianism becomes diffused as Kanticism, it no longer becomes recognized as a moral philosophy. The legal positivists are able, to some degree, to deny any links to moral philosophy insofar as the key tenets of Kantianism—the notions of rationality, of order and fairness—are preserved in this more amorphous, background set of views that can be taken for granted or assumed by legal scholars (and where troubling, specific differences can be dropped). In light of this facilitation, I will show how, for all of its denial, legal positivism remains very much connected to, and even dependent on, its disavowed legacy in Kant.

To make this argument, I focus on Hart, and, in particular, his famous work *The Concept of Law*, perhaps the most canonical text in contemporary legal positivism. I focus in this chapter on Hart and legal positivism more generally instead of contemporary natural law theory precisely because of the distancing move from moral philosophy that Hart epitomizes. Whereas natural law philosophers (of whom probably the most important contemporary example is Ronald Dworkin) are openly interested in questions of truth and universality (and hence have a more direct and obvious link to Kant), it is the legal positivists' move to reject, or at least distance themselves from, these notions that make them interesting to me.[11] From a Benjaminian position, the natural law theorists' connection to idolatry is more readily apparent. What is more complicated is the legal positivist position that already seems to reflect a kind of Benjaminian sensibility, moving away from idols and toward law as a human contrivance. It is this apparent similarity that I would like to both reject and complicate or subvert in this chapter.

Not Being a Kantian

In thinking about Hart's legal positivism and its relationship to Kantianism, we see immediately the distancing move. For one thing, Kant is hardly ever mentioned by name. In *The Concept of Law*, Hart mentions Kant only once, in a footnote (and then only to note a distinction that Kant makes between juridical and ethical laws).[12] Rather than see this as evidence that Meyer is incorrect in her views about the pervasive influences of Kantianism in law—including in terms of legal positivism—I would say, on the contrary, that it suggests that Kantianism has become so pervasive as to become an invisible backdrop to law, particularly in terms of the legal positivist tradition.

More to the point, in this chapter, I will argue, looking at Hart's work in particular (but also supplying examples from other thinkers like Joseph Raz and Scott Shapiro), that the assumption and resulting invisibility of Kant in legal thought allows a functional division of labor in the application and effect of law. Here law itself can be seen as being totally or partially divorced from moral and ethical questions even as those moral codes remain in place as a backstop to prevent a total collapse of ethics. Such a division of labor ensures that a certain, consistent, and—from the point of view of Kantianism—ethical practice remains at least possible. Allowing for heinous regimes like Nazi Germany to count as being "lawful" even while decrying their iniquity, a thinker like Hart (for example in his debates with Lon Fuller on this very question) can see the law as being neutral with respect to any ideology, even the Kantian ideology that makes such a position tenable in the first place.[13] I will argue that without the firm knowledge that Kantianism condemns a regime like Nazi Germany in no uncertain terms, Hart would be unable to allow the law as such to retain its seeming neutrality.

In terms of how this argument about legal positivism and its occult relationship to Kantianism intersects with the interests of this book, I will argue that a surface similarity between positive law and some of the ideas I have been attributing to Benjamin is misleading, at least when we do not (as I will at the end of this chapter) "force" our reading toward a greater alignment between these thinkers (once again favoring a Benjaminian direction). In his move toward legal positivism, Hart may well be looking to a notion of law that has been stripped of its idealistic—and therefore idolatrous—aspects (although Hart would certainly not put it that way). For Hart, as we have already begun to see, the practice of law must be removed from messy entanglements with troubling moral questions (that is, questions about truth). The irony here is that this very preference for avoiding messiness is itself a legacy of Kant's influence on law more generally. By formally removing itself from all moral theories—even Kantian theory—Hart's legal positivism has the appearance of being just something that human beings come up with and do on their own. How then is this any different from the kind of anti-idolatrous notions that I have been ascribing to Benjamin?

The answer lies exactly in the occult relationship between positive law and its occluded source—Kantianism.[14] By denying its roots in Kantian philosophy (that is, by itself creating a sublime distance between itself and its own origin, paradoxically treating Kantian philosophy itself as the source of contamination in this case), Hart's legal positivism has no way to engage with or even recognize its own idolatry. As we will see, a thinker like Hart will not deny the centrality of Kantian philosophy to legal jurisprudence (even if he doesn't call it by its name). Yet, by insisting on a difference between such a theory and the actual practice of law—a difference based in particular in the law's *failure* to be what Kantian doctrine would insist that it be—Hart produces a different sort of failure, akin to the very same sublime operation that we saw in Kant's own work. By failing to be Kantian, Hart reproduces the Kantian failure to be true and, in this way, also reproduces the Kantian error (at least when we read Kant himself without a Benjaminian lens) of thinking that this failure cannot itself be a bearer of idolatry, of false truth posing as its own overcoming.

Yet, when we read Hart in a different light, such a failure becomes the basis, as already suggested, of a connection with Benjamin after all—not a surface similarity but a deeper and more lasting one. As with the subjects of the previous two chapters, rather than simply condemn Hart as an idolator despite his best efforts to avoid such entanglements, I will attempt to recoup from his work a way to think about it as being similar to or in constellation with Benjamin. When we think of legal positivism in a conspiratorial, Benjaminian sense, we might come to find ways in which the failure to be Kantian can succeed in an unanticipated manner, further enriching our understanding of a Benjaminian theory of law in the process. Hart's failure to be Kantian can be grafted onto Kant's own (happy) failure to be Kantian, an internal form of resistance to the stated intentions of both authors. A different way to put this is that it is exactly by holding onto a remnant of Kant, however denied, that Hart himself can be shown to have a radical possibility. As with Kant's turn toward religion, what appears in Hart to be a move in an idolatrous direction (i.e., Hart's lingering connections to Kantian moral theory after all) becomes the basis for a real resistance to idolatry in Hart's work. At the end of this chapter, I will argue for a different kind of legal positivism, one that a conspiratorial reading of Hart makes possible and which represents an attempt to push Hart's gesture away from moral law into a full break with, and a radical subversion of, that (idolatrous) conception of law.

A Useful Illusion: Hart's *Concept of Law*

Hart's *The Concept of Law* is a fascinating book. It surely drove his intellectual enemies crazy because it seems to concede so much to other positions (and, in particular to the notion of natural law, with which legal positivism is usually contrasted) as well as to Hart's own imperfections, even as it is masterful and definitive. Hart tells us boldly from near the beginning of the book that "we shall follow [John] Austin [his earlier predecessor, along with Bentham in formulating legal positivism much as we (and Hart) have received it] in an attempt to build up . . . the idea of law. We shall not, however, hope, as Austin did, for success, but rather to learn from our failure."[15] I don't read this as any kind of humility—even false humility—on Hart's part. True to his larger vision that the law, precisely in its imperfection, is unlike a strictly moral understanding (i.e., that it is a creature of the very empirical world that Kantian philosophy seeks to shun, as Meyer too implies), Hart's rhetorical style similarly embraces the virtues of failure, of what he calls the "open-texture" or contingency and malleability of both law and language.[16] Thus, for Hart, even, or perhaps especially, when a practice or idea fails to convey the ideal it is meant to stand for, there are many useful and pragmatic results nonetheless.

Hart gives numerous examples of such an approach throughout the body of *The Concept of Law*. In one example, when considering what incalculable quality the law possesses that makes it something more than a mere set of predictable rules to be mindlessly applied by judges, Hart takes on a critic's voice (something he does wonderfully well) to speak of the mystifying elements of law:

> Can there really be something over and above these clear and ascertainable facts, some extra element, which guides the judge and justifies or gives him a reason for punishing? The difficulty of saying what exactly this extra element is has led these critics of the predictive theory to insist at this point that all talk of rules, and the corresponding use of words like "must," "ought," and "should," is fraught with a confusion which perhaps enhances their importance in men's eyes but has no rational basis. We merely *think*, so such critics claim, that there is something in the rule which binds us to do certain things and guides or justifies us in doing them, but this is an illusion even if it is a useful one.[17]

Although, as noted, Hart is ascribing this view to a critic (and hence, to a notion he presumably doesn't agree with), the concept of a "useful illusion" may be very helpful to better understand Hart's own, actual position insofar as it suggests a way of thinking that, although not correct, has important and beneficial consequences. Indeed, in the sentences that immediately follow this passage, Hart seems to embrace at least the spirit of this criticism:

> All that there is, over and above the clear ascertainable facts of group behavior and predictable reactions to deviation, are our own powerful "feelings" of compulsion to behave in accordance with the rule and to act against those who do not. We do not recognize these feelings for what they are but imagine that there is something external, some invisible part of the fabric of the universe guiding and controlling us in these activities. We are here in the realm of fiction, with which it is said the law has always been connected. It is only because we adopt this fiction that we can talk solemnly of the government "of laws not men."[18]

Here we are back in Numa's territory once again, but Hart has squeezed the disguise (the "useful illusion") that allows us to believe in law almost down (but crucially not entirely down) to nothing. Indeed, Hart offers a defense for why we need some disguise, even if it is a very thin one. There is a value, he tells us, in not recognizing our feelings about law "for what they are"; the belief in some external guidance, some meaning for the universe, is valuable for law. Even while distancing himself from actually agreeing with or believing in these notions (in part by putting these ideas in the mouths of "critics" and other rhetorical figures that are distinguished from what is presumably Hart's own position), we see that for Hart they nonetheless help to sustain a sense of the law that seems necessary for its functioning. Hart tells us: "It is only because we adopt this fiction that we can talk solemnly of the government 'of laws not men.'" If we are too aware that our laws are made, enforced and judged by fickle and protean human beings, rather than by discernible and eternal laws, we probably wouldn't obey, wouldn't be capable of law, at all.

In something of the same vein, Hart goes on to write:

> In the vast majority of cases that trouble the courts, neither statutes nor precedents in which the rules are allegedly contained allow of only one result. In most important cases there is always a choice. . . . It is only the tradition [i.e., Blackstone's] that judges "find" and do not "make" law that conceals this [choice], and presents their decisions as if they were deductions smoothly made from clear pre-existing rules without the intrusion of the judge's choice. . . . [A]ll rules have a penumbra of uncertainty where the judge must choose between alternatives.[19]

We see here, once again, the operation of a "useful illusion" in terms of the way that rules are thought to apply in law. The chaotic and contingent human element in jurisprudence—the very element that Hart seeks to recuperate in his argument that legal and moral systems are not identical—is present but masked by fictions and beliefs that allow the law to be regarded, as it must, as impartial, neutral, and fair.

Yet, for all its status as a "fiction" or "useful illusion," Hart gives a bit more force to the rules-oriented side of things than might be inferred from the previous statements. Despite his interest in the contingent aspects of judging, for Hart there must be a balance between a belief in rules that is so literal that it eliminates human judgment entirely and a belief that rules are meaningless and everything comes down to the (necessarily arbitrary) decision of individual judges and other legal actors. Hart writes, "Formalism [the belief that law follows set and predictable rules] and rules-skepticism [the idea that the law is "merely" a series of judicial actions that retroactively become seen as legal or just] are the Scylla and Charybdis of juridical theory; they are great exaggerations, salutary where they correct each other, and the truth lies between them."[20] In this way, for Hart it is the divergence, once again the failure to exactly pinpoint what law is, that keeps law from either ossifying into dogma (formalism) or dissolving into meaninglessness (rules skepticism). Such an opposition is "salutary" despite being false; it too serves as part of the larger "useful illusion" that sustains the practice of law.

Hart consistently seeks to maintain this balance that keeps the law loose and in play, undetermined by either the presence or the absence of rules. Even as he argues for "a fringe of open texture, instead of a variable standard"[21] in law, Hart also tells us that "every rule may be doubtful at some points [but] it is indeed a necessary condition of a legal system existing, that not every rule is open to doubt on all points."[22] He further speaks of the "prestige gathered by courts from their unquestionably rule-governed operations over the vast, central areas of the law" as a way to allow for the creative side of law, the unpredictable "fringe" in which a kind of rules skepticism prevails, to proceed without danger.[23]

Given the balance he seeks between rule and freedom, Hart makes the peculiar argument (one that I will explore the implications of momentarily) that while the content of law could be just about anything (that is, not determined, not according to "natural" or any other kind of preexisting law), the outcomes of that decision must be treated with a kind of reverence. For all of its contingency, we must treat the law *as if* (to use a Kantian locution) it were in fact the manifestation of some higher law. However, for Hart the reverence comes not from the preordained or the natural but rather from the inner workings and logic of the legal system:

> It is important to notice that the dominant status of some easily identifiable action, event, or state of affairs may be, in a sense, conventional or artificial, and not due to its "natural" or "intrinsic" importance to us as human beings. It does not matter which side of the road is prescribed by the rule of the road, nor (within limits) what formalities are prescribed for the execution of a conveyance; but it does matter very much that there should be an easily identifiable and uniform procedure, and so a clear right and wrong on these matters.[24]

"It Could Be Otherwise"

In directly considering the relationship between law and morality, Hart shows that a seemingly simple and clear principle of justice such as "treat like cases alike" is required to "remain an empty form."[25] It must be empty because more fundamental questions like "what is like and what is unlike?" are not settled questions. Looking at the example of racism (Hart frequently cites examples involving the legality of racial segregation), Hart shows that the law cannot resolve moral questions over which there is no fundamental agreement (this in and of itself sets the law apart from morals in his view). The law is perfectly capable of being used for unjust and immoral causes without ceasing to be law. Even the question of whether one kind of human being is a legal person is not a settled question (he cites Huckleberry Finn, Nazi Germany, and the South Africa of his day as examples of excluding certain groups of people from the category of humanity). For Hart, it is the form of law and not its content that determines how law can be sustained even in areas of profound disagreement.

In thinking further about whether there is anything "natural" about law, any bottom-line minimum moral standard that must apply to make law function, Hart both cites and seems to duplicate Hobbes. He offers certain criteria that constitute "the *minimum content* of Natural Law."[26] These criteria include human vulnerability (the fact that we are all mortal), approximate equality (the fact that "no individual is so much more powerful than others, that he is able, without co-operation, to dominate or subdue them for more than a short period"),[27] limited altruism (the fact that we are not devils but are not angels either), limited resources, and limited understanding and strength of will.[28]

This does sound quite similar to what Hobbes lays out as the basis for natural law in texts like *Leviathan* and *De Cive*.[29] Yet Hart brings his own peculiar twist to this argument as a way to concede far less to natural law theory than he initially appears to (even a version that is as limited and unpalatable to many natural law theorists as Hobbes's). For example, in the case of human vulnerability, Hobbes argues that although it is a "truism" that we are all mortal,

> it is not a necessary truth; for things might have been, and might one day be, otherwise. There are species of animals whose physical structure (including exoskeletons or a carapace) renders them virtually immune from attack by other members of their species. . . . If

men were to lose their vulnerability to each other there would vanish one obvious reason for the most characteristic provision of law
and morals: *Thou shalt not kill.*[30]

For each of his other categories, Hart makes a similar argument. In the case
of limited natural resources he says:

> Again, things might have been otherwise. Instead of being approxi-
> mately equal there might have been some men immensely stron-
> ger than others and better able to dispense with rest, either because
> some were in these ways far above the present average, or because
> most were far below it. Such exceptional men might have much to
> gain by aggression and little to gain from mutual forbearance or
> compromise with others.[31]

For limited resources:

> Again, in this respect, things might have been otherwise than they
> are. The human organism might have been constructed like plants,
> capable of extracting food from air, or what it needs might have
> grown without cultivation in limitless abundance.[32]

The repeated refrain of "things might have been otherwise" is not meant
as speculative science fiction or some kind of backward looking "what if?"
scenario. Hart's intention here is to offer that if this operation is in fact
an example of responding to nature and its conditions, it is nature with
a decidedly small, almost vanishing, *n*. Hart wants to insist that anything
that is could have been otherwise, that nothing is guaranteed, nothing
is permanent (aka "natural"). In his seeming concession to natural law
theory (i.e., in stating that there *is* a "minimum content to natural law"),
Hart has smuggled in his strongest criticism of that doctrine. He demonstrates that to base any idea of law on nature is to enshrine what we
see before us with a kind of inevitability (a plan, a logical purpose or
telos, what Benjamin would call "fate"). To do so gives a false appearance
of being fundamental, a bedrock on which to build legal principles. By
arguing that things "could be otherwise," Hart is extending the contingent, "open texture" of law to nature itself, hence rendering it incapable
of producing the kind of inviolable (i.e., nonempty in terms of content)
rules that Hart opposes.[33]

Hart and Kant

Yet, for all of his engagement with contingency and the "fringe" of law, the form without the content, Hart remains, as I have argued, very much dependent on a Kantian worldview in order to make his understanding of law function. As I have already begun to argue, Hart's distancing himself from Kant complicates our understanding of their relationship, but distancing is still a relationship, preserving a kind of engagement. Even when Hart appears to be detracting from Kantianism and its influence (albeit not by name) in contemporary legal thinking, we see a countervailing acknowledgment of its deeper power. At one point in *The Concept of Law*, Hart asks:

> Does the morality, with which law must conform if it is to be good, mean the accepted morality of the group whose law it is, even though this may rest on superstition or may withhold its benefits and protection from slaves or subject classes? Or does morality mean standards which are enlightened in the sense that they rest on rational beliefs as to matters of fact, and accept all human beings as entitled to equal consideration and respect?
>
> No doubt the contention that a legal system must treat all human beings within its scope as entitled to certain basic protections and freedoms, is now generally accepted as a statement of an ideal of obvious relevance in the criticism of law. Even where practice departs from it, lip service to this ideal is usually forthcoming.[34]

The questions Hart poses here are typically (for him) rhetorical. Somehow, even in conveying the notion that Kantianism (the latter type of philosophy Hart describes) is just another moral system, he asserts that it is, in fact, a basic and fundamental moral view. Although he derides it here as an "ideal" that we generally only pay lip service to, such a view is not so far from Kant's own understanding in the sense that for Kant too, his philosophy is an ideal (albeit one in his view with a far greater impact in the world than Hart would allow).

Such a simultaneous approach to and distancing from Kant occurs quite often in Hart's work. We see an example of this move in Hart's essay "Legal Positivism and the Separation of Law from Morals." Speaking of a situation in which a judge had to decide if an airplane counted as a "vehicle," for example (a situation not anticipated by the earlier drafters of the law), Hart expounds on the nature of legal, as opposed to moral, reasoning:

If a penumbra of uncertainty must surround all legal rules, then application to specific cases in the penumbral area cannot be a matter of logical deduction, and so deductive reasoning, which for generations has been cherished as the very perfection of human reasoning, cannot serve as a model for what judges, or indeed anyone, should do in bringing particular cases under general rules. In this area men cannot live by deduction alone. And it follows that if legal arguments and legal decisions of penumbral questions are to be rational, their rationality must lie in something other than a logical relation to premises. So if it is rational or "sound" to argue and to decide that for the purposes of this rule an airplane is not a vehicle, this argument must be sound or rational without being logically conclusive.[35]

Here, we see that reason—a bedrock of Kantian philosophy and (therefore) packed with presuppositions and moral assumptions—is not disavowed by Hart. Instead, he argues for a unique kind of legal reasoning, which, although it follows different patterns and has a different relationship to logic than moral reasoning, remains a form of reasoning nonetheless.

Even the more conventional, nonlegal notion of reasoning has a vital place in Hart's conception. In this case, this understanding of reason bolsters and supports the law; reason for Hart leads human beings into situations in which they become available for and susceptible to legal subjectivity. For example, in one of the several places in which Hart—in his own version of social contract theory—considers "primitive" humans lack of recourse to formal modes of law (and punishment), he writes:

> Yet, except in very small closely-knit societies, submission to the system of restraints would be folly if there were no organization for the coercion of those who would then try to obtain the advantages of the system without submitting to its obligations. "Sanctions" are therefore required not as the normal motive for obedience, but as a *guarantee* that those who would voluntarily obey shall not be sacrificed to those who would not. To obey, without this, would be to risk going to the wall. Given this standing danger, what reason demands is *voluntary* co-operation in a *coercive* system.[36]

In Hart's genealogy of law, then, we see that behind the assertion that nature "could be otherwise," there is a prior assertion, "what reason demands." Without this, we really could "risk going to the wall." All of his careful attempts to undermine and bracket nature and natural law notwithstanding, Hart is not going to jettison the one guiding principle that allows the law to be decent and moral *most of the time* (not to mention the role of reason in controlling our behavior more generally so that we aren't always in need of the legal system per se). And, just as with Kant, where reason is not itself sufficient, law as sanction provides a backup to ensure that those who are less reasonable will still obey. Yet clearly reason is prior to sanction (and must be for Hart). Even if Hart concedes that the law can serve a perfectly evil cause (his repeated example is Nazi Germany, where sanction is paramount), reason guarantees that such examples will be exceptional and rare and that they will not last forever. Amid the radical contingency that Hart seems to introduce even into the core bedrock of moral law (nature), he nonetheless retains some trace (and, at times, far more than a trace) of the kinds of reasoned orderings that we see in Kant's own work.

Another example of Hart invoking—and relying upon—reason comes when he introduces his discussion of the "minimum content of natural law." He asks—still in a Hobbesian vein—why it is that human beings seek, by and large, to remain alive, why survival is a key and basic moral value for us. At first he makes a philosophical argument that our basic understanding of notions of "danger and safety, harm and benefit, need and function" are all based on a presumed favoring of survival over death in human beings, and that to part from this understanding courts an abyss of nonmeaning.

Hart then turns to a "simpler, less philosophical consideration" for why we favor survival (part of which was previously cited).[37]

> We wish to know whether, among those social arrangements, there are some which may illuminatingly be ranked as natural laws discoverable by reason, and what their relation is to human law and morality. To raise this or any question concerning *how* men should live together, we must assume that their aim, generally speaking, is to live. From this point of view the argument is a simple one. Reflection on some very obvious generalizations—indeed truisms—concerning human nature and the world in which men live, show that as long as these hold good, there are certain rules of conduct which any social organization must contain if it is to be viable. . . . Such universally recognized principles of conduct which have a basis in elementary truths concerning human beings, their natural environment and aims, may be considered the *minimum content* of Natural Law, in contrast with the more grandiose and more challengeable constructions which have often been proffered under that name.[38]

As we have already seen, Hart will go on to show that the "natural environment and aims" of human beings (their vulnerability, their equality, etc.) "could be otherwise," but even before this, or rather alongside this, there comes another presumption, that in whatever context we find ourselves (whether we develop, or might have developed, hard carapaces, plant-like nutritional systems, or immense inequalities in strength and sleeping cycles, for example) we will always turn to reason to discover these natural laws however minimal they might be. Reason remains constant even while nature changes and adapts. No matter what kinds of creatures we end up being, and no matter what kind of arrangements our "nature" leads us to, reason will be there to ensure that we have a "minimum content" of order and fairness (and, here again, in favoring reason over nature, Hart is evincing a more than modest allegiance to Kant, including his lack of interest in the physical facts and aspects of nature). Reason is thus, for Hart, a fallback that saves us from what he regards as a real abyss ("going to the wall"), which would be the consequence of completely embracing the contingency of law.

We see a Kantian approach in Hart more generally when it comes to his understand of the subject's experience of law. Toward the end of his discussion of law and morality, Hart writes:

> In the earlier chapters of this book we stressed the fact that the existence of a legal system is a social phenomenon which always presents two aspects, to both of which we must attend if our view of it is to be realistic. It involves the attitudes and behavior involved in the voluntary acceptance of rules and also in the simple attitudes and behavior involved in mere obedience or acquiescence.[39]

Here, we have something of a version of Kant's two standpoints; only in this case, it is a social division of labor (although Hart concedes that both standpoints can "are to be found often in the same individual").[40] The law is experienced simultaneously as something voluntary, a law that we give to ourselves, and as an external threat (the remnant, perhaps, of Austin's view that law is an "order backed by threats").[41] But it is often different social elements that experience these laws in their different experiential facets:

> Hence a society with laws contains those who look upon its rules from the internal view as accepted standards of behavior, and not merely as reliable predictions of what will befall them, at the hands of officials, if they disobey. But it also comprises those upon whom,

either because they are malefactors or mere helpless victims of the system, these legal standards have to be imposed by force or threat of force; they are concerned with the rules merely as a source of possible punishment.[42]

So, although a given individual can and perhaps will experience the law in these two ways, it seems clear that some members of society will experience the law more in one way (as freedom or autonomy, as a law they choose, that they give to "themselves") and others will experience it in another way (as duty, as a law they dare not disobey). Although he makes allowances that those who experience the law in the second, obligatory way may be "victims" of an unjust law that favors some at the expense of others, it also can serve, in the better examples (and clearly, Hart expects and hopes these to predominate), to preserve the rational many from any "malefactor," to ensure that whatever reason determines as right will not be overly trumped by random and erroneous acts and thoughts. In this way, Hart is showing an allegiance not only to Kant, but to Locke, and we see that his flirtation with contingency is strong but not definitive.

Finally, in thinking about the ways that Hart is subtly (and sometimes not so subtly) Kantian, he even has a version of the "ought" in his work, although here again, he takes pains to argue that the "ought" that comes with law is not the same "ought" that we get from moral philosophy. Hart tells us: "We say to our neighbour, 'You ought not to lie,' and that may certainly be a moral judgment, but we should remember that the baffled poisoner may say, 'I ought to have given her a second dose.'"[43] The "ought" in the case of legal thinking is more like the second version, more a question of efficacy, of process and ordering, than it is a universal and moral duty (Hart writes: "We may say of many a decision: 'Yes, that is right; that is as it ought to be,' and we may mean only that some accepted purpose or policy has been thereby advanced").[44]

Yet here, as with the case of reason, we can see that Hart's legal "ought" is perhaps complementary to, rather than simply different from, Kant's moral "ought." In this case, as we will see more clearly momentarily, the moral "ought" can bolster the law when it fails (even as normally for Hart it is the other way around). At one point in "Legal Positivism and the Separation of Law from Morals," Hart writes (putting this idea in the mouth of his predecessors in legal positivism):

In the case of Austin and, of course, Bentham [we find] the conviction that if laws reached a certain degree of iniquity then there would be a plain moral obligation to resist them and to withhold obedience. We shall see, when we consider the alternatives, that this simple presentation of the human dilemma which may arise has much to be said for it.[45]

Here, the moral "ought" is, as with reasoning, a kind of backdrop against which Hart can safely risk the "fringes" and "penumbras of uncertainty" that for him are the hallmark of a peculiarly legal form of thinking and acting. Hart's complicated dance with Kantianism amounts to his saying, "If I were going to have a moral system associated with my notion of law, it would be Kant's . . . but I don't have one." This kind of characterization of Kantianism is what allows Hart to deny any dependence on moral theory even while granting that the moral theory that isn't being applied to law is given its due in shaping and bolstering society. In this sense, the ultimate "useful illusion" that we get from Hart may be this notion that he is not a Kantian (or, perhaps, a "Kanticist"; ultimately it may come to the same thing as far as an iconoclastic perspective is concerned). Such an illusion is useful because it allows law (with a small *l*) to act as a necessary supplement to Kantian ethics even as the subtractive process by which it is achieved mimics Kantian ethics and the operation of the sublime.

The Failures of Law?

With this backdrop of order, reason, and the failsafe of an "ought," Hart is able to relish and promote the failure of law. As previously noted, the failure in this case—akin to the failure by which Hart distinguishes himself from Austin's successes—is of the law to be perfectly moral (or even moral at all). Very much *unlike* Kant, Hart seems to relish the engagement with the unexpected, the strange, and the local. It is this kind of deformation of, or departure from, moral standards that, in his view, gives law its peculiar (and empty) form. Hart gives us the strongest sense of law's failure to be a moral code (albeit a productive, useful, and necessary failure) in his well-known consideration of laws under Nazi Germany and whether they could properly be considered laws at all. This argument was the basis of a famous debate between Hart and Lon Fuller (already mentioned). In that debate both Hart and Fuller considered the 1949 case of a German woman who, during the Nazi period, informed on her husband simply in order to get rid of him. While the case concerns a set of actions that are clearly examples of moral bankruptcy, Hart argues, both in *The Concept of Law* and in his direct arguments with Fuller (the already cited "Legal Positivism and the Separation of Law and Morals)," that the edicts of the Third Reich must still be considered laws, however "iniquitous."[46]

For Hart, we now can see more clearly the other side of the coin: here law serves to maintain a minimum structure of social order when morality itself has failed (in this way the failure of law to conform to moral standards actually safeguards society against the upheavals that come from a lack of consensus about moral questions or, worse yet, when that consensus comes up lacking). Although law is capable of promoting great evil (and therefore truly failing to be moral), this is a price Hart is willing to pay, and says we all must pay, to avoid the pitfalls of a morally based legal system (where morality can simply be wrong or even evil without any recourse). Separating the law from moral systems ensures that we will never confuse the two (so that formalist types can't think they are being moral when following the law, even in Nazi Germany) and so that some modicum of order is always possible in any society.

Aligning himself in this case with Bentham and Austin, Hart writes of this question:

> Older writers who, like Bentham and Austin, insisted on the distinction between what law is and what it ought to be, did so partly because they thought that unless men kept these separate they might, without counting the cost to society, make hasty judgments that laws were invalid and ought not to be obeyed.[47]

He calls such an outcome a "danger of anarchy" (although he claims that such a view may be "oversimplified)."[48] If everyone were free to judge whether a law was moral or not (and decide whether to follow it accordingly), Hart frets, law would become utterly undone. This seems quite opposed to Benjamin's notion that individual laws are to be "wrestle[d] with . . . in solitude," much less "abandoned" (a question I will return to in the conclusion of this chapter). Although, as already noted, Hart freely admits that law has an "open texture," he doesn't want it to be *too* open. If anarchism (as he understands the term) is an extreme version of Hart's concept of "rules-skepticism," it is one that seems to threaten the entire edifice of law. Here again, Hart allows for a kind of radical negativity at the fringes of law, but such a fringe is made possible by the "prestige" of rule following, the predictable judgments that form the bulk of legal decision.

As with Kant, then, Hart's engagement with negativity is meant to reinforce, rather than undermine, a sense of order. However, Hart seeks to hedge his bets by relying *both* on moral and on positive law. They work, as it were, in tandem (in a kind of "good cop, bad cop" model, almost literally). The "empty form" of law ensures a minimum content of natural law (any more would contaminate the law, preventing the critical appearance of distance). There remains just enough content anyway to ensure that when that empty form gets hijacked, as in the case of Nazi Germany, by an ideology that only poses as moral but is in fact evil, such a disaster will be short-lived and eventually will be overturned. We see then that Hart's distancing from Kant is not quite an abandonment (as it would be for Benjamin); the traces of Kant that remain are sufficient to allow Hart's apparent rebellion from morals not to go too far, not to descend into "anarchy." In this way, for all his appreciation of negativism and disavowal, Hart's "failure" is not utter; he himself ensures that law's failure to be moral does not entirely succeed.

Other Legal Positivists

To complete this discussion of Hart's legal positivism, it is useful to discuss a few other thinkers who subscribe to the same creed. Although Hart is the best known and most canonical of these figures, looking briefly at some of the other thinkers in this movement will show that the occult Kantianism I have spied in Hart is not limited to him but is emblematic of legal positivism more generally. Among other major legal positivists, Joseph Raz is perhaps best known. Raz, like other legal positivists who follow Hart, defends Hart from attacks by natural law theorists (and, in particular, from Ronald Dworkin), especially in terms of claim that wherever there are "legal gaps" (that is, when the law does not have a clear answer and judges must decide by other means), it reveals the extent to which judges are guided by morality after all.[49] For Raz, in fact, moral values can be among many factors that go into making legal decisions when the law is not clear or is in conflict with itself, but the decisions themselves remain critically framed within a legal context.[50]

Despite this (Hart-style) slight concession to natural law philosophers, Raz leans pretty hard the other way (harder than Hart does himself) toward a strict legal positivism. He seeks, for example, to exclude a "right" to civil disobedience derived from the dangerous idea that moral codes can trump legal ones and that laws can be challenged on such grounds.[51] He also considers the right to conscientious objection, which he considers to be a "private act" meant only for individuals to avoid obeying a law they find to be immoral (as opposed to civil disobedience, which is public and seeks to "change public policies").[52] Although he considers the arguments for conscientious objection to be more persuasive than those for civil disobedience, he proclaims himself not entirely sold even on this point and describes his own views of the issue as being "inconclusive."[53]

Ultimately, Raz says that any right that puts the law in a subordinate position vis-à-vis the conscience is to be resisted as much as possible. He suggests that one way to do this is to avoid making laws that clearly trump moral codes:

> The main device for protecting freedom of conscience is and must in any case be the avoidance of laws to which people are likely to have conscientious objection. A state which does not impose an obligation of public worship according to state religion will not have to deal with objection to such a duty. Freedom of conscience and the pluralistic character of a state are guaranteed by its self-restraint from dictating action in areas known to be subject to sensitive moral convictions.[54]

In his attempts to have the law avoid conflicts with moral codes, we see the huge pull that morality continues to have on legal authority. What is interesting to note is the extent to which, in his attempts to avoid choosing morals over law, Raz has instituted a kind of morality (and a Kantian one at that) as the basis for such avoidance. The values of pluralism, liberalism, and humanism are not seen here as having themselves any certain moral character but are rather portrayed as being neutral, fair, and rational. In this way, the occult moral doctrine of Kantianism is revealed, once again, through an act of occlusion. In Raz's view that we should be liberal rather than moral, we see a distinction that produces a particular moral order in the guise of keeping all moral orders at bay.

In his quite recent book *Legality*, Scott Shapiro gives his own belated answer to Dworkin's attacks on Hart and legal positivism more generally through his idea of a "planning" model of law.[55] He writes that, rather than serving to realize preexisting moral codes, "the interpretation of law is nothing but the interpretation of plans"[56] and further that planning serves to "structure legal activity so that participants can work together and thereby achieve goods and realize values that would otherwise be unattainable."[57]

Like Raz, Shapiro challenges Dworkin's idea that in "hard cases" (where, once again, existing law doesn't give much guidance) judges turn to moral truths to answer the silence of the law. Shapiro argues that Dworkin presents a false choice in such cases between judges doing what the law demands and creating law out of whole cloth. He argues that even many legal positivists have bought into a false dichotomy, writing that these authors

> imagined that if judges are finding the law in hard cases, then they cannot be making it. In truth, however, judges can do both. They can apply the law by acting as morality requires them to do and enforce preexisting rights by deciding for the morally entitled party. Yet they can also make new law and create new rights by recognizing that one of the two parties to the suit should win. Under one description "deciding for the morally entitled party," the decision is legally mandated; under another "deciding for the promise," it is legally unregulated.[58]

This argument once again appears to cede a great deal of territory to natural law theory, but it does so only by subsuming what is for natural law theorists a definitive and all-subsuming category into just one iteration of legal decision making.

For all of Shapiro's advocacy of a legal positivism that is divorced or free from moral codes, here again, we find not so much the definitive abandonment of morality and norms but an accommodation to them. In *Legality*, Shapiro goes on to argue that hard cases, far from posing a challenge to legal positivism, are critical for the creativity and applicability of law. His planning model of law seeks for maximum flexibility to be offered to future judges according to the social values and conditions of their own time. Arguing against strict legal formalism, Shapiro writes:

> As Hart emphasized long ago, by repressing the existence of borderline cases [once again, those cases that cannot be anticipated, that do not easily fit into areas of settled law], formalists deny judges the prospect of shaping the law in accordance with social aims and consequences. They squander the moral opportunity afforded by the penumbra.[59]

Scott also makes a similar case against interpretive methodologies that seek "plain meaning of statutes."[60] Such readings, he argues, "will lead to absurdities, and strictly applying the law come what may will lead to morally monstrous results."[61]

In these "moral opportunities" and "morally monstrous results" we see that there continues to be, for Shapiro, as for Hart and Raz, a division of labor between moral codes and the law. Shapiro too relies on a background of moral categories in order to be able to safely reduce legal decision making to the local and the particular (even as he is perfectly willing to demonize moral thinking). In contrast to Benjamin, this turn to the local is not divorced from, but rather relies upon and engages with, a prior moral (and Kantian) arrangement.

We can see some evidence of this division of labor when Shapiro returns to the question that vexed Hart as well, of whether morally wicked regimes like Nazi Germany and the United States before it outlawed slavery can be said to have properly legal systems. More specifically, he asks if judges in such systems have the authority to defy the laws of their own countries. By way of an answer, Shapiro tells us:

> Even in systems where judges are *legally* obligated to apply the law come what may, legal positivism does not claim that judges are thus *morally* required to apply the law come what may. To the contrary, this inference is mandated by natural law theory. Legal positivism, as we have seen, is predicated on the conceptual distinction between legal and moral obligation and denies that there is always a moral obligation to obey the law. A good positivist judge, therefore, would not confuse the constitutionality of the fugitive slave law with its moral validity and would resist the authoritarian demand to heed the law simply because the law said so.[62]

Here we see a way for the judge to have the best of both worlds. Legality protects judges from moral codes they do not agree with (and for Shapiro it is important to recognize that Nazi Germany and the antebellum United States did see themselves as having and following moral codes). At the same time, morality itself allows the judge not to follow the law when such bad moral codes are being applied. Scott tells us that there is a difference between being constitutional and being moral, but in either case, a kind of basic and prior (Kantian) moral code permits and even requires the judge to navigate between these poles of authority.

Hart and Benjamin

This discussion brings us back to Hart himself. If, in Hart's view, we must choose to consider Nazi Germany as being "lawful" in order to avoid the "dangers of anarchy," it seems to me this alone makes anarchism worth a second look. If the failure of law is only meant to be partial, to distinguish it but not entirely break from a moral (and Kantian) order—and not only for Hart, but as we have seen for other legal positivists as well—perhaps we ought to push harder on Hart's assertion that law is most itself, most distinguished from moral codes, when it fails. It is here that we begin to see why the occult links to Kant and his own appreciation for failure, far from condemning Hart to an irremediable idolatry, are part of how we can recuperate Hart. Pushing farther on Hart's concept of failure in both a Benjaminian and a Kantian direction (the latter when he himself has been read via Benjamin) allows us to rethink Hart's apparent similarity to Benjamin in a way that is far more subversive, more in keeping with the reading I have undertaken with other thinkers in this book.

But before I do so, I would first like to consider this apparent similarity itself. I want to show why, despite his turn to a human-centered notion of law, when left to his own devices (that is, when not read through a Benjaminian lens), Hart remains very much ensconced in idolatry. In terms of the resemblance between these thinkers, let me note, first of all, that Benjamin begins the "Critique" by remarking, "The task of a critique of violence can be summarized as that of expounding its relation to law and justice. For a cause, however effective, becomes violent, in the precise sense of the word, only when it enters into moral relations."[63] In other words, Benjamin's project seems not unlike Hart's in that he too begins by distancing himself from moral thinking (only, as we will see, Benjamin's act of distancing is far more extreme than Hart's; it's an entirely different order of distancing). If violence is the marker of mythic law, then any engagement with moral thinking is by definition mythic and, hence, leads only to more violence.

In response to his opening query, Benjamin too seems to flirt with a kind of Kantian solution by arguing, "With regard to [law] it is clear that the most elementary relationship within any legal system is that of ends to means, and furthermore, that violence can first be sought only in the realm of means, not in the realm of ends."[64] Here Benjamin does indeed sound very much like Kant, arguing that violence is part of the empirical world, the "realm of means" (as opposed to the noumenal/heavenly "realm of ends").

Yet, immediately after this apparent feint toward Kant, Benjamin feints in an entirely different direction (one that is very different from Hart as well):

These observations provide a critique of violence with premises that are more numerous and more varied than they may perhaps appear.

For if violence is a means, a criterion for criticizing it might seem immediately available. It imposes itself in the question whether violence, in a given case, is a means to a just or unjust end. A critique of it would then be implied in a system of just ends. This, however, is not so. For what such a system, assuming it to be secure against all doubt, would contain is not a criterion for violence itself as a principle, but, rather the criterion for cases of its use. The question would remain open whether violence, as a principle, could be a moral means even to just ends. To resolve this question, a more exact criterion is needed, which would discriminate within the sphere of means themselves, without regard for the ends they serve.[65]

Here we see another example of Benjamin's own approach to the question of means. For Kant—at least Kant when he is not read in constellation with Benjamin—one must eschew the question of means entirely in order to pursue a just end. For Hart, one can simultaneously pursue a notion of just (i.e., legal) means and just (moral) ends, as long as one recognizes that the two forms of "justness" involved are quite different and at least formally (or avowedly) unrelated. For Benjamin, on the other hand, as already noted, the entire notion of a "just end" is itself impossible for human beings to know. He writes that one would think that "a critique of [the notion of just means] would then be implied in a system of just ends. This, however is not so." We must abandon ("abzusehen," again) the very notion of ends, Benjamin tells us (insofar as they are certainly idolatrous, no matter what we decide) and focus on "a more exact criterion . . . which would discriminate within the sphere of means themselves, without regard for the ends they serve." This is another example of what Benjamin calls, later in the "Critique," a case of "pure means" (the same set of means, I argued in the last chapter, that Fenves reads into Kant himself).

Contrasting natural and positive law, Benjamin reinforces this point when he writes:

This thesis of natural law, which regards violence as a natural datum, is diametrically opposed to positive law, which sees violence as a product of history. If natural law can judge all existing law only in criticizing its ends, then positive law can judge all evolving law only in criticizing its means. If justice is the criterion of ends, legality is that of means. Notwithstanding this antithesis, however, both schools meet in their common basic dogma: just ends can be attained by justified means, justified means used for just ends. Natural law attempts, by the justness of the ends, to "justify" the means, positive law to "guarantee" the justness of the ends through the justification of the means.[66]

Here Benjamin is recognizing the potentially idolatrous nature of both natural and positive legal theory. Although they seem "diametrically" opposed, we see that positive law is not, as we have already seen in our reading of Hart, free of some relation, however guarded, to the very same ideals that animate natural law.[67]

For all its self-proclaimed distance from morality, Benjamin ties positive law (and, thus, by extension, legal positivism as well) directly to Kant:[68]

> Even the appeal, so frequently attempted, to the categorical imperative, with its doubtless incontestable minimum program—act in such a way that at all times you use humanity both in your person and in the person of all others as an end, and never merely as a means—is in itself inadequate for such a critique [of violence]. For positive law, if conscious of its roots, will certainly claim to acknowledge and promote the interest of mankind in the person of each individual. It sees this interest in the representation and preservation of an order imposed by fate. While this view, which claims to preserve law in its very basis, cannot escape criticism, nevertheless, all attacks that are made merely in the name of a formless "freedom" without being able to specify this higher order of freedom remain impotent against it. And they are most impotent of all when, instead of attacking the legal system root and branch, they impugn particular laws or legal practices that the law, of course, takes under the protection of its power, which resides in the fact that there is only one fate and that what exists, and in particular what threatens, belongs inviolably to its order.[69]

Here, again, Benjamin invokes the idea of fate (as already noted in previous chapters), a background of predetermination that is so utter that it compromises even endeavors to directly address questions of human freedom and justice. If positive law is "conscious of its roots" (i.e., its roots in a predetermined order), it will recognize that it does not escape the same mythic (and hence, violent) context any better than Kantianism itself. In the face of such a totalizing idolatry, anything less than a full-bore attack on the entirety of law is "most impotent." At the same time, even a complete attack on law also risks being impotent unless it can discard some of the most basic conceptions of human freedom, individuality, and law, unless, that is, it can engage in the kind of radical iconoclasm that both Kant and legal positivism seem to embrace but which neither actually delivers upon.

To put this in a nutshell: Although Hart promises a means-based method that does not trouble itself with ends, the fact that those ends remain in place (however much they are denied) indicates that with Hart we are not dealing with "pure means." Having not truly broken with moral ends, Hart's means remain decidedly impure, within the realm of violence and myth and bound by a sense of fate that cannot be denied.

In speaking of the "impotence" even of positive law, Benjamin is treading directly upon one of the most basic claims we saw in Hart, that positive law, for all its failures, offers at least a potent and effective way to run a society. Even (or especially) if the laws that are promulgated are imperfect, Hart's claim is that positive law offers a way to avoid the pitfalls that any morally oriented approach to law would otherwise fall into. For Benjamin, the most obvious proof that even positive law is impotent in this regard is the vital role of the police in enforcing and producing law:

> The assertion that the ends of police violence are always identical or even connected to those of general law is entirely untrue. Rather, the "law" of the police really marks the point at which the state, whether from impotence of because of the immanent connections within any legal system, can no longer guarantee through the legal system the empirical ends that it desires to attain at any price. Therefore, the police intervene "for security reasons" in countless cases where no clear legal situation exists. . . . Unlike law, which acknowledges in the "decision" determined by place and time a metaphysical category that gives it a claim to critical evaluation, a consideration of the police institution encounters nothing essential at all. Its power is formless, like its nowhere-tangible, all-pervasive, ghostly presence in the life of civilized states.[70]

Here we see the ultimate product of putting one's faith in a "form without content." The formlessness Hart seeks, the radical aporia that he approaches in half and partial measures, works itself out, not so much in a free process of judgment but by the random and arbitrary brutality of the police. It is the police who fill in the gap between the (metaphysical) moral law and the (empirical) legal process that Hart sees as the basis for positive law. That "formless" void, the fringe or "penumbra of uncertainty," is, from a Benjaminian perspective, the place where the desire for order and "empirical ends" of the state or legal system becomes filled after all. The negative or failure, that sought-after experience of freedom (from empirical facts for Kant, from moral law for Hart), becomes a "positive" in this way, but it is a positive that is the opposite of any conceivable vision of freedom. For Benjamin, the police are the truth of the contemporary legal system; they are the arbitrary and brutal face of mythic law (and violence).

Steering toward Charybdis: Another Positive Law

At this point, we seem to have come to a dead end in positive law; as we have seen, the engagement with the negative for Hart, as for Kant (at least when the latter is read on his own), is not truly negative, not truly failed but only partially so. Hart's iconoclasm is incomplete because he retains too much faith in his ability to resist idolatry in all its myriad forms; he believes that the distancing moves he makes amount to being free from what he is distancing himself from. Not unlike Kant, Hart has not seen that the very vehicle by which he combats, or breaks free from, the idolatry of moral thought—that is, in his case, the law—is itself potentially idolatrous, reflecting some of the very problems that drive him to seek an alternative notion to truth and morality in the first place. That Hart and Kant share this characteristic seems strange, insofar as they initially appear to be diametrically opposed in terms of their relationship to empiricism. As already noted, for Kant, human beings wrongly ascribe truth to the empirical world. By a sublime experience of removal from that false sense of truth, we intuit the moral law. For Hart, it would appear at first glance to be the opposite. The apparent truth is some kind of moral code (in which Kantianism is itself the privileged category) and law serves as a way to tie us back into the empirical world, not as a truth but as a pragmatic way to get things done in the face of moral uncertainty. Yet in both cases, I have argued that the sense of removal from truth does not succeed in breaking with idolatry (although only Kant employs this language). Too much trust in a sense of negativity and subtraction (the sublime experience) as being itself intrinsically pure of idolatry has let these thinkers compromise with truth claims that they might otherwise formally reject.

As a result of this convergence, Kant and Hart come much closer to one another than one would initially suspect. In the end, Hart's laws are not all that different from laws that one would expect from transcendent sources (with a few, hopefully rare, exceptions like the laws of Nazi Germany). We see the taint of Kantianism (or "Kanticism") in Hart's insistence that the law always be consistent, that it be as universal as possible, that it be uniform in character, and, above all, that it be worked out according to the dictates of reason.

But what if we pushed harder on Hart as we did with Kant in the last chapter? What, if anything, can Hart tell us about a different notion of positive law, one that is far more iconoclastic, even more welcoming of the failure of law to be true (the real failure, not merely the sublime experience itself)? What if, that is, we read Hart's work as containing not only an occult Kantianism but an occult Benjaminianism as well? Here, as in the previous chapter, the very exercise of engaging in and seeking out failure (which, as I have argued, can be read as Hart's version, however altered, of Kant's sublime) can be amplified, enhancing the iconoclastic possibilities that are endemic to Hart's approach to law.

Such an endeavor is worthwhile because there is much in Hart that is useful for our purposes. The basic idea that Hart presents of a positive form of law that is expressly human, that is disconnected from all forms of natural or divine sources, is important for an iconoclastic legal project. One area that is worth thinking about further in this regard is Hart's notion of the "fringe" of law, its "penumbra of uncertainty." If the reader recalls, for Hart this fringe can be a relatively unscripted and creative place because of the "prestige" of the great bulk of law that is regular and rules oriented. He tells us too, as we saw earlier in this chapter, that "formalism and rules skepticism are the Scylla and Charybdis of juridical theory." To amplify the failure of law is to undo the careful balances and "useful illusions" that constitute the bulk of Hart's work. What if we radically unmade this balance? What if we stripped law of the "prestige" of rules formalism? What if we committed ourselves to Charybdis and went to "the wall?"

In fact, embracing Charybdis would not be quite what we are doing, and Hart himself helps us to understand why. Seen from the perspective of balance, rules skepticism is Hart's term for a belief that rules are only what legal authorities say they are. He tells us that the belief in rules as having meaning and a truth of their own (formalism) is a "salutary" balance to this tendency. But without this balance, rules skepticism would turn into something else; it would become a set of "pure means" cut off from the ends of legal formalism. So long as law is engaged in the shadow of reason and the moral truth (i.e., so long as it is bound within "fate"), the "fringe" can never be more than that, something marginal and perhaps vaguely threatening as itself (so that taken by itself it becomes "Charybdis," a horrible monster, paired with the equally horrible "Scylla" of ossified rules of law). Such an understanding of law must operate in relation to a set of truths (i.e., idols) that make it seem arbitrary and random by contrast; it remains bound within an economy of instrumentalism and violence. But if that shadow is removed, however temporarily, the fringe could be seen as coming into its own; it could become a zone of real creativity, of responsibility and politics that has no preordained judgment, no sense of what it would have to do or be. In such a situation, rules would not be purely arbitrary because the very notion of arbitrariness is itself a product of the false dichotomies that constitute phantasmic legal theory. Instead of being arbitrary, we would have rules that are self-chosen, which is something different. Relatedly, the "ought" that comes along with these new understandings of rules would be radically different than the "ought" we get from moral law (just as Hart himself suggests, minus the radical implications). The "ought" of a law of pure means is one that is similarly directed to our own possibilities rather than to a submissive relationship to a series of false ends; it would (finally) entail a secular practice of law.[71]

Benjamin can be of service here as well. If Hart expresses a fear of a "danger of anarchy" by removing too much of the obligatory side of law, Benjamin offers a more specific concern about avoiding what he calls "childish anarchism." In the "Critique" he writes (in a passage, part of which was already cited in chapter 1): "Nor, of course—unless one is prepared to proclaim a quite childish anarchism—is [a critique] achieved by refusing to acknowledge any constraint toward persons and by declaring 'What pleases is permitted.'"[72] Benjamin offers that neither such a "childish anarchism," nor a resort to Kantian categorical imperatives, nor positive nor natural law, as we understand them, can resolve the problem of mythic law. So if the kind of anarchy that we are seeking to apply to law is neither "childish" nor "dangerous," not a free-for-all where all do whatever they want (and the world, of course, goes to hell in a handbasket), what kind of law, what kind of (nonchildish) anarchy are we talking about?

As a partial answer (more of which is to be elaborated in the conclusion), I would say that the anarchism we might embrace here is the anarchism that comes from the failed sign of law, that is, the anarchy of "rules skepticism" (aka "Charybdis") and the enhancement of the penumbra as a zone that has turned its back on the ends of law. The law and politics that are produced through such failure would be based on those aspects of law that remain after it has been deflated, after it has subjected to the strictest possible iconoclasm. We already got a sense that "small *l*" law can survive its encounter with the Second Commandment from the consideration of Badiou and his notion that turning to one single law "can even be supported by recollecting the content of the old law."[73] A law that has utterly failed to be true—that is, a law that has passed through the acid bath of the Second Commandment and become "pure means"—is a potential guide for, or even ally to, our anarchic political community (as also noted in the previous chapter). Such a notion of law wouldn't be utterly unrelated to the notion of law that currently exists; it's the same law, only now it has collapsed on itself. This is why turning to canonical figures like Kant and Hart is both useful and necessary for thinking about a different form of law; the "old law[s]" are not erased but rather reoccupied and recuperated. Kant and Hart both help to provide the content (despite a preference on their part for a pure form), the actual materials and the basis from which we can navigate toward a different notion of law and, in this way, contribute to a Benjaminian legal project.

Accordingly, and in keeping with Hart's contribution, we could think of a form of positive law that is truly "positive," a form of law that emerges when we "decapitate" Kantian theory and Hartian legal positivism, sundering their (idolatrous) ends. Although we saw with both Kant and Hart (when read on their own terms) a tendency to smuggle in the very truth (the "false positive") they sought to avoid, when we subject them to a Benjaminian reading, this false negation is itself negated, leading (as any fifth-grade math student can tell you) to a positive. In this way, we achieve a "sublime of the sublime" or a "subtraction from the subtraction," a real failure of these operations.[74] The form of "positive" law that emerges is positive only in relation to the truth that it has been broken from. It is not "true" or "just itself," some fresh start in the empirical world that leaves us free of a long legacy of enlightenment and terror (the two are inextricably linked for Benjamin). Rather, this positive is merely "old law," in a new guise; it is located in a history, it has a relationship to all that has gone before. Such a law exists as a remnant, but it can be recuperated both from its connection to truth, however unacknowledged, and from "dangerous" and "childish" forms of anarchy in order to make a nonidolatrous (and nonchildish) anarchist legal practice possible.[75]

It is for this reason that I see Hart's secret relationship to Kantianism (or his "failure" to not be a Kantian) as constituting, not so much a betrayal of his legal positivist principles, as a way for those principles to finally become possible. The unacknowledged ends that animate Hart's work—his denials and disavowals notwithstanding—would remain just that if it we did not make an explicit connection between Hart and Kant. In order to create a law of "pure means," those ends have to be addressed; the idolatrous promise that the notion of the moral law contains has to be overcome, shown to truly fail. In this way, Hart's own attempts to be free (or freer) from the moral law can be enhanced. Hart's connection to Kant, then, becomes the path by which his legal positivism can become something more radical; by reading Hart, Kant, and Benjamin in constellation, we get the mechanism by which Hart's own law becomes merely and finally positive.

One of the biggest differences, as I see it, between this alternative conception of positive law and Hart's own conception (that is, his conception when he is not read in constellation with Benjamin) is his distance from Benjamin's notion that law is to be "wrestled with" and perhaps "abandoned." The sense of consistency and order that for Hart are a hallmark of canonical law would have to give way to something far more dynamic. Hart himself seeks a balance between stasis and dynamism, but in this new version of positive law, we see a definite preference for the latter category. Each application of law would be a struggle, an agonic process. Sometimes old laws would be applied, sometimes they would be altered beyond recognition and sometimes they would be "abandoned." And the application of a law one time would not mean that it would be applied the same way the next time. In this way, there would be no "precedent," just a series of histories, of stories that had no demand for repetition; there would be no sense of these laws as being a manifestation of "justice," no sense of progress toward some ideal (and idolatrous) end.

Yet such a practice would still always have guidance, always retain some sense of an "ought"; we would not have to reinvent the wheel each time we engaged with law. The bedrock of this other positive law would be, as we have already seen in previous chapters, the single law that we must never break or abandon: the Second Commandment. Our engagement with this law prevents us from sliding down into a bad (or "childish") anarchism, one that is purely whim and destruction. We would remain beholden to law, would remain constituted as legal subjects. Our relationship to this law would similarly keep us from heading toward an ossifying formalism or dogmatism in law ("Scylla"), because the Second Commandment is, as previously noted, inherently subversive of such approaches.

In such a context, the practice of law would be radically different, but not absolutely different from what Hart envisions. We would remain responsible; we would seek to "treat like cases alike" (albeit with a shifting determination of "likeness"), to practice a kind of mutual forbearance. But these judgments would always be preceded by an ongoing struggle against the idols that these concepts generally bring along with them.

Hart himself suggests some of the difficulties we would face in such a situation: how do we in fact determine what is "like" and what is "unlike?" What counts as a rule as opposed to a suggestion? Who counts as a person, a member of our polity? Hart shows us that nothing can be taken for granted, that language is capable of a great slipperiness (an "open texture") that bedevils our attempts at engaging in law in ways that avoid randomness and brutality. But with a different orientation to positive law, this slipperiness or open texture would be, not the basis by which we are always defeated in our attempts at producing justice, but rather the context that makes our creativity and our responsibility possible in the first place. It is the slippages, the openness and the fungibility of both language and law, that serve, ultimately, as the basis for our resistance to idolatry. The failures of language and law alike, as we have seen at several points in this book, are, as Benjamin tells us, our most critical allies in evading idolatry. To embrace this spirit (as Hart does, but only partially, not enough) is to encounter a positive that is not so much solid and tangible (because to think that risks returning us to idolatry yet again) but liquid and endlessly complex. *This* positive law is, perhaps, what we can derive from Hart; it is what happens when we lop off or subvert the "ends" (even occult ends) that Hart relies on despite his own insistence on the opposite being the case. In this way, we can, from deep within the heart of canonical law, think about "an unsurpassably spectacular gesture," a deep and critical subversion of law. With such an act, we can think about how we would practice law if we were truly left to our own devices, abandoned by saviors (exposed as idols) and therefore bereft of all hope for truth and justice, with no one, finally, to turn to but ourselves and our own determinations.

In the following chapter, I will leave aside close engagements with particular theorists (with the exception of C. L. R. James) and seek to apply this study of the Second Commandment to an actual political event (taken in the Badiouian sense), the revolution in Haiti at the turn of the nineteenth century. I will treat this event as an example of an actual community engaging in collective acts of subversion and iconoclasm in ways that both illuminate this project and show that it can and has been done.

FIVE

The Haitian Revolution

One Law in Action

So far in this book I have been dealing with the idea of following one law on a purely theoretical basis. In this chapter, I would like to change gears somewhat, not to abandon theory by any means, but to engage in thinking about an actual event where we can look at the practice of following the Second Commandment. That event, the focus of this chapter, is the Haitian Revolution at the turn of the nineteenth century. The Haitian Revolution, although a very complicated and often problematical case, offers, I will argue, one of the clearer examples of what following one law looks like, not so much in terms of offering a practice of political or legal anarchy (although, as I will show, there are certainly moments of both sorts of anarchy, and not just in the pejorative sense) but rather in exemplifying what it looks like when law is not overridden by, but instead becomes resistant to, idolatry.

The case of Haiti and its revolution offers us an example of how moral and political—and, hence, idolatrous—values can be rendered into weapons against the idolatry they otherwise produce in political subjects. By looking at how a group of impoverished and utterly marginalized slaves engaged with "universal" and "natural" (read French) law in ways that thwarted and usurped the power and authority of that law, we see an example of the power that comes from obeying the Second Commandment. In the Haitian resistance to European economic, political, and ideological power, we see an instance of turning (mythic) law against itself, as it were.

What is left in the wake of such resistance is a legal space that is surely not free or saved from idolatry; the aftermath of the Haitian Revolution attests to the lingering power of phantasmagorias of various forms. Yet at least for a time, this revolution offered a power of resistance—an anarchic power, I will argue—that can be employed against even the most overwhelming forces (including its own phantasmic tendencies). When we think about our contemporary predicament, about the weakness and failure of the Left in our own time, about the seeming absolute power of capitalism and the states that foment it, we can look to the Haitian revolutionaries as proof that no power is unbeatable and no situation is so dire that it cannot be changed (via "a slight adjustment").

In order to think further about such a possibility, after a general overview of the Haitian Revolution and its meaning and importance, I will look at how the ideals of the French Revolution were received, first by the revolutionary leader Toussaint Louverture and some of his generals, and then by the community of ex-slaves themselves, those who fought for and created a Haiti that was permanently free of the threat of slavery (although the country was subsequently to be gravely punished for that freedom).[1] By looking at how these various actors engaged respectively with the rhetoric and ideals that came from the French Revolution—ideals that were never intended to include or even affect the Haitian slaves—without succumbing to that ideology, we can see an example of the Second Commandment in action. We see the refusal of idols even as those idols continued, in some strange and deflated fashion, to be believed in long after being exposed as such. My task here will be to explain how this unique set of events came about, how false liberal rights went on to produce true radicalism, a radicalism set precisely against the liberal values that inspired the Haitian Revolution in the first place.

A Purposive Misunderstanding

The Haitian Revolution took place roughly between 1789 and 1804 with a long period of ferment and slave uprisings followed by an increasingly organized, and successful, resistance to European control. At the time of beginning of the revolution, Haiti (then known as Saint-Domingue) was one of the richest and most lucrative colonies in the world. This one colony, part of the French-controlled Caribbean Antilles, produced 40 percent of Europe's sugar and 60 percent of its coffee.[2] A brutal slave system was kept in place to sustain this level of production, and it seemed to most contemporaries that slavery in Haiti would go on indefinitely.[3] In his own reflections on the situation in Haiti just prior to the revolution and its aftermath, C. L. R. James writes in *The Black Jacobins*, his justly famous account of the revolution,

> Men make their own history, and the black Jacobins of San Domingo were to make history which would alter the fate of millions of men and shift the economic currents of three continents. But if they could seize opportunity they could not create it. The slave-trade and slavery were woven tight into the economics of the eighteenth century. Three forces, the proprietors of San Domingo, the French bourgeoisie and the British bourgeoisie, throve on this devastation of a continent and on the brutal exploitation of millions. As long as these maintained an equilibrium the infernal traffic would go on, and for that matter would have gone on until the present day. But nothing, however profitable, goes on forever. From the very momentum of their own development, colonial planters, French and British bourgeois, were generating internal stresses and intensifying external rivalries, moving blindly to explosions and conflicts which would shatter the basis of their dominance and create the possibility of emancipation.[4]

James's account of the French Revolution pays special attention to the interplay of forces between Europe and Haiti. As he documents, the revolutions in France and Haiti were mutually reinforcing. James asks:

> What has all this [i.e., the French Revolution] to do with the slaves? Everything. The workers and peasants of France could not have been expected to take any interest in the colonial question in normal times, any more than one can expect similar interests from British or French workers to-day. But now they were roused. They were striking at royalty, tyranny, reaction and oppression of all types, and with these they included slavery. The prejudice of race is superficially the most irrational of all prejudices, and by a perfectly comprehensible reaction the Paris workers, from indifference in 1789, had come by this time [1792] to detest no section of the aristocracy so much as those whom they called "the aristocrats of the skin." On August 11th, the day after the Tuileries fell, Page, a notorious agent of the colonists in France, wrote home almost in despair "One spirit alone reigns here, it is horror of slavery and enthusiasm for liberty." Henceforth the Paris masses were for abolition, and their

black brothers in San Domingo, for the first time, had passionate allies in France.[5]

It was the original promise of freedom, as spelled out in the 1789 Declaration of the Rights of Man and Citizen, among other documents produced by the early French Revolution, that inspired a set of uprisings across the Caribbean and, more specifically in Haiti, a sustained resistance to, and overturning of, the system of slavery.[6] And it was in turn the example of those slave uprisings that inspired the masses in Paris; the image of slaves fighting for their freedom made the concept of freedom itself highly tangible, an explicit and attainable image that clarified matters for the French workers. Although these transatlantic revolutionary relationships are mutual, for James, it is the Haitian Revolution that was the source of radicalization (an idea I will return to at the end of the chapter). The slaves of Haiti received abstract (and idolatrous) ideas from France and reexported those ideas in the form of a radical new notion of freedom from exploitation, reversing (both literally and figuratively) the colonial relationship.

This radicalization occurred despite the fact that from the outset, the French revolutionary leadership, with a few important exceptions, were adamantly opposed to extending "universal" rights and freedoms to a large category of people, the Haitian slaves included. The leaders of the French Revolution (even including a figure like Robespierre) were still bourgeois. They were still interested in transatlantic trade, still interested in the value produced by a colony like Haiti, still competing with Great Britain for global political and economic domination, still willing (often extremely willing) to maintain slavery.[7]

We see here the complicated dynamic between false (and idolatrous) liberal-derived notions of universal and natural rights, and the slaves' engagement with those ideals for purposes that are diametrically opposed to such intentions. In his own analysis of the Haitian Revolution, Illan rua Wall offers us a critical insight into how, not only leaders like Toussaint Louverture, but the Haitian slaves in general, received the complicated legacy of the French Revolution:

[The Haitian slaves] (mis)understood the meaning of the idealistic phrases [such as the Declaration of the Rights of Man and Citizen]. It was a misunderstanding, of course, because the ideals of the revolution were hardly meant to apply to women and Jews, let alone slaves! However, the slaves *knew* that they were to be excluded from these declarations; theirs was not a mistake of ignorance. Thus, when they took up the words, they did so out of a *purposive misunderstanding* of the implicit logic and therefore they do not represent some sort of *tabula rasa* on which the enlightenment norms were projected, but rather active, thinking subjects who resisted "enlightenment" with its own norms.[8]

In his notion of purposive misunderstanding," Wall offers us a helpful way to think about the functioning and importance of the Haitian Revolution. The term, in its very apparent self-contradiction, suggests the kinds of engagement with idolatry that can escape totalization. In a sense, we always "misunderstand" the nature of idolatry; our understanding of truths that seem to present themselves as natural and unavoidable is always suspect, always a "miss." Yet to speak of "purposive" misunderstanding suggests something different, a way to engage with idolatry that does not lead to just more phantasm.

Here we must be careful because one could easily think that by being "purposive" one is in control of an engagement with fetishism that otherwise offers no agency. To argue along such lines suggests that it is possible for human beings to lift themselves out of idolatry through a sheer act of will. But this is not what Wall is referring to by his use of this term. He acknowledges that the Haitians tended to really believe in the rights that were expressly denied to them. They treated the idea of "universal rights" with as much reverence as the French did, if not more. Wall notes an example that is also cited by various authors from Laurent Dubois to Carolyn Fick (and which comes from an earlier account) about the personal effects of a Haitian rebel who was captured and executed by the French. Dubois quotes from the account of the incident and then comments:

> "When they searched his body, they found in one of his pockets pamphlets printed in France, filled with common-places about the Rights of Man and the Sacred Revolution; in his vest pocket was a large packet of tinder and phosphate and lime. On his chest he had a little sack full of hair, herbs and bits of bone, which they call a 'fetish.'" The law of liberty, ingredients for firing a gun, and a powerful amulet to call on the help of the gods: clearly a potent combination.[9]

The suggested equation between a "fetish" made of hair, herbs and bone with the ideologies of the French Revolution is telling (even if based on the happenstance contents of one person's pockets). To think of the notions of human rights, freedom, and equality as fetishes is note their double quality as both alluring and false. Wall notes this quality directly: "Rights were both a weapon against the existing international and national colonial order and also a projection of what might occur after the violence had subsided. They were both a political rupture and a projected social pacification."[10] We see here that it is possible to resist an ideology even while fervently believing in it. The idea of "purposive misunderstanding," then, becomes less a notion of deliberate misreading than a more complicated—and potent—mix of belief and misbelief, of misreading, devotion, and subversion all at once. Later, in the conclusion, I will revisit this complex position by looking at the notion of misinterpellation. Playing off Althusser's concept of interpellation, the term "misinterpellation" refers to the subject who answers a call—in this case a call for freedom and rights—that is not meant for her but to which she responds nonetheless (with results that are subversive for the authority structures that make the call in the first place). We see here that, given such subject positions, it is possible to be bound by the phantasmagoria in one sense even as it is resisted in another. It is this ability to both "believe" in and thwart such an ideological system that is the focus of this chapter.

Wall makes one other point that is helpful for thinking about resistance that is both part of and subversive to the phantasmagoria. He notes: "Haiti . . . present[s] the actual revolt of the objects themselves. Haiti is a slave revolt, as such it is 'the property' itself that is challenging the 'property system.'"[11] Here, at least in symbolic terms, we see the idea that "objects" (i.e., slaves) can revolt against the idolatry that they are part of. This is consistent with Benjamin's own idea that objects are both sources of fetishism and the means by which that fetishism is overcome, as discussed in previous chapters.

In the specific case of Haiti, we are not, of course, dealing with literal objects but with human beings who have been objectified (but then again, in Benjamin's view objects are also "objectified" for the purposes of fetishization). In any case, for Benjamin, under conditions of phantasmagoria, everything that can be represented, human beings very much included, is commodified, turned into a source of, and a site for, fetishism. By the same token, human beings too resist and reveal the failure of that fetishism; this is why we are able to obey the Second Commandment. While for Benjamin such acts of resistance and subversion are a constant force in the world (partaking in a "*weak* messianic power," as he puts it), as I will argue further in the conclusion to this chapter, in the case of the Haitian Revolution this process takes on a special, uniquely subversive, connotation (as Wall suggests too).[12] In Haiti the question of commodification and its defiance, the means by which idolatry is combated (by its own mechanisms), is rendered exceptionally literal and readily exportable, a source, as we have already seen, of radicalization of other movements, other places, and other times. Here human beings who have become literally and visibly commodified (as slaves) show how all human beings (who are commodified in more subtle and complex forms) can resist and upend their own relationship to fetishism.

With these thoughts in mind, let me turn to a consideration of some of the specifics of the Haitian Revolution. As noted, I will first turn to Toussaint Louverture and his understanding of the "universal" rights bestowed (or not) by the French Revolution, before considering the larger Haitian community of ex-slaves and their own reception of these principles. As we will see, when we move from the revolution's leader to the larger ex-slave community, we also move closer to an anarchist, collective response to the problem of idolatry. This is not to take away from Toussaint's genius as a military and political leader but only to note, as already suggested in chapter 3, that there is, in the collective subversion of mythic law, a greater power, both of subversion itself and of the kinds of resistance it produces. As will become clearer, the engagement with a "weak" messianic power can be very powerful indeed.[13]

The "Hesitations" of Toussaint Louverture

In his own considerations of Toussaint, C. L. R. James directly tackles the strange duality of the revolutionary leader's approach to French and universal law. James cites Toussaint as writing, "I took up arms for the freedom of my colour, which France alone proclaimed, but which she has no right to nullify. Our liberty is no longer in her hands: it is in our own. We will defend it or perish."[14] Here we see an idea that will be quite persistent in Toussaint's writings and sayings, the idea that French law is true, even if the French themselves pervert it. In a sense, this notion permits Toussaint to hold two contradictory thoughts in his head: first, the idea that the freedoms and rights proclaimed in the Declarations of the Rights of Man and the Citizen are universal and true, and, second, that the actual practices of France as a colonial power are not in keeping with those rights (or, if they are, they are corrupted by a few bad individuals). France is thus at once a shining source of truth and a source of the corruption of that truth, a perfect and altruistic nation and an imperialist power out for its own benefit.

In a similar vein, James also cites Toussaint as writing:

Men of good faith . . . will not be able any longer to believe that France, who abandoned San Domingo to herself at a time when her enemies disputed possession . . . will now send there an army to destroy the men who have not ceased to serve her will. . . . But if it so happens that this crime of which the French Government is suspected is real [i.e., the crime of seeking to reinstate slavery in Haiti], it suffices for me to say that a child who knows the rights that nature has given over it to the author of its days, shows itself obedient and submissive towards its father and mother; and if in spite of its submission and obedience, the father and mother are unnatural enough to wish to destroy it, there remains no other course than to place its vengeance in the hands of God.[15]

We see more clearly here how this kind of duality is perpetuated. If France is both "father and mother," Toussaint shows how such parents can distort their own natural roles and authority. Yet there remains a higher authority that sets up the role of parents and children in the first place: God and the idea of nature that God's order produces.[16] With this belief system in place, Toussaint is both able to believe in something called freedom—and ascribe this idea to the French Revolution in very clear terms—even while not trusting the French one bit.

James writes of these sorts of statements:

This strange duality, so confusing to his people, who had to do the fighting, continued to the very end. And yet in this moment of his greatest uncertainty, so different from his usual clarity of mind and vigour of action, Toussaint showed himself one of those few men for whom power is a means to an end, the development of civilization, the betterment of his fellow-creatures. His very hesitations were a sign of the superior cast of his mind.[17]

For James, the fact that Toussaint "hesitates," his juxtaposition between belief and calculation, is a mark of his unique status and also, at least by implication, the source of his power. It seems as though only someone who truly believed in freedom (and seemingly could only believe in such a thing insofar as it was articulated for him by the French) could fight for it so boldly. At the same time, his simultaneous suspicions prevented this belief from hampering his ability to fight and scheme effectively.

In admiring his "hesitations," his straddling of two contradictory frames of mind, James favorably compares Toussaint to some of his generals, whose point of view was more in keeping with the desires and interpretations of the general ex-slave population (that is, less tolerant of the whites, as well as the plantation economy that Toussaint worked hard to maintain even after slavery was abolished). Immediately following the previous quote just cited, James writes: "Dessalines and Moïse [two of Toussaint's most trusted generals] would not have hesitated."[18]

For James, Toussaint's only real failure was his unwillingness to explain to the ex-slave community why he was doing what he did, why he appeared to favor the plantation owners, the whites, and the French over his own community when he had substantive reasons behind his actions. Toussaint's "unrealistic attitude to the former masters, at home and abroad, sprang not from any abstract humanitarianism or loyalty, but from a recognition that they alone had what San Domingo society needed. He believed that he could handle them."[19] In discussing the compromises that Toussaint made with whites and colonists, James compares him to the Bolsheviks:

> If he kept whites in his army, it was for the same reason that the Bolsheviks kept Tsarist officers. Neither revolution had enough trained and educated officers of its own. . . . The whole theory of the Bolshevik policy was that the victories of the new régime would gradually win over those who had been constrained to accept it by force. Toussaint hoped for the same. If he failed, it is for the same reason that the Russian socialist revolution failed, even after all its achievements—the defeat of revolution in Europe. Had the Jacobins [in France] been able to consolidate the democratic republic in 1794, Haiti would have remained a French colony, but an attempt to restore slavery would have been most unlikely.[20]

Of Toussaint's killing of the immensely popular black general Moïse for insubordination, James wrote: "Toussaint recognised his error. . . . But so set was Toussaint [on stamping out the wilder aspects of the uprising, which he associated with Moïse] that he could only think of further repression."[21]

James's high opinion of Toussaint is not shared by all the scholars who write on the Haitian Revolution. Carolyn Fick, among other scholars, is much harsher on Toussaint. She agrees with James that Toussaint "made the fatal error of not taking concrete and vigorous measures to dispel [the rumors that he was aiming to restore slavery in collusion with the Europeans]."[22] But she also goes much further in her criticisms. Unlike James, who seems to accept Toussaint's desire to maintain plantations after the end of slavery as necessary, Fick writes:

> Nothing required [Toussaint] to reintegrate former white colonists as economic partners in building a new social and political order. In fact, by doing so, he contributed to the alienation of the black laborers and reinforced their alienation with a rural code that emptied their freedom of any practical substantive meaning. Even worse, he executed the one leader they trusted implicitly [i.e., Moïse], in whom they saw their own aspirations represented, and upon whom Toussaint could have counted for swift, organized mass resistance.[23]

In terms of how Toussaint understood, or represented, his own perspectives, we see, for example, that in his *Mémoires*—his account of his final struggle with General Leclerc, the French military leader who was dispatched by Napoleon to retake the colony and ultimately restore slavery via "special laws"—Toussaint gives his own justification for reimposing the plantation system on the ex-slave population:

> If I made my fellow Haitians [*mes semblables*] work, it was to give them a taste of the price of true liberty without license; it was to stop the corruption of morals; it was for the general good of the island [*le bonheur general de l'île*], for the interest of the republic. And I effectively succeeded in my task because in all the colony one doesn't see a single man who isn't working, and the number of beggars has been reduced to the point where one sees only a few in the cities and none at all in the countryside.[24]

Here we see that at the end of his life (he wrote these memoirs while imprisoned in France), Toussaint continued to demonstrate a strong allegiance to the enlightenment ideals that spurred the French Revolution (and hence, his own), despite all that he had suffered at the hands of France. It may be that over time, the careful balance that we find in Toussaint's "hesitations" began to tilt toward the phantasmagorical. Here, as is so often the case in revolutionary movements, an open-ended revolutionary spirit began to resemble—at least in the way that Toussaint conceived of things—the very regime it had replaced (a hallmark of idolatrous forms of politics).

Toussaint's *Mémoires* (written by his own hand) are some of the longest extant records of his own words, but they are complicated by the fact that he is in a desperate situation; he is reduced to being a spectator of the revolution in Haiti (now led by Dessalines, who goes on to become Haiti's emperor, Jacques I), worried about his family, and in worsening health. It is hard to know what Toussaint's intentions were in writing this document. The overriding theme of the *Mémoires* is his own continued loyalty to France and the perfidy of General Leclerc, whom Toussaint continually charges with violating France's great laws. He writes, for example,

> I observed that the intentions of the [French] government were peaceful and good toward myself and those who had contributed to the goodness that the colony enjoyed. General Leclerc surely had neither followed nor executed the orders that he had received, since he came to the island like an enemy and engaged in evil solely for the pleasure of doing so.[25]

At the same time, there is a mixture of pride and defiance even amid his repeated subjugation to France (and, especially, to Napoleon). He begins the *Mémoires* by asserting:

> The colony of Saint-Domingue, of which I was the commander, enjoyed the greatest tranquility; culture and commerce flourished there. The island had achieved, to a splendid degree, a position that had never been seen before. And all of that, I dare to say, was due to my own efforts.[26]

We see this same complicated mix of emotions in many places in the *Mémoires*. Toussaint, for example, seeks to understand why Leclerc went to war against him (refusing to believe that he was under Napoleon's orders). At one point, Toussaint asked some French soldiers that he had taken prisoner why this was the case:

> They said that they feared the influence that I had on the people and they didn't have anything but violent means by which to destroy that influence [*et qu'on n'employait tant de moyens violents que pour la détruire*]. That made me think anew. Considering all the evils that the colony has already suffered, the houses destroyed, the assassinations committed, even violence against women, I forgot all the wrongs regarding myself to think only about the good of the island and the interests of the government. I determined to obey the orders of the first consul.[27]

We see here evidence of the "hesitations" that James spots in Toussaint, but in the context of his imprisonment, Toussaint seems hampered rather than strengthened by his mixed response to France and its laws. He continues to hold the law in highest regard, but his ability to subvert that law is acknowledged mainly in retrospect. He ends the *Mémoires* with an openly idolatrous treatment of Napoleon that in its own way may be both a recognition of the first consul's power and also a testament (given all that Toussaint has done and been) to the emperor's falseness and vulnerability as an idol of power:

> First consul, father of all military figures [*les militaires*], integral judge, defender of innocence, pronounce on my situation; my pleas are very profound; bring [to Haiti] the salutary remedy to prevent them from never improving [*portez y le remède salutaire pour les empêcher de jamais s'ouvrir*]; you are a doctor; I count entirely on your justice and fairness![28]

In the very hopelessness of his plea to Napoleon, we see a potentially subversive statement about the strength and also the vulnerability of idols; when they are exposed as such, we might learn not to turn to them for salvation, not to count on them despite the endless run of promises, of hailing and interpellation that we receive from them. Here Toussaint practices a form of resistance (at least potentially), a misinterpellated subject enacting (in this case) his revenge upon the authority that brought him to subjectivity in the first place. We see in Toussaint's engagement with idolatry both the powers and the costs of such an endeavor. His "purposeful misunderstanding" of supposedly universal rights is not, as we have seen, a masterful performance in which Toussaint is able to control his responses at all times. Seeing this leader in action, we get a sense that, for better or worse, he absolutely believed on some level in the universal laws he thought he was obeying. And this belief, it seems, may have been necessary for the very impossible success that he brought. It was impossible for a black man of his time, a former slave, to rise up and defy not one but four powerful imperialist nations (France, Britain, Spain, and the United States). But somehow—and this is the true miracle of Toussaint—he was able to do so exactly because he believed what they believed. He believed that he was authorized by a power that could not be resisted; he believed in his own universal agency. He turned the sense of fate (to use a Benjaminian locution) and its sense of inevitability against those who normally wielded such power. By taking that agency away from those that originally conceived it, Toussaint did indeed turn the fetishism of the Enlightenment into a weapon against itself. In doing so, he obeyed, in his own limited fashion, the Second Commandment. Even if, in the end, that careful balance was undone and he was returned, at least to some extent, to the phantasm he had both resisted and obeyed all of his life, it is possible to read Toussaint at the end of his life as recognizing both what he had done and how he had done it. Yet, for all of his subversion, ultimately Toussaint cannot be read as fulfilling the radical possibilities of the Second Commandment; in his hesitations, in his partiality, he does indeed perform miracles, but these are miracles that are, at least to some extent, in keeping with, and not ultimately destructive to, the world of phantasm.

The Former Slaves

For their own part, the former slaves of Haiti had a much different experience of the freedom and equality promised by the French Revolution than did Toussaint or any of his generals.[29] Although a man like Toussaint had no formal education, his position of power and his desire to present himself in ways that accorded with French universalism put him in a unique position vis-à-vis the larger community of Haitian ex-slaves. From the beginning, the ex-slaves of Haitian had their own understanding of events in France. Much of the initial response to the French Revolution occurred through rumors circulating throughout the French-speaking Caribbean. As Dubois and Garrigus note, rumors that the French king had freed the slaves and that the recalcitrant plantation owners had kept this a secret caused an initial mobilization.[30] In his own account of their reception of the French Revolution, James argues that the Haitian slaves caught the gist, if not the specifics, of events in France:

> [The slaves] had heard of the revolution and had constructed it in their own image: the white slaves in France had risen, and killed their masters, and were now enjoying the fruits of the earth. It was gravely inaccurate in fact, but they had caught the spirit of the thing. Liberty, Equality, Fraternity.[31]

In fact, for James, the true lessons from the French came, not from the revolutionaries in Paris, but from the local French planters whose response to slave uprisings was brutal and swift:

Revolutionary literature was circulating among [the slaves]. But the colonists were themselves giving a better example than all the revolutionary tracts which found their way to the colony. De Wimpffen asked them [i.e., the white plantation owners] if they were not afraid to be perpetually discussing liberty and equality before their slaves. But [the planter's] own passions were too violent to be restrained. Their quick resort to arms, their lynching, murders and mutilations of Mulattoes and political enemies, were showing the slaves how liberty and equality were won or lost.[32]

Here we begin to see that however they interpreted abstract notions of rights and freedoms, the slaves' material conditions were an education in their own right. Something had radically changed in the slaves' lives; factions of whites were in opposition to one another, and a general sense of possibility and change was in the air. The slaves had the notion, however they interpreted it, that throwing off their bondage had suddenly become a real possibility.

Carolyn Fick, who is one of the best chroniclers of the slaves' own position vis-à-vis the revolutionary spirit at that time, writes that marronage, the escape from and resistance to slavery, was an integral part of slavery itself. While marronage did offer moments of disruption and the possibility of escape for individual slaves, it did not pose an existential threat to the institution of slavery.[33] This all began to change by 1791 as events in France had a strong effect on the Caribbean context. Fick tells us:

From the very beginning of the colony under Spanish rule, throughout its long history under the French, until the abolition of slavery in 1793–94, slaves defied the system that denied them the most essential of social and human rights: the right to be a free person. They claimed that right in marronage. But it was not until 1791 that this form of resistance, having by this time acquired a distinctively collective characteristic, would converge with the volatile political climate of the time and with the opening of a revolution that would eventually guarantee that right. That marronage had become an explosive revolutionary force in 1791 was due as much to the global context of revolutionary events as to the persistent traditions of resistance which, necessarily, remained narrower in scope.[34]

Thus, even if the slaves were doing what they done before, rising up and resisting their oppression, the changed context of their situation meant that they were now not merely resisting from within the system but defying it entirely.[35] This is in keeping with the idea, which I will discuss in greater detail at the end of this chapter, of reading the Haitian Revolution as a Badiouian event (albeit from a Benjaminian perspective). Here acts of resistance that might once have been part of "business as usual" had become radically different, a form of subversion with an entirely new set of meanings and consequences. This is akin to James's point that in the context of the 1790s, the Haitian slave owner's actions were no different than they had been before: brutal repression of any uprising. But in these revolutionary times, such actions occurred in a new context; rather than perpetuating the status quo (as they always had done before), the brutal acts of the slave owners offered the slaves a lesson in how to defy and upend the slavery system once and for all.

Here we see that the question of the slaves' (and then ex-slaves') reception of French revolutionary ideas does not come in a purely intellectual, abstract context.[36] It is the effect of those ideas, the radically different environment that they created in both France and Haiti, that upended the usual effects of idolatry and the phantasmagoria and created a context in which resistance was not only possible (as it always had been through the system of marronage) but effective in permanently eradicating the institution of slavery in Haiti.

For Fick, it is the experience of the collective uprising in this new, revolutionary context, that is itself transformative of the Haitians from slaves into a free community:

> The real significance of their movement, in the early days as well as throughout the revolution, was the profound impact of self-mobilization, of the popular organization and the obtrusive intervention of the slaves—on a massive scale—on a revolutionary process already several years in motion.[37]

As Fick tells it, a collective sense of agency and decision arose among the ex-slaves in Haiti, a result of their experiences and their own rising sense of possibility. As with James too, Fick describes the "masses" as having a distinctly different agenda than Toussaint. While Toussaint thought that his reimposition of the plantation system was necessary, "the one sector of Saint Domingue society in which Toussaint would have found his most logical and most natural ally, the mass of black laborers, stood in fundamental opposition to his own social and economic philosophy."[38]

For Fick it wasn't just that the ex-slaves didn't like what Toussaint was doing to them, but rather they had their own, alternative views on specific issues ranging from a policy on whites, economic and social methods of organizing the island, and even a sense of what freedom was or meant to them. In terms of a policy toward the whites, as already noted, the general community of ex-slaves was much less favorable toward working with or even allowing whites to remain on the island. Even Dessalines, who for James, Fick, Dubois, and others, is far more antiwhite than Toussaint, continued to fight for Toussaint and the French in repressing uprisings by ex-slaves for an inexplicably long time. His own combination of loyalty to Toussaint and a sense of his own position—and the need to maintain it— may have made him act against his conscience, but act he did. Furthermore, James tells us, among other sources, that Dessalines too promoted and oversaw the plantation system in Haiti and that he "whipped blacks in his province, and Toussaint threatened to take away his command at the least complaint."[39] The ex-slaves themselves were generally and always against any accommodation with whites whatsoever (not to mention opposed to any ill treatment of themselves by anyone, whatever their skin color).

In terms of their attitudes toward economic and social policies, here too Fick notes a divergence between the ex-slave population as a whole and their leadership:

> As to the attitudes and aspirations of the black workers, . . . politically this popular consciousness reflected a profound cleavage between the policies, the economic orientation, and general philosophy of a supreme revolutionary leader and the deep-rooted aspirations of his people. Personal attachment to the land, and popular claims to small individual holdings and to the parceling of sequestered plantations, was a powerful current that Toussaint knew well enough, but it was not what he envisioned for Saint Domingue's future.[40]

Against the latifundia style imposed by Toussaint, and other leaders (but especially by Toussaint), the ex-slaves preferred individually or family-farmed smallholdings of land. For Fick, this preference may have stemmed from the slave experience itself, insofar as this was

> at once an extension of that small autonomy they had acquired under slavery with their kitchen gardens and marketing experience, and at the same time the beginning of a consciousness that later became manifest in the formation of a class of small, more or less self-sufficient, peasant producers.[41]

Perhaps most crucially, this experience of small landholding was, for the ex-slaves, their own definition of freedom, in contradiction to what freedom was supposed to mean in the documents and (bourgeois) ideologies of the French Revolution and even for Toussaint himself:

> Freedom for the ex-slaves would mean the freedom to possess and till their own soil, to labor for themselves and their families, with no constraints other than their own self-defined needs, and to sell or dispose of the products of their labor in their own interest. Or, to put it another way, freedom would consist largely in subsistence farming based upon individual, small proprietorship of land, in direct contradiction, at that, with the demands of a colonial economy utterly dependent upon large-scale production for external markets.[42]

This alternative notion of freedom is rooted in the material practices (and perhaps collective histories) of the ex-slaves. In this environment, this preference tended to distort and subvert the "universal" freedoms that were the original spark for the Haitian Revolution. This notion of freedom did not involve—as the "universal" form of freedom demanded—switching from literal slavery to a wage system. Even if Toussaint was scrupulous about making sure the workers were treated fairly in their postslavery plantations, forbidding them to be whipped and demanding that they receive a part of the profits they produced, the ex-slaves still preferred (quite understandably) their own economic system to his.

Although their version of land tenureship and production may, once again, not have been any more "authentic" or truly "free" a form of production than either the slave or wage system, in its very resistance to global capitalism, the smallholding land tenure system represents a subversion of the effects of bourgeois ideals.[43]

For Fick and Dubois both, the divergences between the leadership of the ex-slaves and the ex-slaves themselves points to an unregulated collective response that I would label as anarchic (although neither of them do). Fick tells us that although at first "popular leaders thoroughly embodied the aspirations of their followers, as the slaves and their leaders were united around the single objective of freedom," eventually that agreement began to break down.[44] "The black workers continued to resist, but on their own, in a generalized, inarticulate movement of protest and discontent over the constraints perpetuated by the new labor system that replaced slavery."[45]

For Dubois, one source of this extraordinary resistance may have also had to do with ancestry and tradition. He notes that many Haitian ex-slaves were from (actually were born in) the Kongo region of Africa. He tells us, quoting John Thornton,

> In Kongolese political culture, there was a long-standing conflict over the nature of kingship, between traditions that emphasized a more authoritarian form of rule and others that limited the power of kings and promoted more democratic forms of rule. Such traditions drove conflicts in which many of those enslaved in Saint-Domingue would have participated. Indeed, the Kongo might even "be seen as a fount of revolutionary ideas as much as France was."[46]

Regardless of their background and traditions, however, the experience of the revolution itself changed the perspective of the Haitian ex-slaves' preferences (whatever they may have been before). As Fick tells us:

> An irreversible transformation had occurred in the lives of these slaves. In less than a year, many of them had travelled the distance from obedient servant to armed auxiliary of mulattoes and free blacks in a movement that was not of their own making, finally to emerge as agents of their own freedom, and on their own footing.[47]

As knowledge of Napoleon's "special laws" (i.e., his intention to reimpose slavery) became more widespread, this spirit of independence grew in the ex-slaves to the point where their resistance to French rule led them to oppose even their own leadership (especially Toussaint, who became a prisoner of the French in any case):

> Popular resistance now began to coalesce into insurrectionary movements. While the rapid formation, or reemergence, of massive maroon bands and strong centers of aggressive, armed rebellion characterized the resistance of the black in the North . . . it was often the concerted acts of resistance, carried out by small numbers or groups of individuals, that prompted the formation of similar movements in the South and the creation of a network of resistance, whose aim was to proselytize, to gather additional recruits and supporters, to call meetings and assemblies, and to devise plans of action.[48]

We see here a generalized form of resistance that has taken root and which was so powerful that even a massive invasion of the island by Napoleon's troops could not reimpose French control. It is impossible not to be moved by stories told by James and others about the degree to which the conviction to fight the reimposition of slavery transformed the ex-slaves. Men, women, and children fought with an absolute determination, and nothing could stop them in their desire to drive the French soldiers back into the sea. In the face of a massive intimidation campaign by the French, neither terror nor death held any power over the community:

> Far from being intimidated, the civil population met the terror [of the French] with such courage and firmness as frightened the terrorist. Three blacks were condemned to be burnt alive. A huge crowd stood round while two of them were consumed, uttering horrible cries. But the third, a boy of 19, bound so he could not see the other two, called to them in creole, "You do not know how to die. See how to die." By a great effort he twisted his body in his bonds, sat down and, placing his feet in the flames, let them burn without uttering a groan. . . . With the women it was the same. When Chevalier, a black chief, hesitated at the sight of the scaffold, his wife shamed him. "You do not know how sweet it is to die for liberty!" And refusing to allow herself to be hanged by the executioner, she took the rope and hanged herself. To her daughters going to execution with her, another woman gave courage. "Be glad you will not be the mothers of slaves."[49]

It wasn't just bravery in facing the gallows, however, that defeated the French; the ex-slaves fought, both for their generals like Dessalines and on their own (sometimes against said generals), in the mountains and plains of Haiti, ultimately succeeding in protecting and maintaining their hard-won freedom.

Freedom and the Second Commandment

In thinking about Toussaint and his "hesitations" vis-à-vis the larger community of ex-slaves, we can see that the people he commanded did not share Toussaint's firm belief in the liberal rights that came from France. Yet, in their own way, the ex-slave community too displays a duality insofar as the freedoms that they came to enjoy had their origin, to some extent, in those very same doctrines. Although I would argue that the ex-slaves practiced a far purer (that is to say, more iconoclastic) form of the Second Commandment than Toussaint, it was he in particular who helped create a situation in which it was possible for them to experience, at least in moments, their own full (and anarchic) self-expression as legal and political subjects.

If the ex-slaves took the "freedom" and the "equality" that was promoted in France and ran with it, transforming it into something that was very much of their own devising, they nonetheless also engaged in the original, phantasmic forms of these rights (albeit transformed as rumors and dreams of their own). Just as marronage became revolution, so too did the ideas generated from within the oppressive system that bound them become the means by which that system was subverted and overtaken by its own devices. Such an insight reinforces the fact that in effect the subversion of a phantasm does not come from "without" the phantasmagoria but through and from the phantasm itself.[50]

The ex-slaves are not operating, therefore, in a political space that is free from phantasm and idolatry any more than Toussaint. But their resistance to idolatry, that is, their engagement with the Second Commandment, is greater than his because they have simplified their relationship to representation (and idolatry) down to its pith. What for Toussaint is a complex engagement with ideas of freedom and equality, a love-hate relationship with France and the Enlightenment, is for the ex-slaves boiled down to a simple premise—their refusal, at all costs, to be reenslaved. This recalls Badiou's notion, already cited in chapter 2, that through the encounter with the Second Commandment, the law becomes "reduced to a single maxim that must not be carved onto stone."[51] In the case of the ex-slaves, that maxim can be summarized as "We will never again be reduced to slavery." With such a denuded and basic conviction as the anchor for the entire spectrum of their resistance, the ex-slaves' engagement with phantasms is necessarily also more limited; the ex-slave population as a whole therefore proved itself to be much less persuaded by the blandishments of Enlightenment thought than Toussaint himself (an idea I'll return to shortly).

This simplicity, this denuding of idolatry to the point where it is no longer totalizing and determinant (so that their response is not a "hesitation," as with Toussaint, but a full-throttled subversion), spread, as already noted, from the colony to the metropole. James tells us that it is the experience of the slave uprising in Haiti that helped to radicalize the masses in France. James is careful to argue that the radicalization of the Haitian masses happened first (he offers two subsequent chapters of his account of the radicalization of the masses. The first is called "The San Domingo Masses Begin" and the second is called "And the Paris Masses Complete"). It was only after they witnessed the experience of the slaves in Haiti, when the idea of freedom became as tangible, as legible as casting off of actual chains, that the Parisian masses were able to subvert their own phantasms. They too were inspired (or misinterpellated) by a form of freedom that was not really intended for them as a means to upend their own subservience to phantasm, to the idolatries of nascent capitalism in France.

This resistance even applied, as already noted, to the ex-slaves' own relationship to their leaders. Whether the phantasms they resisted came from France or from Haiti, we see a consistency on the part of the broad population of ex-slaves that suggests, once again, the anarchic tendency inherent in obeying the Second Commandment. The more this commandment gets obeyed, the more various kinds of centralized power and authority are dissipated, allowing a communal political response instead.

The Haitian ex-slaves, because they were, as Wall tells us, both object and subject, occupied a hybrid position between idolatry and the "freedom" that this idolatry promised but never delivered. By showing how an idol like freedom can be the basis for its own resistance, for producing, if not "authentic" and "true" freedom, then at least a freedom that serves, a freedom that is not part of the intentions of phantasmic capitalism, the slaves of Haiti show us all not only that it is possible to subvert idolatry, to obey the Second Commandment, but further that it *has been done*. This, not just in small individual moments (something that Benjamin informs us happens all the time, at every moment), but in a widespread and collective movement that changed the whole world.

Reading Haiti as an (or the) Event

For all of these reasons, I would argue that the Haitian Revolution is not simply an event, to use a Badiouian term, but possibly even *the* event. I don't say this to belittle or downplay other great revolutionary moments, other breaks with phantasms. Nor do I want to romanticize or glamorize the Haitian context. The revolution was compromised, partial, halting, and incomplete, to be sure, just as other revolutions have been; its aftermath is just as problematical, perhaps more so, than so many others. But there are a few aspects about the Haitian Revolution that make it worthy of consideration as an event that is especially potent in terms of both thinking about how to obey the Second Commandment and the effect that this event has upon us in our own time, and in our own struggle.

As already discussed, the fact that the Haitian Revolution was about slavery is vitally important. Although the Haitians wanted neither slavery itself nor a capitalist wage system, the former model is far more impervious to the seductions of the phantasmagoria than the latter. As we know all too well, it is entirely possible for a wage earner to consider herself free; the blandishments of liberal capitalism provide plenty of fodder for such thinking. An actual slave, on the other hand, knows she is not free (some ironic statements by Rousseau notwithstanding).[52] The very concept of "freedom" is itself, in the phantasmagorical context, a pure delusion. Yet in the case of Haiti this delusion was denuded down to its most basic form, to the pith of representation. Here the literalness of the notion of freedom cannot be reduced any further (no more idolatry can be squeezed out of such a concept). In the hands of Haitians casting off their slavery, freedom became something tangible and legible (if still not "true"), perhaps forever altering the meaning and possibility of the term "freedom" in the process. This case offers the clearest example I can think of of Benjamin's concept of turning an idol (in this case, the concept of freedom) into a weapon against itself, leading to subversion rather than just more delusion.

The case of the Haitian Revolution also suggests what a community marked by "pure means" might look like; after the initial lure of (phantasmic) ends, the complex mix of resistance to, disappointment in, and exposure of those ends left the ex-slaves in the position of being very much on their own, not at all on the path they may have initially set out for. The "freedoms" and decisions that they took on their own suggest what a life (and law) of "pure means" offers. Here we get a very small glimpse of a true secularity, a radical aloneness.

As such, the Haitian Revolution also offers us an unusually clear example of what it looks like to obey just one law (a law of "pure means"). In Haiti this law was reduced to the "single maxim" of resisting slavery. The "no" of the Galician Jews and the general strikers becomes here an absolute no of resistance to phantasms (recognizing that this resistance is not entirely independent from, but always in struggle with, phantasms).

The revolution also constitutes a refusal to engage in "looking forward," in promises of utopias and other such lures. In this regard, such a moment can also be related to a revolution that was near and dear to Benjamin's own heart, the Spartacist uprising in Germany in 1918–19. That revolution was, after all, also named after the leader of a much earlier slave uprising, and, as Benjamin tells us, it shared with the Haitians a backward-looking rather than forward-looking emphasis. In "On the Concept of History" Benjamin writes that the Spartacists "complete . . . the task of liberation in the name of generations of the downtrodden."[53] Like the Haitians, then, the Spartacists do not move toward a promised redemptive future (and, in that way, remain ensnarled in idolatry). Benjamin compares the Spartacists to the

Social Democrats who "preferred to cast the working class in the role a redeemer of *future* generations" and thereby "cut . . . the sinews of its greatest strength."[54] Both revolutions (i.e., the Haitian and the Spartacist), then, can be seen as serving the Second Commandment particularly insofar as they resisted from their inception any forms of idolatry disguised as future salvation. Turning their back on the future as they do, both revolutions turn their back on ends as well and thus facilitate their transformation into "pure means."

By following the Second Commandment, the Haitians became immune, however temporarily, to the blandishments of the phantasmagoria, and in that immunity they discovered a power they could not otherwise have possessed. This event, then, remains a lodestone, a source of strategy and power for any conspiracy or revolutionary action; its coming into possibility becomes the basis for a larger possibility, a manifestation of our relationship to a "*weak* messianic power" that allows us never to be totalized, never defeated even by the most determined and powerful of foes.

The question of how the Haitian Revolution relates to other events leads us to another, and related, reason that the Haitian Revolution is especially transgressive, possibly *the* (as opposed to an) event.[55] It was in some ways *more* impossible than any of the events Badiou speaks of in *The Communist Hypothesis*. Perhaps the term "more impossible" sounds ludicrous, but what I mean by here is that the coming into possibility of the event in Haiti contributed vitally and tangibly to the coming into possibility of all those other events that followed in time. Its possibility made those events *less* impossible. The crystallization of opposition represented in the casting off of slavery was a kernel that was available to and influential upon these other revolutions even when they were not directly (or even indirectly) aware of that effect. Insofar as the Haitian Revolution provided the impetus for the radicalization of the French Revolution, as we have already seen, it was a central influence on the revolution that itself became the global model of revolution per se. As such, the radicalism of the French Revolution became a vehicle for the even greater radicalism of the Haitian Revolution that was smuggled within it. This radicalism—this resistance to the phantasmagoria—was imported outward through time and space. In this sense it is the Haitian Revolution that made possible the Paris Commune, France's May 1968, the Cultural Revolution in China, and the Spartacist movement as well, among other cases (arguably, it is the spirit of Taksim Square, of Tahrir Square and Zuccotti Park).

It would be a disservice to Benjaminian thought to make this argument too strongly causal and temporal; for Benjamin, influence works into all directions. It moves forward, backward, and sideways through time (as we understand and experience it). But in the constellation of revolutionary moments, I would still privilege the Haitian Revolution as having a special status, a node that reinforces (and, in turn, gets reinforced by) other nodes, a first among equals of evental situations. At the very least, given the mutual fueling of the Haitian Revolution and the French Revolution, we could call it the event of the event (insofar as the French Revolution has the status of being *the* revolution, the model for all that was to follow), similar to the "sublime of the sublime" (the negation of the negation) discussed in the previous chapter.

One of the most telling aspects of the Haitian Revolution, one that further distinguishes it from other events, is the fact that it was largely silenced and forgotten (and quite actively so) for the next 150 years. The fact that a society of slaves had defeated one of Europe's greatest powers (and, in fact, had defeated three of the main imperialist powers of the day) is remarkable, to put it mildly. But what is even more remarkable is that for a long time, this fact was hardly ever remarked on outside of Haiti itself. It is really the work of scholars like C. L. R. James and many who followed him who reminded the world of what had happened in Haiti (Wall speaks of the "absence of Haiti," and Sibylle Fischer speaks of the revolution being "passed over in silence").[56] Today it is fairly commonplace to discuss this revolution and its significance, but it was not always like this. There have been attempts to forget other events too, of course; the bourgeoisie would obviously have preferred to forget (and attempted to erase the memory of) the Paris Commune and other such events, but they were largely unsuccessful in these attempts because of the ongoing presence of Communist parties and workers' movements and histories that were written, published and disseminated within the metropole itself. But the Haitian Revolution was so stunning, so impossible, that it was too subversive, too dangerous to discuss. The revolution was remembered in slave communities in the Americas, and in Haiti too, always posing a threat to capitalism and imperialism's claims of absolute power. Hence its silencing elsewhere.

The fact that we can speak of it so openly today without capitalism falling apart does not mean that it is any less a dangerous moment for the phantasmagoria. Instead, it speaks to the ability of capitalism to absorb almost any threat to itself, turning it into a commodity of sorts. But even such a commodification does not lessen the impact of the Haitian Revolution because, once again, at its core lies a nugget—the single maxim of saying no to slavery—that cannot be further commodified, cannot be denied or overwritten. The story of Haiti, whether spoken or not, remains a permanent and dangerous threat to the phantasmagoria in all of its power (more dangerous than ever perhaps insofar as it has been absorbed into its fabric).

If a reader thinks this means that only a slave revolt can defeat the phantasmagoria, that any struggle less simplified, less basic in what it asks for, will founder in the miasma of false freedoms and truths that constitute our world today, I would argue that we always have the story of the Haitian Revolution before us. Exactly because for Benjamin time does not divide us but offers us ways to make transtemporal connections and conspiracies, I would argue that if we accept the Haitian Revolution as *the* event, or as the event of the event, we import all of its radicalizing, all the clarity that it offers into our own time and our own struggles.

As such, as *the* key event, the Haitian Revolution offers us the critical value of following the Second Commandment to the fullest possible extent (not entirely, of course because in such a case, the revolution would just become another phantasm). This revolution may not be the only model we have for such a consideration: one other example that comes to mind immediately is the engagement with anarchism in Spain in the 1930s. That event also serves as an especially potent form of subversion of idolatry, offering its own constellations, its own radical example, but that argument remains for another day.[57] If we look at the Haitian Revolution as *the* event, our own ability to resist the phantasmagoria is strengthened; our own resolve becomes strengthened in a way that may otherwise seem out of reach. We too can better learn, not only the possibility of following only one law, but our own ability to actually follow it.

Conclusion

How Lawful Is One Law?

At this point, I have made various arguments for the possibility of obeying only one law. This is not to say that other laws could never be followed, but rather that only one law must be obeyed or engaged with at all times and without exception. Such a stance changes our relationship to law more generally from subject to author. This is the stance promised by thinkers ranging from Kant to Hobbes, but in my view, by reading this promise through a Benjaminian lens it comes into fuller fruition. When we can "wrestle in isolation" with such laws, when we can at times "abandon" or turn our back on law, when it becomes truly a decision and not a duty (at least not a duty in the ordinary sense of that word), we can say that we have finally become the authors of law that we were always meant, or said, to be. The one element that keeps this authorship from itself turning either into a *Lord of the Flies* (or "childish") anarchism, or a formula for a new, and possibly worse form of mythic violence, is the Second Commandment, "the law of the break with law." This is a rule that must not be broken if we are to avoid being ruled by rules, relegated to being authors of law in name alone.

In the previous chapter, an example of the Second Commandment in action was examined, the case of the revolution in Haiti. In looking at this example, I did not mean to suggest that the Haitian Revolution was somehow an ideal case, an anarchist paradise or a perfect leftist movement. It would be foolish and out of keeping with the historical record to make this claim. When it comes to following the Second Commandment, one should not look for ideal cases (since there won't be any) but simply for a case that best illustrates how it might function. I have chosen the Haitian Revolution and argued that it is perhaps uniquely suited, but other moments, including the previously noted Spartacist uprising, the Paris Commune, or Spanish anarchism in the 1930s, are all examples of this possibility. Even in our own time, the magical year of 2011, which saw resistance and uprising all over the world, from the Arab Spring to Occupy Wall Street, as well as the current struggles in Turkey and elsewhere, suggests the ongoing possibility of resisting and thwarting fetishism and established forms of power and law.

But even with these examples, we are left with many questions about the Second Commandment, not just as a form of resistance, which it always will be, but also as a way of life, a daily practice that can be the basis of politics. As we have seen throughout this book, the resistance to idolatry is something that occurs at all times and in all places, but this in and of itself is not a basis for a full-fledged political alternative to global capitalism. Such resistance is a feature of capitalism in the same way that marronage is a feature of slave systems: it is vital, but it does not necessarily challenge that system. In some ways it can be read as being part of how that system continues (by allowing at least some modicum of an alternative).[1] We can read the existence of such resistance as evidence that the phantasmagoria can never be totalizing, but the case of the Haitian Revolution, among others, gets us to ask a different question, a question about how this resistance can be made more consistently, more subversively, more devastatingly so that it becomes a basis for something more than just resistance, so that it alters the very nature of our political practices (as the Haitian Revolution did).

In this final, concluding chapter, I want to look at the notion of an anarchist community that maximizes the resistant power of the Second Commandment. To do so, I want to answer three questions about what such a sustained practice would look like. First, would the law remain violent? If mythic law is violent, as Benjamin tells us, is there a way to have a law that isn't similarly violent? Do we find in Benjamin's own work a way to understand how law can transcend its troubling relationship to mythic violence and violence more generally? The second question is what happens to the subject of "law" when the dutiful/idolatrous aspects are undermined in favor of the elective/resistant aspects of law. What does the subject become when she is finally in charge of her own law? What, by extension, does a community become when it collectively "wrestles" with the law? The final question is this: In a society based on following only one law, would the law still command? Would it effectively get us to obey, in any sense, or would it leave us each to do as we please, effectively (and problematically) lawless? Does law become merely a subset of politics at this point, or does it retain some essentially "law-like" features and, if so, what are they? To get at this last question, I will engage in speculation about what a community that held a sustained anarchic practice (that is, an ongoing engagement with the Second Commandment) might actually look like.

I will mainly revisit texts that have already been encountered, Benjamin, Kant, Hart, among others, but I will also consider one other author not yet discussed. Simon Critchley's *The Faith of the Faithless* is a book that engages with many of the same ideas that I have been engaging with here; religion, idolatry, law, even divine violence. Critchley helps us to think particularly about the question and possibility of avoiding violence, and in this case too, I will attempt to read him through a Benjaminian lens, adding him to the constellation of thinkers that constitute this book.

Law and Violence

The first question to address is whether a practice based on only one law can escape the seemingly inevitable connection that Benjamin makes between law and violence more generally. In looking at our relationship to, or imitation of, divine violence (a complex question, as I will soon show) are we merely exchanging one form of violence for another, and, if so, is nonviolence even possible?

In the "Critique," Benjamin's answer is definitive: "without doubt" (*ohne Zweifel*).[2] He offers the revolutionary general strike as an example. Contrasting the revolutionary general strike with the political strike (which is, once again, just a case of bargaining rather than overthrowing the state), Benjamin writes:

> Whereas the first [political, liberal] form of interruption of work is violent, since it causes only an external modification in labor conditions, the second [the revolutionary strike], as a pure means, is nonviolent. For it takes place not in readiness to resume work following external concessions and this or that modification to working conditions, but in the determination to resume only a wholly transformed work, no longer enforced by the state, an upheaval that this kind of strike not so much causes as consummates.[3]

Given this possibility of nonviolence, how do we think further about obtaining such a goal? Is such nonviolence possible only in flashes, or is it possible in the long run, in the general practice of law as such?

Crypto-Marcionism and the Law

One temptation in thinking about the possibility of nonviolence is to give up on law altogether. If law is so saturated with violence, wouldn't it be better to do away with law once and for all? One scholar who helps us think further about this notion is the aforementioned Simon Critchley. His recent book, *The Faith of the Faithless*, is in part an argument against what he calls "crypto-Marcionism," a way of thinking that offers such an escape from law and violence, based on the heretical ideas of Marcion of Sinope (ca. AD 85–160). In arguing against Marcion, Critchley seeks to foreclose a response to the violence of law that prematurely rejects any legal and moral responsibilities. In his view, the temptation of such a creed is widespread; he includes thinkers ranging from Agamben, Badiou, and Heidegger—especially Agamben—in the ranks of contemporary crypto-Marcionists.

Critchley tells us that Marcion interprets Paul as offering a complete break with (Jewish) law, effectively sundering the Old Testament from the New and basing Christianity on faith alone.[4] For Critchley, such a way of thinking turns to utopian notions of a humanity that bear no taint of original sin and hence are no longer in need of law. Speaking specifically of Agamben's version of crypto-Marcionism, Critchley writes: "Agamben characterizes the Messianic as a lawlessness that, in a sovereign political act, suspends the legality and legitimacy of both Rome and Jerusalem."[5]

I considered Agamben's supposed rejection of law in chapter 1. Recall that in that chapter, I argued that Agamben's apparent antilawfulness disguises a more nuanced relationship to law. For Critchley, however, there is no such nuance. Critchley tells us that Agamben to some extent bases his own rejection of law on Benjamin himself, focusing on the distinction Benjamin makes in the "Critique" between law and life.[6] By ridding us of law (the crypto-Marcionist position), Critchley argues, Agamben (via Benjamin) seeks to allow us our life. Yet as I read him (and Critchley would certainly agree with this) Benjamin offers no cover for any kind of Marcionism (whether of the cryptic or overt variants). Although it is true that Benjamin tells us that divine violence "purifies the guilty, not of guilt, however, but of law," to read such a statement as ridding us of all law collapses divine violence and the kinds of law it operates by with mythic violence and ordinary human law.[7] It is only the latter sort of law that is "purified" by acts of divine violence (by definition, since divine violence is not going to eradicate, but rather constitute and manifest, divine law).

Critchley's opposition to such crypto-Marcionism stems from his own particular reading of Benjamin. Looking at the same passages as Agamben, Critchley argues that the fact that divine violence leaves us remaining guilty suggests a debt or obligation—and a legal one at that—that we cannot avoid.

Critchley sees this same tendency to connect law and guilt in his reading of Paul as well:

> For Paul, we don't escape from the law. This is also why Paul's Jewishness is essential. If the law was not fully within me, as the awareness of my fallenness and consciousness of my sin, then faith as the overcoming of the law would mean nothing. If, with Marcion . . . we throw out the Old Testament, then we attempt to throw away our thrownness and imagine that we can distance ourselves *from* the constitutive flaw of the law, from our ontological defectiveness. If we throw out the Old Testament, then we imagine ourselves perfected, without stain or sin.[8]

Such a reading reinforces the notion that we remain bound by law; the fact that we are left with guilt is a sign that we are left with (some form of) law too. We cannot be purified of law entirely insofar as our guilt is a testament to our fallenness, a condition that cannot be denied without resort to a yet deeper idolatry.

"Mystical Anarchism"

For Critchley, Marcionism's rejection of law leads to a mistaken and utopian form of anarchism, what he calls "mystical anarchism." The principal example Critchley offers of this creed is Marguerite Porete and her "Movement of the Free Spirit" in medieval France. This movement offered that through an inward movement, one could, in effect, encounter—or even "be"—God. Looking at *The Mirror of Simple Souls*, a writing attributed to Porete that describes how this encounter with God (the Lacanian term "misencounter" might be a better word) actually works, Critchley writes:

> The abyss that separates the Soul from God cannot be byssed [*sic*—he probably means bypassed] or bridged through an act of will. On the contrary, it is only through the extinction of the will and the

annihilation of the Soul that [a state of maximum proximity to God] can be attained.[9]

Quoting from *The Mirror of Simple Souls*, Critchley further writes: "the Soul . . . does not see God. Rather . . . 'God of his divine majesty sees himself in her, and by him this Soul is so illumined that she cannot see that anyone exists, except only God himself, from whom all things are.'"[10] This is Marcionism (of a sort) because through this process, we are no longer bound by law and sin; the soul can essentially rid itself of itself and leave in its place only God (but only temporarily; for Porete, the true merger with God only happens after death).

Even without Critchley's help, we can see why this kind of anarchism, however appealing and radical it may appear, cannot serve our Benjaminian purposes. The entire experience seems to be an ecstatic and mystical version of the Kantian sublime; this is transcendence, the belief that we can escape ourselves, even temporarily. Here, we see ample ground for idolatry, a mistake (which will be revisited shortly) wherein we merge ourselves with God's agency and escape "mythic" law only to inscribe ourselves in it all the more by collapsing our own agency with that which we (erroneously) attribute to the divine. Such a move does not, cannot, avoid violence because it does not recognize that the very idea of the divine—even including the most intense personal experiences of (being or knowing) God—can be the source of our (mythic) violence.

We see here more clearly why we must not abandon law entirely; we recognize our need, that is, for the Second Commandment. Without the bindingness of law, a sense of guilt and fallenness, our own limitations and all too human (in)capacities, there is nothing to prevent us from turning to phantasms of ecstatic union, of freedom from guilt and law (and violence), just as Critchley fears. The presence of law, our requirement of it, humbles us, and in the process safeguards us—at least potentially—from this kind of ultimate phantasm.

Acting in God's Name

Up to this point (minus some quibbles about Agamben) I am in lockstep with Critchley, and, indeed, I find his work to be richly illuminating of the kinds of pitfalls and temptations of visions of lawlessness and "true freedom" that we must avoid in our quest for nonviolence. I begin to part company with him in his own positive agenda, where Critchley offers that we can achieve nonviolence—at least in some form—without avoiding law.

In terms of his advocacy for a nonviolence that remains within law, Critchley once again seeks to make his position clear by first showing what he is against. Critchley's great opponent in this case is not Agamben but Žižek.[11] Against the mystical anarchism Critchley attributes, at least indirectly, to Agamben, he sees Žižek as practicing (something that Žižek would probably agree to as well) a kind of old school Leninism and, along with it, what he sees as a dangerous embrace of violence.[12] This, then, is the position opposite from Agamben: if we are going to accept a need for some form or kind of law (a question Žižek is more ambiguous about than Critchley), we must also learn to live with a certain (sometimes quite high) level of violence.

Here again, as with Agamben, Critchley argues that Žižek bases his position on a misreading of Benjamin and, in particular, the "Critique" (in fact, the same passages cited by Agamben and by Critchley himself are also cited by Žižek). In this case, Critchley tells us that Žižek's (mis)reading is based on a consideration of the role of divine violence in Benjamin's work. Critchley tells us that Žižek looks to Benjamin's notion of divine violence as a way to justify his Leninism, wherein the Communist Party assumes the role of divine violence for the sake of revolution. Critchley writes:

> Divine violence is understood theoretically as "the heroic assumption of the solitude of the sovereign decision." Žižek illustrates this with the questionable examples of the radical Jacobin violence of Robespierre in France in the 1790s and the invasion of the Brazilian dispossessed in the 1990s.[13]

According to this reading of Žižek he is not just an old school Leninist but an old school idolator as well (although Critchley doesn't actually use the language of idolatry himself. He does, however, call Žižek an "obsessional fantas[ist]," which doesn't seem much better).[14] To think that the Jacobins acted with "divine violence" seems like a formula for justifying anything in the name of God; in other words, it suggests more business as usual, more mythic law in the name of its supposed undoing.

Actually, Žižek's point is more subtle and complicated than this. In the pages of Žižek's book *Violence* that contains the passage Critchley cites about a "heroic assumption of . . . sovereign decision," Žižek writes:

> Divine violence is precisely not a direct intervention of an omnipotent God to punish humankind for its excesses, a kind of preview or foretaste of the Last Judgment: the ultimate distinction between

divine violence and the impotent/violent *passages a l'acte* of us, humans, is that, far from expressing divine omnipotence, divine violence is *a sign of God's (the big Other's) own impotence*.[15]

For Žižek, then, the actions of the Jacobins can be considered "divine violence" in the sense that the leadership, according to Danton's formulation, is "terrible so that the people will not have to be." By taking on the responsibility for violence, the Jacobins prevent the sansculottes from having to engage in what Žižek calls a "direct 'divine' violence" themselves.[16] The Jacobins effectively take responsibility for the fact that their actions are *not* commensurate with God, that there is no "big Other" for whom they can attribute their actions (and thus remain ethically "off the hook" for their deeds). Žižek goes on to write (including the line that Critchley quotes from):

> Divine violence should thus be conceived as divine in the precise sense of the old Latin moto *vox populi, vox dei*: *not* in the perverse sense of "we are doing it as mere instruments of the People's Will," but as the heroic assumption of the solitude of sovereign decision. It is a decision (to kill, to risk or lose one's own life) made in absolute solitude, with no cover in the big Other. If it is extra-moral, it is not "immoral," it does not give the agent license to kill with some kind of angelic innocence.[17]

Quoting directly from Benjamin's "Critique" (in a terrain that we are now very familiar with ourselves), Žižek tells us that when we act, when we "wrestle in solitude" with a divine commandment, we do so without guarantees that what we are doing is actually right, that our moves are sanctioned by God. Žižek sees the Party as "heroic" because it takes on the "solitude" that Benjamin speaks of; it takes on the burden (and the guilt) of political action.

Because they share a common text, Žižek's argument has many points of commonality with Critchley (minus the notion of the party's "heroic role"). Both authors look to Benjamin's notion that the Sixth Commandment against killing serves "not as a criterion of judgment, but as a guideline for the actions of persons or communities who have to wrestle with it in solitude." In his own comments, Critchley also focuses on the shift of responsibility from God to human actors, but in his case that responsibility takes on an individual, and anarchist (but not mystical), coloring:

> The point is that we are doubly bound: both to follow the thumbline of the divine commandment and to accept responsibility for

choosing not to follow it. We are bound both ways and doubly responsible. The commandment is not a decree that is to be followed once and for all, the moment it is made. On the contrary, the commandment is something we struggle with, that we wrestle with [Critchley reminds us that the name "Israel" means "struggles with God"]. The moral commandment is not an *a priori* moral law from which we derive the *a posteriori* consequences. In many ways, the situation is always the reverse: we find ourselves in a concrete socio-political-legal situation of violence, and all we have is a plumb line of nonviolence, of life's sacredness. There are no transcendental guarantees and no clean hands. We act, we invent.[18]

In reading the same passages in the "Critique," both Žižek and Critchley stress our personal responsibility, our not knowing what God asks of us even as we seem to be acting in God's name.

Yet, for both Critchley and Žižek, the distinction between God's will and our own can be hard to maintain (or at least harder than it is for Benjamin). Of the two of them, Žižek is definitely less careful about keeping this distinction perfectly clear. Immediately after his discussion of acting "with no cover in the big Other," Žižek seems to forget this distinction, moving into the kind of phantasmic reading of divine violence that Critchley ascribes to him more generally. He writes:

When those outside the structured social field strike "blindly," demanding and enacting immediate justice/vengeance, this is divine violence. Recall, a decade or so ago, the panic in Rio de Janeiro when crowds descended from the favelas into the rich part of the city and started looting and burning supermarkets. This was indeed divine violence. . . . They were like biblical locusts, the divine punishment for men's sinful ways.[19]

Here there is no equivocation for Žižek, no space between God and human action: "This was indeed divine violence," a punishment for sin. It seems that for Žižek, when a community takes on the "direct 'divine' violence" for itself without the intervention of a party or state (that is without the heroic assumption of that awful responsibility by Leninists), any sense of not perfectly embodying God's agenda falls away (but he doesn't condemn such a move; indeed he seems to celebrate it).

This stance is everything that Critchley does not like about Žižek yet even Critchley himself is prone to this same conflation, albeit in slightly more subtle ways. As might be expected, Critchley tends to use the term "divine violence" to refer to the political movement that he prefers (as do I): anarchism. Speaking of the "anarchism of divine violence," Critchley suggests that anarchy (at least the right sort of anarchy) may itself be a form of divine violence.[20]

> Divine violence is a violence against violence that releases the subject from its (de)formation by law. . . . Such is the potentiality, but only the potentiality, of a transformation of the condition of mere life—or bare life in contemporary bio-politics—into a praxis of life's sacred transience, what we might call a provisional anarchism.[21]

Although this might seem to conflate human and divine agency, for Critchley there is always a division between the two:

> What is divine about divine violence? The name "God" is not the super-judicial source of the moral law. On the contrary, "God" is the first anarchist, calling us into a struggle with the mythic violence of law, the state, and politics by allowing us to glimpse the possibility of something that stands apart, an indefinite demand that cannot be fulfilled, that divides the subjectivity that tries to follow it.[22]

For Critchley, such a demand is infinite, even "ridiculous," because we are not up to the task. Speaking of Christ's statement in the Sermon on the Mount "Be ye therefore perfect, even as your father which is in heaven is perfect' (Matt. 5:48)," Critchley writes: "He does not imagine for a moment that such perfection is attainable, at least not in this life. Such perfection would require the equality of the human and the divine."[23] For Critchley, the fact of our imperfection, our nondivinity, seems to allow us to engage in "divine violence" without resort (although, once again, Critchley would not quite put it this way) to idolatry. But such a stance risks, in my view, the very error that Critchley espies in the work of Porete and mystical (I'd say "mythic" instead) anarchism more generally, a sense that human imperfection itself safeguards our experience of the divine, ensures that we know what properly belongs to "us" and what belongs to "God," hence blurring the distinction between the two realms.[24]

Reading Benjamin in Constellation with Himself

If both Žižek and Critchley think of divine violence as something humans can do in ways that may blur human and divine agency, the blame for such a reading may in part be laid on Benjamin himself. In the "Critique," Benjamin is far from always clear on this question. For example, he writes:

> This divine power [i.e., the power of divine violence] is not only attested by religious tradition but is also found in present-day life in at least one sanctioned manifestation. The educative power, which in its perfected form stands outside the law, is one of its manifestations.[25]

Here it certainly does sound like human beings are capable of engaging in divine violence even in relatively mundane ways. The German term Benjamin uses for "educative power" is "erzieherische Gewalt" with "erzieherische" having connotations of family education, upbringing, and so forth, the very kind of private life activities that for Benjamin (as Critchley notes) are analogous to a politics of anarchism.[26] Benjamin goes on immediately after that, however, to write:

> These [manifestations] are defined, therefore, not by miracles directly performed by God but by the expiating moment in them that strikes without bloodshed, and, finally, by the absence of all lawmaking. To this extent it is justifiable to call this violence, too, annihilating; but it is so only relatively, with regard to goods, right, life, and suchlike, never absolutely, with regard to the soul of the living.[27]

Here we can see both why one could be justified in thinking that for Benjamin human practices (and particularly anarchic ones) are, in fact acts of divine violence (although Benjamin doesn't say this outright) but also why it is vital to keep a distinction between human acts and acts of God separate. In the very next sentence that follows, Benjamin shows us exactly why this distinction is crucial:

> The premise of such an extension of pure or divine power is sure to provoke, particularly today, the most violent reactions, and to be countered by the argument that, if taken to its logical conclusion, it confers on men even lethal powers against one another. This, however, cannot be conceded.[28]

This, then, is the crux of the question. If we think we act on behalf of God, we are given a kind of carte blanche to do as we please, to kill and dominate as we will. With the divine sanction such a blurring of boundaries suggests, we can even think that when we are killing we are doing so in a way that is "nonviolent" (insofar as we are acting not for but *as* God). Here, words become our servants, a way to convey images that we approve of; we have reentered the maw of the phantasmagoria.

Throughout this book, I have been arguing against this very danger; this conflation is exactly what we must avoid if we are to make sense of Benjamin's understanding of law. If we cannot keep our own actions and intentions separate from divine ones, we can never escape mythic law, never escape violence. Benjamin's text here is not unlike the situation he goes on to next describe, one in which "the question 'May I kill?' meets its irreducible answer in the commandment 'Thou shalt not kill.'"[29] We, the readers of this text too, are left to "wrestle in solitude" with the meaning of these words. Rather than definitively assert the boundary between divine and mythic power, Benjamin leaves us to experience both the temptations to ride over that distinction, and the requirement to resist; the rest is left up to us. Benjamin reminds us that the Jews "expressly rejected the condemnation of killing in self-defense"; here, the black-and-white nature of text ("Thou shalt not kill") does not lead to a single and inevitable conclusion. By extension, we readers are invited to similarly treat the "Critique" as a fluid, even dangerous text (another text to "force" or subvert, another text that is not immune to its own forms of fetishism).

In his own reading of this question, Critchley links the ambivalence that he reads in Benjamin to Derrida. In terms of the relationship between violence and nonviolence in particular, Critchley writes:

> For [Derrida] responsible political action can only consist in the negotiation between contradictory, irreconcilable, and yet indissociable demands. On the one hand [here Critchley adopts a phrasing much used by Derrida himself], political action has to be related to—on our terms—a moment of the infinite demand or the Biblical command if it is not going to be reduced to the prudential, pragmatic needs of the moment. Action needs to be articulated in relation to a notion of the infinite that exceeds the finitude of any context. But, on the other hand, such an infinite demand cannot—or, for Derrida, *must* not—be permitted to *program* political action, where specific decisions would be algorithmically deduced from incontestable moral precepts. Action is guided by taking a decision in a situation that is strictly undecidable, and where responsibility consists in the acceptance of an ineluctable double bind.[30]

Here, the ambiguities of the text are reflected in a larger set of (Derridean) ambiguities; Critchley's response is similarly ambiguous. Like Derrida,

Critchley turns to paradox and the impossible as ways to understand and negotiate with what Benjamin's text may require of us.

In my own response to the complex and seemingly contradictory or "impossible" meanings of the "Critique of Violence," I read Benjamin differently. Rather than seeing divine violence as an ambiguous trap where we must act even though we have no idea what to do—where we are infinitely responsible even though we are also infinitely limited in what we can conceive and act upon—I would say that divine violence is instead a means that allow us to act in ways that are not predetermined. It is a force that makes decision possible where none was possible before. Insofar as phantasm in the form of fate deeply scripts us and limits our options in myriad—and invisible—ways, the struggle with phantasm gives us, if not "agency," then at least a space to act where preordained choices lie broken and shattered before us. Rather than read Benjamin as ambiguous, therefore, I see the text as permitting our own reading and our own decision (as a model for our own political practices that are no longer rendered "impossible" by the phantasmagoria).

In light of this understanding, I would argue that our own ability to be decisive, to engage in struggle with idolatry, is best supported by reading the "Critique" as arguing that human beings can never engage in divine violence themselves. This seems to me to be the only way to keep the distinction between human actions and divine actions absolutely distinct. If we know that we are *not* agents of divine violence, our temptation to blur our agency with God's becomes that much better resisted and our fidelity to and engagement with the Second Commandment is enhanced.

Here, I want to reiterate that even Benjamin himself can be a source of potential idolatry and even he has to be subjected to a reading by his own methods; even Benjamin must be read in constellation with himself. When we read Benjamin in this way we see that divine violence is not something that humans do. Rather, we can say that God's acts of divine violence create a context in which our own action, our own response, is possible (and where our response is something different, not an act of divine violence itself).

This might seem a small point, a semantic quibble about acting with or thanks to divine violence when we resist the violence of mythic law. But I think it is a critical distinction to make. If we allow divine violence itself to become (as with Žižek) a name for what we decide is a punishment for sin or (as with Critchley and Derrida) a name for an undecidability that leaves us in impossible situations, we diminish the critical iconoclasm that makes Benjamin such a subversive thinker (even to himself!).

Of course, to be fair, neither Žižek nor Critchley seeks the carte blanche authorization that comes with more traditional notions of acting with divine authority. As we have seen (and based on their mutual readings of Benjamin), they both insist that the subject who acts is not innocent, does not have "clean hands." They insist that we all bear responsibility for what we do. Yet if there is no formal separation between human action and divine violence, there is no way to ensure that dirty hands become clean after all (as Critchley, with some plausibility, claims happens with Žižek).[31] When we realize that it is our responsibility not only to follow but to uphold the Second Commandment, to apply it in all cases and to all subjects (that is, when we accept our responsibility as authors and not merely subjects of this law), we see that such a stance cannot be set firmly as a principle in any one text and thereby become something that we simply obey. Instead, our duty to the Second Commandment must be an ongoing commitment, not undecidable, not impossible (each time we wish to follow it, we must decide anew to do so).

A Nonviolent Violence?

The previous chapter, on Haiti, offered one view of what the practice of an ongoing commitment to the Second Commandment might look like. Now I want to argue in the strongest possible terms that the actions of the revolutionaries in Haiti were *not* acts of divine violence. Instead, my claim is that the divine violence that for Benjamin is happening at all times and all around us created a context in which something like the Haitian Revolution became possible. To reiterate a claim I made earlier in this book— something discussed at much greater length in the preceding book in this trilogy, *Divine Violence*—God serves, messianically, to unmake the idols we have set up in the name of the divine. Furthermore—and as a result—the very tools by which phantasms are spread are also themselves in a constant state of revolt against the powers they serve. This is why it becomes possible for the slaves of Haiti to mishear and misunderstand the call for freedom that came from France; representation is a fickle and unstable forum, and the totalization of phantasms is never actually possible. In light of these inherent forms of resistances, these acts of God, it becomes possible for the human subjects of the phantasmagoria to respond (to become responsible), to engage with the one law that ties us to these acts of divine mercy. If the first set of actions (by God) is an example of divine violence, the question becomes what to call our own actions that are in response (and thanks to) those divine acts.

The Haitian Revolution may have not been an act of divine violence, but it wasn't an act of mythic violence either. May we (therefore) call this a nonviolent revolution? The very notion seems absurd in the sense that it was, as any perusal of *The Black Jacobins* will attest, a supremely violent event (taking the term "violence" in its normal, everyday sense in English). Is it possible to think about nonviolence in connection with the Haitian Revolution in any way that doesn't seem to simply be more doublespeak, a false sense of engaging in revolutionary action with "clean hands" when they are anything but?

We can ask similar questions if we return to Benjamin's own argument that the revolutionary general strike is somehow "nonviolent." Benjamin calls such an action "nonviolent" even when it seems as if the revolutionary strike, like all political actions aimed against capitalism and the state, sometimes involves a behavior that we would ordinarily call violent. How do we think about such an apparent paradox?

Critchley himself, in his own musing on the subject of nonviolence, acknowledges that one cannot renounce violence altogether if one truly wants to engage in revolutionary action. He speaks admiringly, for example, of Dietrich Bonhoeffer, the German theologian who began as a pacifist in his opposition to Hitler. When it became apparent that such nonviolent action was not going to work, Bonhoeffer showed a "willingness to become guilty."[32] Critchley also speaks (specifically in terms of Levinas) of "walk[ing] a Benjaminian tightrope of nonviolent violence," producing a complex admixture of violent and nonviolent responses.[33]

Critchley does a superb job of drawing out some of the implications of what nonviolence looks like in Benjamin. Quoting from the "Critique," Critchley writes:

[For Benjamin] such a nonviolent resolution of conflict is indeed possible in what he calls "relationships among private persons," in courtesy, sympathy, peaceableness, and trust. This leads Benjamin to conclude that "there is a sphere of human agreement that is non-violent to the extent that it is wholly inaccessible to violence: the proper sphere of 'understanding': language."[34]

Critchley refuses to decipher what Benjamin means in the above passage in terms of language, but it seems fair to say that Benjamin understands language as a mutual and (generally) peaceful shared agreement about meaning, something that happens mostly through anarchistic and collective means.[35] Critchley also points out that for Benjamin resolutions of conflict can be settled "peacefully and without contracts" and "on the analogy of agreement between private persons."[36]

This nonviolence, a kind of anarchist fabric that underlies our common practices, coexists with (and is usually eclipsed by) the decidedly violent context of mythic law. For Benjamin, as we have already seen, our lives occur against a backdrop of ubiquitous violence. Even progressive, worker-oriented movements often partake in this violence. Thus, for example, in his discussion of the (nonrevolutionary) political strike, Benjamin tells us that we normally consider such an action to be "nonviolent." Yet such a strike constitutes "only a 'withdrawal' or 'estrangement' from the employer." It therefore in fact does engage in a violence after all because "it takes place in the context of a conscious readiness to resume the suspended action under certain circumstances that . . . only superficially modify it."[37] We are violent for Benjamin not only when we physically hurt someone but just as critically when we help to sustain and reproduce the phantasmagoric conditions of global capitalism. Against the specter of violence evoked by states and parties, individual or group acts of violence that involve knives, fists, and guns, Benjamin juxtaposes a much deeper and more pernicious violence, the violence of phantasm, of faux reality and relentless commodification.

The question to ask at this point is whether the peaceful coexistence Benjamin (and, by extension, Critchley) looks for does more than endure this larger violence. Is a larger practice of political nonviolence possible and, if so, would it still be effective? To anticipate my final question for this conclusion: would such a recourse be lawful?

Critchley's own answer is yes; he speaks, as we have seen, of a "nonviolent violence." He further states (still on the attack against Žižek):

What Žižek dreams of is a guilt-free perfection of sublime violence, where the infinite pierces the finite in a divine act. It sounds exciting. My view is different: politics is action that situates itself in the conflict between a commitment to nonviolence and the historic reality of violence into which one is inserted, and which requires an ever-compromised, ever imperfect action that is guided by an infinite ethical demand.[38]

In this context being "nonviolent" does not mean refraining from hurting people, but means instead (as Critchley so ably puts it) doing "violence to violence," turning (as we saw in the case of the Haitian Revolution) the means of phantasms into weapons against them.

Here I am largely in agreement with Critchley, but I am a bit more cautious about the use of an oxymoronic term like "nonviolent violence." Without a greater attention to iconoclasm, such a term risks, once again, sounding like one of those propagandist euphemisms such as "climate change" or "ethnic cleansing." I know that Critchley has no intention of engaging in such malign usage, but I could imagine an awful (and idolatrous) political leader who would speak of mass killings as "nonviolent violence" or something of that sort, backed by an elaborate philosophical justification (perhaps even borrowed from Benjamin). The term "nonviolent violence" too is redolent of the ambiguity that I see Benjaminian theory as resolving rather than fomenting. Furthermore, if we think we are committing "nonviolent violence," it might be a lot easier to imagine that we have clean hands (instead of what Critchley calls "dirty hands all the way down") than if we acknowledge our own relationship to violence.[39] For these reason, unlike Critchley, I would avoid speaking of "nonviolent violence" and speak instead of "nonmythic" (or "antimythic") violence, a space Benjaminian theory makes possible between divine and mythic violence.

I think of antimythic violence as a supplement to and facilitator of the nonviolent and anarchist politics that Benjamin envisions (and Critchley appreciates). By labeling such actions "antimythic," we are reminded of the ongoing centrality of iconoclasm in our engagement with the Second Commandment. And we are also reminded that these actions are neither divine nor mythic but are located in a space that is made possible by the former and required in response to the latter. To the question of whether we could ever dispense with antimythic violence and proceed to a world marked by pure nonviolence, I would say that for Benjamin the answer must be no.[40] To acknowledge our own violence is to acknowledge that we remain, as ever (and as Critchley notes too), guilty, fallen and partial to the temptations of phantasms as subjects of law. If we cannot do without law, we cannot, in a sense, ultimately do without violence either (so that a purely nonviolent politics would not, by definition, be lawful either). At the same time, our violence can be directed not against one another but against that which is truly violent, the apparitions of state and police violence that otherwise overwrite our nonviolent, anarchist practices.[41]

Love, Again

For all of their differences, Critchley and Žižek share a trait of not insisting on the strong iconoclasm that Benjamin offers. This might be the reason that both of these thinkers choose, not unlike Badiou, Agamben, Hardt,

Negri, and many others, to turn to love as a political solution to the problems of violence and its connection to law. In *Violence*, after citing a stirring speech by Robespierre, Žižek tells us that the status of divine violence "is radically subjective, it is the subject's *work of love*."[42] He goes on to write:

> The notion of love should be given here all its Paulinian weight: *the domain of pure violence*, the domain outside law (legal power), the domain of violence which is neither law-founding nor law-sustaining, *is the domain of love*.[43]

Critchley too looks to a power of love as a way to guide our actions (only in a different, even opposite direction, than Žižek supposes). Like Badiou, he turns to Paul and the commandment to "love thy neighbor as thyself" as a way to bypass the entanglements of law and violence. He writes: "This is why faith and the commandment of love that it seeks to sustain is not law. It has no coercive, external force. . . . The Commandment to love is mild and merciful but, as Kierkegaard insists, 'there is rigor in it.'"[44]

It is curious that, after his eloquent stance against Marcionism and the urge to avoid law, that Critchley would turn to a force like love as an alternative. Just after inveigling against mystical anarchism, Critchley turns to love, a force that is deeply caught up with the very mysticism he criticizes. As previously noted several times already, love, as it has been articulated over the last few hundred years (and then some), is replete with the longing for union, a dark history of enforced community, hierarchy, and other aspects that Critchley is otherwise critical of. Žižek's turn to love may make more sense (in that it is less contradictory to what he is trying to do), but I see it as no less an indication of his own move, in his case a deliberate one, against iconoclasm, at least of a certain (Jewish) sort. In either case, I see turning to love as ensuring (or at least failing to prevent) our ongoing entanglement with mythic violence. Love is entirely of a piece with phantasm; it is its sweetest (but therefore most pernicious) of faces. As I see it, what you get from divine violence is not love, but its opposite, a celestial indifference that leaves you to your own devices. In the face of that indifference, human beings are finally able to act on their own in ways both violent and nonviolent. More to the point, in such circumstances, human beings can engage with the Second Commandment to deploy antimythic violence, leaving them able to undertake at the same time a practice of political nonviolence that is far more sustained, far more engaged than under the usual conditions of phantasmagoria.

Misinterpellation and the Subject of Law

Related to this extensive conversation about nonviolence and its possibility is a question about subjectivity. What kind of subject do we become when we take on the authorship of law? What happens to us when we finally receive a power that has been promised to us by liberalism all along (but never delivered upon), a power to engage with law and not simply suffer under it? In thinking about this question, it seems to me that a radical shift in interpellation takes place. Normally, we think of interpellation as the command that gives the subject her identity. This is a totally passive state where the subject is formed entirely by her relationship to the authority figure. Althusser supplies us with a famous image of interpellation via the example of a police officer shouting in the street to a passerby, "Hey, you there!" The individual being addressed turns around and, Althusser tells us, "by this mere one-hundred-and-eighty-degree physical conversion, he becomes a subject."[45]

This well-known description has its echo—but also its challenge—in Fanon's own experience of being similarly "interpellated." In this case, Fanon speaks of being addressed (if not as directly) by a young white child on the streets of Lyons. The child says "Tiens, un nègre" ("Look, a negro"), which Fanon experiences as a self-shattering moment.[46] Up to that time, Fanon had been raised to think of himself as a French subject; he had not thought of how he was different. His experience of being in this case interpellated replaced one phantasmic identity ("a Frenchman") with another ("un nègre").

In Fanon's case, this interpellation led him, not to further subservience, but to radicalization and resistance. Clearly then, interpellation does not always work the way it is intended to. The extreme form of this dysfunction—that is, the most subversive mechanism of interpellation—arrives in the already mentioned case of misinterpellation, when the subject answers a call that wasn't intended for, or addressed to, her. In thinking of this possibility, specifically in terms of the previous discussion of the Haitian Revolution, I see misinterpellation as a potentially radical and iconoclastic force that unmakes or reshapes our subjectivity as we engage in a new relationship to law.[47] It transforms the passive subject of interpellation into an unexpected, undesired interloper. Even as misinterpellation originates from within the phantasm (the call for freedom, or for any other kind of subjectivity comes from within the phantasmagoria), it breaks from the internal logic of idolatry and invites the subject's own unscripted response. Here the failures of representation, which are usually glossed over and denied by phantasm, become too glaring to ignore.

We see even in Althusser's famous essay on interpellation a hint that something like misinterpellation is possible:

> Why [does the interpellated individual become a subject]? Because he has recognized that the hail was "really" addressed to him, and that it was *really him* who was hailed; (and not someone else). Experience shows that the practical telecommunications of hailings is such that they hardly ever miss their man: verbal call or whistle, the one hailed always recognizes that it is really him who is being hailed.[48]

The critical phrase here for my purposes is "they hardly ever miss their man [or, presumably, woman]." If the act of interpellation, of hailing, "hardly ever misses" its intended individual, that means that once in a while they do miss. Once in a while, it is possible that the hail is not "really" addressed to someone and that it is not "really [he or she] who was hailed." Althusser also evokes this possibility in the next paragraph: "Somewhere (usually behind them) the hail rings out: 'Hey, you there!' One individual (nine times out of ten it is the right one) turns around, believing/suspecting knowing that it is for him."[49] My interest here is in the one time out of ten that the hailing is wrong, the effects and interpretations are misdirected, the business as usual of subject formation misfires.

In the previous chapter, I discussed an example of misinterpellation in terms of how the Haitian slaves "purposively misunderstood" their call to freedom by the Declaration of the Rights of Man and Citizen. The Haitian slaves who responded were not the subjects of that document's call. Nor, in their mistaken reception of that call, did they receive the (liberal, false, idolatrous) freedom that the framers of that document intended. The Haitian slaves were, in effect, misinterpellated; they erroneously received a call that formed them as subjects, but subjects of an entirely different, and radically subversive, sort.

Such misinterpellation is, I would argue, the basis by which we can understand what happens more generally to the subjectivity of a set of persons or communities that dedicate themselves to following the Second Commandment. Given that the Second Commandment invites the breakdown of phantasms, phantasmic subject formation is similarly affected. The phantasmic forms of authority become like Badiou's "old law," a deflated and reduced ruin. Rather than further our subjection, as we saw in the last chapter, the call (in this case the call of freedom) becomes a weapon against its own originators; the siren call of phantasm no longer works the way it is supposed to. Perhaps because phantasmic interpellation does not let up and mythic law remains a force that we must always contend with (whose call we will always hear), we could also refer to misinterpellation as counterinterpellation, a call to a different, anarchic, and antimythic form of subjectivity that corresponds to our engagement in antimythic violence.

Unsummoned

A very helpful source for thinking further about misinterpellation comes from a parable by Franz Kafka. Kafka illuminates Benjamin more than any other writer I know. Recall that Benjamin says of Kafka, "No other writer has obeyed the commandment 'Thou shalt not make unto thee a graven image' so faithfully."[50] Kafka is thus not only Benjamin's muse in general, but in particular guides him (and us) in following the Second Commandment.

Kafka's parable "Abraham" tells us that in addition to the well-known Abraham, Kafka "could conceive of another Abraham."[51] Whereas the famous Abraham was surely intended to be summoned by God's call, this other one is not:

> But take another Abraham. One who wanted to perform the sacrifice altogether in the right way and had a correct sense in general of the whole affair, but could not believe that he was the one meant, he, an ugly old man, and the dirty youngster that was his child. . . . An Abraham who should come unsummoned! It is as if, at the end of the year, when the best student was solemnly about to receive a prize, the worst student rose in the expectant stillness and came forward from his dirty desk in the last row because he had made a mistake of hearing, and the whole class burst out laughing. And perhaps he had made no mistake at all, his name really was called, it having been the teacher's intention to make the rewarding of the best student at the same time a punishment for the worst one.[52]

This Abraham, "an ugly old man" with a "dirty youngster," is the true hero (or subject) of this parable, the one who is not called and yet who responds. Kafka tells us that this Abraham has faith insofar as "he would make the sacrifice in the right spirit if only he could believe he was the one meant."[53] But Kafka makes it very clear that he is *not* the subject God meant to call, or, if God did call him, it was only as a joke or punishment, a way to show up a bad student (and showcase the teacher's pet by contrast).

Kafka tells us this unsummoned Abraham makes "a mistake of hearing." This mistake" is the same misinterpellation, I would argue, that got the Haitian slaves to "misunderstand" their own call to freedom. They were not called, but they came nonetheless. The unloved, worst student comes from his "dirty desk" to receive a prize. And a prize he does receive (even if none was intended for him).

If we think of the God of this story as a phantasmic deity or manifestation of fate, a keeper of the orders and hierarchies of global capitalism, we see that the calling to sacrifice is a way to continue those hierarchies, to teach everyone a lesson about his status, about who is on top and how things are done. But the true, subversive implication of this story lies in the inability of this false God to perfectly control this environment. It is not certain if this God meant to call the worst Abraham or not. If the calling was deliberate, it was not for the purposes that this Abraham imagines it to be. We can see this as a potential moment of divine violence when the true God, acting through the screen of this phantasm, ensures that the ordering and delivery of the false God's summonings do not work quite as planned. There is a divinely inspired failure in the communications systems of the phantasmagoria; in the cracks and fissures created by such failures, misunderstandings, mishearings, and misreadings can occur (not just the *méconaissance* or misrecognition that Althusser speaks of, since this actually enables rather than disables the production of phantasmic identity by disguising the operation of interpellation itself).[54]

If we think about the subject of the Second Commandment, we can see that such a subject is the product of these misunderstandings, mishearings, and misreadings. This subject, the unsummoned, undesired Abraham, at the bottom of the hierarchy, may have arrived at the front of the classroom by accident, but once he is there, there is no telling what will happen (as when Toussaint arrived on the world stage). This Abraham can do maximum damage insofar as no one expected him, no one wanted him to show up. The arrival of this Abraham is the event that Badiou speaks of, a product of the *weak* messianic power that Benjamin describes (and which is so important to Critchley as well). Having shown up in ways that were neither anticipated nor desired, this subject's every action is a blow to phantasmic power (as we saw in the case of the Haitian slaves who radicalized, or potentially radicalized, the world through a chain of revolutionary misresponses). If the interpellated subject is formed in respect to power and authority, to becoming who she or he is in response to the call, the misinterpellated subject is inherently set against this system, a subject of "pure means."

When we realize further that the act of misinterpellation is not an event that only occurs once in a while, at some dramatic, historical juncture (like the call to the Haitian slaves by the French Revolution or God's call to Abraham) but is in fact occurring at all times, at each time that we receive our subjectivity, we can see that we are always being so (mis)called; we do not have to wait for this misinterpellation to reach us. Each of us is this other Abraham, and every moment (as Benjamin tells us) is a moment when we can exercise our new, unexpected, unwanted, and maximally powerful counter-authority. Indeed, as already noted, Benjamin tells us that "every second [is] the small gateway in time through which the messiah might enter."[55] Benjamin's messiah, far from being a delivering God who "saves" us once and for all, is instead a space of misunderstanding in which our own unwanted, unexpected agency continually becomes possible, however wrongheaded and deluded it remains. Into this space of misinterpellation walks the subject who obeys only the Second Commandment.

Does One Law Command?

The final question to ponder is perhaps the hardest of all, at least in terms of thinking about Benjamin's legal theory as a practicable possibility; how much command, how much "law" is there when we follow the Second Commandment? When we think about what it means to obey only one law, an immediate impression is that we are not obeying any others, that chaos and "anarchy" (in the pejorative sense of the word) will reign. How can there be any sense of order or commandment, how can there be any sense of a "rule of law," when it seems as if we can—and will—do "what pleases"?[56] This specter of a society gone mad, of killers and rapists having their way without punishment, of law being a personal decision or whim, is perhaps the greatest barrier to taking Benjamin's legal theory seriously as an approach that might actually be desirable. Even if he sets himself explicitly against such "childish" anarchism, it seems as if a system of law in which only one law had absolutely to be obeyed invites precisely this general collapse, the absence of law and, hence, the death of politics as well. Wouldn't it be better, a reasonable person could ask, to live with our phantasms in exchange for a basic security, a sense of protection and peace that can only come with mythic forms of law?

There are a number of responses to this concern. The first, a variant on what I've said before, is that to look to mythic violence as a form of protection is akin to the peace Rousseau imagined Odysseus and his followers "enjoying" in the lair of the Cyclops.[57] If mythic violence is the source of a prevalent lawlessness, why would we turn to it for a solution or for our safekeeping? In his understanding of the police and the army, Benjamin warns us that the peacekeepers we turn to for protection are, in many ways, our worst enemy. It is not just that police can be random and corrupt, but also that the very fact that we put so much store in them suggests that we have abandoned our own role as legal and political actors. As with the question of sovereignty more generally, giving away this power means essentially hoping that those who have been entrusted with it will in fact do what we would like them to do. Even when we think that they do this (and that is a question often driven by our perspective, our race, national identity, class, religion—or lack thereof—gender identity, sexual orientation, and so forth), it remains the case that we ourselves are mere spectators to our own legal and political environment.

Another point to make is that when we encounter the "slight adjustment" that for Benjamin is the hallmark of messianic interference in idolatry, we are not in a "brave new world" where anything goes. We are still in the same world (the one we've always lived in), only minus the overriding organization of our reality by the phantasmagoria. To be sure, we still will be living in a world marked by delusion and interpellation, but it is one where the breakdown, the misreading and mishearing of those calls, would be maximized. Such a world is not radically different; it is not a utopian paradise. Instead it is this world when our own anarchic self-governance is no longer eclipsed by phantasms of state, society, and so forth. This is a world where the idols of liberal global capitalism become (not unlike the case of liberal calls of freedom in Haiti) deformed, malfunctioning, and better resistant to capitalism's own idolatry.

Above all, we don't have to worry about a turn to a devastating lawlessness when we follow just one law if we note the critical role of the Second Commandment itself. Recall that Badiou tells us that "the law of love can even be supported by recollecting the content of the old law."[58] If, once again, we substitute the words "Second Commandment" for "law of love," we can read this passage as a way to remind us that the Second Commandment does not wipe out law (with a small *l*); it permits such law to remain only in a deflated and denuded form. Recall too that Badiou tells us that this law (once again, substituting the Second Commandment for the commandment to "love thy neighbor") "gives to the faithful subject his consistency," thus assuring us that the unmaking of law as we know it is the absolute unmaking neither of law nor of the consistency that we vainly look for in such law.[59] Without these critical aspects of the Second Commandment, we would have nothing to prevent the nightmare scenarios of people running amok, and I would probably agree that phantasms are better than nothing (although that would be a dreadful decision to have to make). But with the Second Commandment we have what indeed amounts to a command—a rule that we ought not break.

Let me spend some time examining the quality of this "ought," to compare it with its Kantian equivalent, building on the conversation that began in previous chapters. How is this "ought" different from Kant's? Or how does Kant's "ought" change when read through a Benjaminian lens (and if it does so change, does it remain an "ought" at all)? If we are going to call this ought a "commandment," what does that entail when our entire relationship to command itself has been radically upended?

The "Ought" of the Second Commandment

The key characteristic of Kant's ought is that it is simultaneous to and identical with freedom. It is both our binding duty and freely chosen, reflecting a split subjectivity in Kant between our "higher" (noumenal) and "lower" (phenomenal) forms of self. When we reread Kant in constellation with Benjamin, when we substitute our "choice" as misinterpellated subjects for the choice freely made by our noumenal selves, we can also reread the benefits of such freedom in a new, subversive context. Speaking of freedom in the *Groundwork of the Metaphysics of Morals*, Kant tells us:

> Freedom of the will, although it is not the property of conforming to laws of nature, is not for this reason lawless: it must rather be a causality conforming to immutable laws, though of a special kind; for otherwise a free will would be self-contradictory. Natural necessity, as we have seen, is a heteronomy of efficient causes; for every effect is possible only in conformity with the law that something else determines the efficient cause to causal action. What else then can freedom of will be but autonomy—that is, the property which will has of being a law to itself?[60]

The idea of freedom being "the property that the will has of being a law to itself," that is to say, freedom as autonomy (a law we give to ourselves), is critical for our purposes. The subject of the Second Commandment is similarly autonomous, with one vital exception. The one law that we cannot take to ourselves, that cannot be part of our autonomy, is the Second Commandment. This one law must remain entirely external to us. If the Second Commandment were part of our autonomy, if it were truly self-given as law, it too would be subsumed into the internal phantasms that constitute the basis of mythic law and authority. Instead, the Second Commandment serves as a tether, an externality that allows us maximal freedom in our context as fallen, guilty subjects.

While we are heteronomous as regards the Second Commandment, this one law becomes the source of our autonomy vis-à-vis all other law (in this way we receive a heteronomously derived autonomy, not quite what Kant had in mind, to be sure). All other laws, all other commandments, we can say are self-chosen, but the Second Commandment is different.

In the case of the Second Commandment, it's not so much that we "choose" or "don't choose" to obey it but rather that we either recognize ourselves as being in its orbit or overwrite that recognition with our own phantasms.[61] It's not up to us to choose such a law, it's always there whether we will it or not. Other laws are to be "wrestled" with or even "abandoned," but we cannot abandon the Second Commandment; when we try, it is we ourselves who get abandoned.

In this sense, we see a ghostly echo of Kant's formulation of the subject of law, but it is the reverse of the way Kant himself describes it. Here, rather than having us freely choose the noumenal, higher law and be subject to that law as phenomenal beings, it is as phenomenal beings that we have "free choice" (however partial and temporary that may be). As far as we relate to the Second Commandment itself (what could be considered the one "higher" law), we are absolutely bound and subject; we are commanded.

As for the force of this ought, although it is a "*weak*," power, we see that as subjects of the Second Commandment, we are utterly transformed by our obedience to and engagement with it. As we saw in the case of the Haitian slaves, this subjectivization offers us a new kind of power and authority. This is the ought that comes, in their case, from the conviction (or "single maxim") that "we will never again be reduced to slavery," the same kernel of resistance to phantasm that proved more powerful than the armies of France and Britain combined.

The position of the subject who resists the phantasmagoria can be seen as analogous to, or an extension of, the example of the Haitian slaves. Hearing the siren call of false promises of individuality, freedom, and "positive" law, the subject is called, but every act of interpellation is always also an act of misinterpellation. Under conditions of phantasm, we are all being drawn toward rights we are never meant to possess; we are always being miscalled. The subject of phantasm too can determine a single maxim, in this case: "we will never again be reduced to the thrall of phantasm"; this conviction can serve as the basis for a new kind of agency, a new kind of "ought."[62]

We can see the difference between this ought and the more ordinary ought that comes with mythic law. We "ought" to follow mythic law because if we don't we might get caught, punished, and so forth. The ought of the Second Commandment, on the other hand, is not based on probability; it is not a gamble about getting caught. Nor is it a struggle with inner morality, with feeling bad if we do something wrong (even if we "get away with it"). If we disobey the Second Commandment we *will* certainly be resubmitted to the thrall of phantasm. If we obey it our reward is similarly instant. There is nothing speculative or internalized about this kind of ought (and it will be recalled that for Benjamin, we are never free from guilt and responsibility no matter what we do).

In this sense, I would argue that the ought of the Second Commandment is far stronger than any kind of morally derived (or Kantian) ought. The greater force (violence?) of the ought of the Second Commandment comes from the fact that it is, finally, something that allows our own decision. Such a decision does not come from the phantasms of sovereign decisions, nor from a sense of "higher" metaphysical moral truth, nor as a command from a idolatrous understanding of God, nor even from a sense of "what pleases" (since the allure of phantasm always insists that it offers the greatest pleasure, the thing that we most desire, almost by definition). When we recuperate the authority of our own decisions, our own ought, in the silence (and indifference) that follows the divine unmaking of those phantasms, our commitment to this capacity is unlike any other.[63] Once we have been able to make this choice, why would we ever choose anything else?

Authors of Law: Imagining the Lawfulness of an Anarchist Community

What we get from this ought, as opposed to the pseudo-oughts of mythic law, is the capacity for politics. Normally what passes as politics is simply a manifestation of phantasm, delusions of political engagement and representation that are nothing of the kind. With our obedience to the Second Commandment, we get our own possibility of acting, of deciding, of "wrestling" with law and duty, of breaking, at last, from the dictates of fate. But this leads us to a final, critical issue: How law-like would it be to only obey one law? In the division that so many thinkers see between law and politics, does law disappear when legal decisions become, as we have seen above, deeply political, not predetermined and not determining but open and contingent?

Law will not and cannot disappear in any anarchic society (I certainly do agree with Critchley on that score). In such a context, law, in the form of the Second Commandment, remains separate and even prior to politics. But what about the rest of law? What about the practice of daily life under the circumstances of a sustained obedience to the Second Commandment? What would such a practice look like? Would it be possible to speak of "law" in that context at all?

It would probably be easier to start with the ways that the practices of a community explicitly oriented around obeying the Second Commandment—that is, the practices of a community of anarchists— *wouldn't* be "law-like," at least according to traditional jurisprudential notions (some of which have already been discussed earlier in this book). Such a law would not constitute, for example, a case of "orders backed by threats," as Austin has suggested.[64] There is no one to order and no one to threaten to bolster our devotion to the one law; God, to the extent that there is divine interference in our legal ordering, does nothing but unmake our idols. Nor does such a vision of law follow Kelsen's notion of conditional orders whereby nothing is based on moral codes but rather on conditional statements (i.e., "If you break this law, this is what will happen to you").[65] Much of the actual practice of law under conditions of obeying just one law would not be conditional at all. At any given point a very different set of decisions might be made; everything would be shifting and in flux, not a standard set of action and responses.

H. L. A. Hart is very useful (especially when read in constellation with Benjamin) for thinking about the positive valence of a society that obeys only one law, the ways that it would still be "law-like" or lawful. In *The Concept of Law*, Hart tells us that law has three facets that we always look for: first, it is in some sense obligatory. Second, it corresponds to a belief system (be it about morals, justice, or other such notions). Third, it is characterized by rules.[66] Each of these presumptions, he argues, turns out to be far more complicated than we might suspect. In terms of rules, for example, Hart asks, "What *are* rules? What does it mean to say that a rule *exists*? Do courts really apply rules or merely pretend to do so?"[67] In other words, are rules anything other than the name that covers arbitrary decisions by legal actors? Hart's willingness to deeply question our assumptions about law helps us to better imagine what a society that had a decidedly looser relationship to law (that is, a greater devotion to the "open texture" of law, to embracing Charybdis) might look like.

My argument here is that, with the tether offered by the Second Commandment, our relationship to law (with a small *l*, local and "positive" law) would be radically altered but not unrecognizable, not entirely unrelated to what Hart looks to in law more generally. As already stated, insofar as it can be said to already exist amid and between the overwritings of phantasmagoria, the anarchist community I am trying to envision here is not really that different from the communities we already live in; it would just be a "slight adjustment" from our current practices (but that slight adjustment itself contains huge and radical significance). The slight adjustment in this case would be a move from being, not just subjects of law (which we would, of course, remain as subjects of the Second Commandment), but authors as well. What would it look like if we were authors of the very laws that we follow? What would the fabric of this "lawfulness" be like? Let me look to Hart's notion of law as a way to engage in a thought exercise: imagining an anarchic community (but really, it is just the communities we already have, minus the preponderance of phantasm) and how law would operate in such a context.[68]

In terms of whether such laws would oblige, as I see it, the answer would be yes; a decision made by the anarchist community I am trying to envision here would be binding (and hence, obligatory).[69] It might be that a given community would have multiple levels of different forms of obligation, some overlapping, some not. Yet if one agreed to something, one would be considered to be bound by that agreement.[70] At the same time, this bindingness would not have the same quality as what such a term usually entails.[71] Normally, a community acts in order to fulfill certain ends, and so all of its acts collectively add up to a kind of weight or precedent that collectively predetermines what the community will do next.

In his study of Rousseau, *Fugitive Rousseau: Slavery, Primitivism, and Political Freedom*, Jimmy Casas Klausen suggests that an anarchic community, a fugitive community that coexists with, but also resists, repressive forms of politics, denies both the temporality and the spatiality of ordinary (that is sovereign, phantasmic) decisions its own internal politics. He writes:

> As Rousseau understands it, sovereignty necessarily varies: "sovereignty, which is only the exercise of the general will is, like it, free, and is not subject to any kind of engagement. Every act of sovereignty, like every instant of its existence, is absolute, independent of the one that precedes it; and the sovereign never acts because it wanted, but because it wants." . . . A sovereignty disanchored from

precedent thus enables diasporic fugitive peoples to respond to changing political environments by admitting mutability into the general will itself.[72]

Here we see one version of how such a community would act. As noted previously, what we call precedent would, in this context, only mean the story of decisions that have been made at different points in time; it would not refer to a set of decisions that come closer to or further from the mark, the "end" that such decisions normally presuppose. In this case there would be no mark, no way to order our decisions at all. The community might— and probably would—change its mind quite often. Individuals would always have the option to dissent and reargue their position. The "decision" itself would not have the force or substance (i.e., the "truth" as determined by the people) to weigh down and resist alteration; it would just be the name for what a community decided to do at one particular moment in time.

It's tempting to say that in a community dedicated to fighting against idolatry many of the bases for violent opposition would be removed. But, as I've said before, this is not a utopia but simply the way we practice politics now minus the certainty of collective phantasm. I'm pretty sure we'd still have crazy people (maybe they would have a more difficult time selling their madness to others as a form of deep insight, but that is another story). We'd still have people who did not agree for reasons good, bad, and indifferent. In fact, politics and the struggle with law in such a context would be far more difficult for political subjects in the sense that we'd all be making our arguments without the comfort of a sure basis, without a guarantee (at least to ourselves) that what we were saying was right. An anarchist politics is necessarily an agonal one, a messy, ugly business with decidedly "dirty hands." But whatever decision was made would have to be obligatory. Not obligatory as in "true for ever" but obligatory as in "until we make a different decision."[73]

The ludicrous "ideological" warfare of the United States of today between "red" and "blue" ideologies that are merely different versions of the capitalist phantasmagoria (a "liberalism" that sees itself as kinder and gentler but, when pushed at all, exposes its total commitment to market logic, a "conservativism" that prides itself on traditional values when it is radically and utterly in the thrall of a capitalist logic that chews up, devours, and excretes all forms of tradition) would not be possible in a society devoted to the Second Commandment. Long-standing and committed obedience to various ideologies denotes the presence of phantasms. Political factions, by definition, would have to be fleeting and shifting in an anarchist community, and I think it would be rare that any one group or person would be the perpetual loser in the decision-making process; if they were, this itself could be a sign of a nascent return of phantasmic categories. At any rate, "law" would be the name for our decisions once they were, in fact, decided, however temporary and shifting they might be.

As for killing and punishment within this community, if we return to Benjamin's own consideration of the Sixth Commandment, we see that to "wrestle in solitude" with such a law is not to dismiss this law, not to treat it as a suggestion. It remains (as Critchley reminds us too) a "guideline" (or "plumb line"), and I don't imagine that it would be taken lightly. We might indeed "abandon" it at times, but I would expect this would occur only in conditions of grave danger to the community. And even then, we might still choose to obey this commandment, as the Galician Jews did when they allowed themselves to be slaughtered. That is a valid choice for Benjamin, but so is resistance, so is fighting back. Killing or harming people in a society when they do not pose this kind of threat seems not so much "wrestling" as acting as if the commandment had never existed. This is why I think it's important to translate Benjamin's phrase as "abandoning" or "turning one's back on" that law rather than "ignoring" it, as his phrase is usually translated into English. When we abandon a law in a particular instance, we do so with a recognition of it. When we ignore it, we just don't care about it one way or the other. In the Benjaminian scheme, we care very much; we take on the agonal decision, at times, to break with such a law (with the exception, of course, of the Second Commandment, which can never be broken or abandoned). The bloodlust we find in our own times, the enthusiasm one often finds for the death penalty (and other ruthless forms of punishment), seems to me hard to sustain when, rather than knowing we were serving a "just cause," we knew instead that the death or harm we were inflicting was purely on us, a decision that might well be wrong and we were entirely responsible for. In the community I am imagining we would have neither a lust for blood nor an absolute edict against bloodshed but rather a shifting, engaged, and difficult relationship to punishment.

Speaking of the question of our actions comforming to moral codes or to a sense of justice, we can see that this too would be radically different in the society I am imagining. There could be no consistent moral codes, no truths that we would turn to for guidance in our decisions. Or, rather, there would be, but they wouldn't have the same valence for us. We would have to imagine, as Benjamin does, that there is a set of clear and unavoidable moral precepts in God's view and that we would have no idea what they were. With the exception, once again, of the Second Commandment itself, such moral precepts would exist only as failed signs, as echoes or gestures toward a higher law that we have no other access to. These failed signs of law ("old law") would haunt our decisions, not so much, as Derrida suggests, because they render our decisions "impossible" (since our decisions would be very possible, happening all the time and precisely thanks to the ongoing presence of divine violence) but simply because they remind us of our fallenness, the dangers we always face of going back into phantasm. Being haunted by truth and higher law as such would keep us, as it were, on our toes, always questioning, rethinking, reconfiguring; it would maintain our loose stance toward representation, and this very looseness, in its own limited way, is perhaps something that we could think of as a form of "justice," perhaps the closest we can come to such a concept.

Finally, as to the nature of rules in such a society, we would see that the very notion of a rule would have to be radically reconceived. "Rules" might mean in such a circumstance just what "precedent" would, once again, the story of the decisions that we have made—not a coherent narrative of applying a uniform standard of laws but rather a shifting and living narrative of decisions, reversals, arguments, and the like. Not unlike the Supreme Court of the United States (which can be read as an anarchist society of nine), today's dissent could become tomorrow's position; our narratives would have their own history, their own weight but would never aspire to have anything like an internal consistency, an allegiance to an unshifting set of laws (unless one thinks of the consistency that is supplied by obedience to the Second Commandment itself). Rather than seeking to perfect the application of true and eternal principles, law would become a store of information about past and present practices for us to draw upon when next we decide.

The One and Only Law: The Power of Weakness

Such a practice of obligations, moral duties, and rules might seem a far cry from what Hart envisions (and, in fact, it is), but this would not be the chaotic free-for-all that we usually picture when we think of anarchy. I agree with Kant when he writes that "freedom is certainly not lawless." Our freedom would be relative; we would have (some) freedom from phantasms and for our own decisions, but we would remain responsible, bound by a set of rules that we had ourselves created (and decreated, and recreated). This freedom would come at a cost, sometimes a terrible cost; we would inevitably make bad decisions. We would surely succumb to phantasms at times. We would remain the same problematical, argumentative, opinionated, representationally obsessed people that we already are. But in a way, this fact might be a comfort: we are already creating our own world, we are already disrupting false laws, we are already producing our own order, our own relationships that are not utterly determined by phantasms. We just need the courage of our convictions. We need to believe that our practices could be sustained without the overarching domination of phantasm, without, that is, replicating Numa's original lie. We need to believe that we can be authors and not only subjects of law, not just one person, but the entire community as a whole. These kinds of beliefs are not themselves pure phantasms (maybe this is part of what Critchley means by the "faith of the faithless") or, rather, they are the stuff of phantasm when it begins to turn on itself; these are the beliefs of misinterpellated subjects, beliefs that are anchored in our devotion to the only law that we really need.[74]

Critchley is very helpful in describing what he refers to as a *meontology*, "an account of things that are not," as a proper basis for our political and legal endeavors.[75] He makes a graceful and compelling argument, stringing together the work of Paul, Heidegger, Badiou, Levinas, and Benjamin, among others. The notion of meontology offers a power based on what is not (what Paul refers to as *hos me*, "as not," which reminds me too of the Kantian "as if"). In a chain of citations, Critchley cites Badiou as citing Paul as writing: "God has chosen the things that are not (*ta me onta*) in order to bring to nought those things that are (*ta onta*)" (1 Cor. 1:28).[76] Such a sentiment can also express the power Benjamin sees in divine violence: a nothing, a purely negative force that unmakes things that are (or at least seem to be) to return them to nothingness. Our corresponding human power, a product of the "*weak* messianic power" that Benjamin refers to in "On the Concept of History" is, I agree, similarly weak, similarly negative, just as Critchley describes it.

But here, once more, I see the power that comes from such weakness and negativity as acting in a different manner than it does for Critchley. In my view it is critical to stress that this power comes to us in ways that are unbidden and accidental. Critchley himself writes (speaking specifically of Heidegger in this case): "Our becoming is not something that we can become. It is not a decision that we can take."[77] But I think this meontological power might be even more unbidden than this implies (misontology might be an even better word for it) insofar as it comes out of the failure of our own efforts at fetishization. In addition, I think it is important to stress that while it may be a "weak" force, the power that it confers upon us (or the power it allows us to see we already possess) is not necessarily weak at all. Sometimes (as the case of Haiti amply demonstrates) it makes us very strong, irresistible, in fact. This power is weak because it is entirely negative or subtractive, but in so subtracting, it allows our own power—the possibility of it—to be more legible to us. It neutralizes another entirely negative power, that of the phantasmagoria, a power similarly based on nothingness (but an entirely different and pernicious sort of nothingness). Canceling out that other power (the negation of the negation), the weak messianic power allows us our own force, our own violence, and even our own nonviolence.

It is for this reason that I agree with Critchley that we need a "faith of the faithless," but I think of faithlessness, once again, somewhat differently than he does. I would once again link this faithlessness to the "faithless" leap that Benjamin describes in the *Origin of German Tragic Drama* when he speaks of how allegory "faithlessly leaps forward to the idea of resurrection" (as discussed in previous chapters).[78] In this passage, Benjamin offers an explanation (albeit a cryptic one) of how, moving toward the subjective, the local, the partial, we are also and simultaneously moving toward the divine. Allegory, the basest of tropes (the clunkiest and the least subtle, as he amply shows), somehow also leads us toward a kind of redemption. By not only embracing but leaping into the failure that allegory embodies, we push toward a deeper failure, a sense, one could say, of meontology itself. We can see this idea of taking "a faithless . . . leap" as a model for our own actions in the face of the phantasmagoria. Here, abandoning all hope for salvation, all of the promises of rescue and fruition that the phantasmagoria offers, we "ought" to throw ourselves, faithlessly, toward the idea of resurrection as a way of inviting the salvation that God always visits us with, the acts of divine violence that reward our faithlessness (which is itself an ultimate expression of iconoclasm). More concretely, we "ought" to dare to live in our communities without the cover of "the big Other," without God or truth or nature or the state. We "ought" to recover what we've always been doing, seeing it now as our own chosen actions. My reading of Benjamin's faithlessness is at once more messianic and more secular than Critchley's. It is more messianic because Critchley comes at this from a completely atheistic perspective and Benjamin does not. As I've argued throughout this book (as well as the two that precede it), Benjamin's theology is a critical component of his politics. We do not need to believe in Benjamin's God, but we do need to acknowledge what this God accomplishes, how this God delivers us, at least potentially, from our own phantasms. And (similar to my arguments about Badiou), at the same time, the Benjaminian view leaves us more alone, more secular, if you will, than even Critchley allows, because what comes, finally is a kind of peace. This is a peace (and probably a letdown, a disappointment, even a despair) that comes when the clamor of phantasmagoria is disrupted, misheard, misrecognized.[79] This "peace," if that is the right word for it, is a welcome silence that we rarely hear; it is the silence of our own abilities, our own choices. If we have the courage to faithlessly believe in this possibility, we can take heart from Benjamin's comment that "divine violence may manifest itself in a true war."[80] This is a war that, it turns out, we have always been fighting (even if we didn't know it). It is a war that we have been losing badly but, insofar as God hasn't given up on us yet (even though we have given up on God over and over again), we can still, just maybe, faithlessly leap into the void of failure that divine violence opens up for us, leaving us radically— and finally—alone.

Notes

1. Niccolò Machiavelli, *The Prince and the Discourses* (New York: Modern Library, 1950), 147.

2. Ibid., 146.

3. Ibid., 147.

4. Victoria Kahn mentioned this idea to me in a conversation.

5. In this book, I will be using the terms "fetishism" and "idolatry" more or less interchangeably although I am aware that these terms have slightly different historical usages. I will also be using "iconoclasm" as a term of opposition to fetishism and idolatry, realizing here too that I am adopting it from other, more specific contexts.

6. This is a term from his famous essay (which will be a major focus of this book) "Critique of Violence," in *Walter Benjamin: Selected Writings*, ed. Marcus Bullock and Michael W. Jennings, 4 vols. (Cambridge: Belknap Press of Harvard University Press, 1996–2003), 1:250.

7. The idea that we must act without divine mandate, even as we remain responsible for truth and justice, is not in and of itself unique to Benjamin. Thinkers ranging from Kierkegaard to Derrida and Žižek make similar points. What I would say is that Benjamin does a better job than any of them in policing the boundary between the human and the divine so that our quality of not knowing is much fiercer, much more absolute for Benjamin than for these other thinkers.

8. Even the much-vaunted democratic origins of the US Constitution are shrouded in a kind of reverent lore that defies too much sharp questioning. Unpleasant facts like the founders' decision to maintain slavery are noted, but somehow this does not lessen (or, more accurately, is not allowed to lessen) the majesty of the founding law. And, as already noted, the US Constitution is itself rooted in the practice of ancient constitutions—of Britain and of Rome. Arendt explains this move by recognizing the terror that comes with starting over, the fact

that with a revolutionary change in government, a true starting over of law and polity, anything could be done in any way. By couching such moments in history and tradition, the gap is avoided, papered over, and moved on from: crisis averted.

9. Hannah Arendt, "Willing," in *The Life of the Mind* (New York: Harcourt, Brace Jovanovich, 1978), 195.

10. Holy Bible, Revised Standard Version (Grand Rapids, MI: Zondervan Publishing, 1971), Exodus 20:4. As Leora Batnitzky tells us, the translations of this commandment matter very much. She compares Martin Buber and Franz Rosenzweig's translation to Luther's. Buber and Rosenzweig translate from the Hebrew (into German) to say, "Do not make any wooden carvings or any figure whatsoever," vs. Luther's "You shall make no portrait nor any analogy whatsoever." She points out that "Luther's translation prohibits any and all attempts at image making while Buber and Rosenzweig's translation prohibits only certain sorts of images: those that remain fixed and permanent." Leora Batnitzky, *Idolatry and Representation: The Philosophy of Franz Rosenzweig Reconsidered* (Princeton: Princeton University Press, 2000), 24. This conversation shows that even this commandment against (certain forms of) representation must itself be represented and, as such, offers many possibilities for its own violation (i.e., further idolatry).

11. I qualify this sentence with "much" because, as I'll discuss shortly, even the Second Commandment cannot be seen as perfectly avoiding fetishism, lest it become the basis for an ultimate and irredeemable fetishism itself.

12. See *Textual Conspiracies: Walter Benjamin, Idolatry and Political Theory* (Ann Arbor: University of Michigan Press, 2011) and *Divine Violence: Walter Benjamin and the Eschatology of Sovereignty* (New York: Routledge/GlassHouse, 2011).

13. For an overview of Benjamin's relationship to Judaism and its contemporary reception in Jewish philosophers of his time, see Gillian Rose, "Walter Benjamin: Out of the Sources of Modern Judaism," in *The Actuality of Walter Benjamin*, ed. Laura Marcus and Lynda Nead (London: Lawrence & Wishart, 1998), 85–117; see also Brian Britt, *Walter Benjamin and the Bible* (New York: Continuum, 1996); see also Daniel Bensaïd, *Walter Benjamin. Sentinelle Messianique: à la gauche du possible* (Paris: Les prairies ordinaires, 2010).

14. Walter Benjamin, "Franz Kafka: On the Tenth Anniversary of his Death," in *Selected Writings*, 2:811.

15. Benjamin, "On the Concept of History," in *Selected Writings*, 4:397.

16. Alain Badiou, *The Communist Hypothesis*, trans. David Macey and Steve Corcoran (New York: Verso, 2010), 215.

17. Walter Benjamin, *The Origin of German Tragic Drama*, trans. John Osborne (New York: Verso, 1998), 233 (henceforth *Origin*).

18. Ibid., 230. For Benjamin, however, Satan is a notably ambivalent figure. He tells us that we have to actually emulate Satan's rebellion, only this time, we rebel not against God but against Satan himself.

19. Ibid., 233.

20. Indeed, as I'll state at the end of this introduction, the term "antifetishist" is not quite accurate since there is a way in which we can never fully escape our fetishism. I use the term antifetishist merely as a convenience, but the term should not be read as an absolute move away from fetishism. As I'll say many times in this book,

to think that one has escaped fetishism entirely is to succumb to a profounder and more intractable form of fetishism.

21. Benjamin, "Franz Kafka," 808.

22. Benjamin, "Concept of History," 390.

23. For example, Benjamin speaks of being "under the eyes of heaven." *Origin*, 232. In fact, properly speaking this isn't a "perspective" since such a term implies something that could actually be seen and viewed by human beings. It is a perspective only by analogy to the human perspective that I describe next.

24. "The Invention of the Devil" ("Die Erfindung des Teufels") in Franz Kafka, *Parables and Paradoxes: Bilingual Edition* (New York: Schocken Books, 1961), 119.

25. This is explored in much greater detail in *Divine Violence*.

26. Benjamin, "Concept of History," 390.

27. And law is such an "antidote" but only in the most radical sense of that word; like the "pharmakon," law is a bit of the poison of phantasm turned into a weapon to unmake or undo its own effects. See the chapter on the pharmakon in Jacques Derrida, *Dissemination*, trans. Barbara Johnson (New York: Continuum, 2004), 98–118.

28. Benjamin, *Origin*, 233.

29. As I'll argue in chapter 4, this rendition of "positive law" is quite different from the usual accounts of legal positivism.

30. Alain Badiou, *Saint Paul: The Foundation of Universalism*, trans. Ray Brassier (Stanford, CA: Stanford University Press, 2003), 89.

31. Benjamin, *Origin*, 233.

32. See, once again, Badiou, *The Communist Hypothesis*, 225.

33. Alain Badiou, *Ethics: An Essay on the Understanding of Evil*, trans. Peter Hallward (New York: Verso, 2001), 45.

34. See Linda Ross Meyer, *The Justice of Mercy* (Ann Arbor: University of Michigan Press, 2010).

35. Jacques Derrida, "Force of Law: The 'Mystical Foundation of Authority,'" in *Acts of Religion*, ed. Gil Anidjar (New York: Routledge, 2001).

36. See, once again, *Divine Violence*.

37. In a more recent article, "Nothing Exists Except an Earthenware Pot: Resisting Sovereignty on Robinson's Island" (*Societies* 2, no. 4 [2012]: 372–87), I argue for reading Derrida in constellation with Benjamin, especially in volume 2 of his *The Beast and the Sovereign*. Here I try to reconcile him with Benjamin (as I do with Badiou, Kant, and Hart, among others in this book). I am also grateful to Bonnie Honig for her comments distinguishing early from late Derrida.

38. Benjamin, "Franz Kafka," 798. The idea of "hope . . . but not for us" is a major organizing theme of *Textual Conspiracies*.

39. In *Textual Conspiracies* I spoke of making an alliance with the signs and objects that constitute the world of fetishes. Insofar as these are all in a continual state of rebellion against the fetishes that we read into them, to ally ourselves with that struggle is enhance our own failure to represent, our own upending of the command of the text to mean one thing only.

40. I am grateful to Nasser Hussain for reminding me of the association between iconoclasm and reaction.

41. This is not to argue that Benjamin's methodology is somehow "universal" and that it transcends his own rootedness in Jewish and European thought—since much of this book is a rejection of the very idea of universalism—but rather that it is one example of an effective methodology, one that might be applied, in very different ways, in other contexts as well.

CHAPTER I

1. For other helpful sources on Benjamin and law, see Marc de Wilde, "Walter Benjamin's Other Law," in *Law's Environment: Critical Legal Perspectives*, ed. U. de Vries and L. Francot (The Hague: Eleven, 2011), 137–54; see also his "Benjamin's Politics of Remembrance: A Reading of "Über den Begriff der Geschichte," in *A Companion to the Works of Walter Benjamin*, ed. Rolf J. Goebel (Rochester, NY: Camden House, 2009), 177–94; Werner Hamacher, "Afformative, Strike: Benjamin's 'Critique of Violence,'" in *Walter Benjamin's Philosophy: Destruction and Experience*, ed. Andrew Benjamin and Peter Osborne (New York: Routledge, 1994), 110–38; Antonia Birnbaum, *Bonheur Justice, Walter Benjamin: Le détour grec* (Paris: Éditions Payot & Rivages, 2008).

2. As Leora Batnitzky tells us, the question of how to combat idolatry, and what idolatry even entails, is fraught. She compares Franz Rosenzweig's opposition to idolatry to that of Hermann Cohen (and, before him, Maimonides). While Cohen sees idolatry as inhering in any engagement with imagery (and, correspondingly, sees philosophy as the solution to idolatrous thought), for Rosenzweig not all images are idolatrous. Images are only potentially idolatrous insofar as they claim to capture and render constant what Batnitzky calls—citing Rosenzweig—the "ever-new will of God's revelation." Batnitzky, *Idolatry and Representation*, 225. She puts the distinction Rosenzweig makes this way: "Rosenzweig argues that the second commandment is as unpagan as the first because both commandments concern the recognition of God's freedom to reveal God's self to the human being. Here, he defines 'religion'—in opposition to revelation (which is anti-religious)—as a kind of 'projective' symbolism that fixes an image of God. To fixate on any one natural experience that has a spontaneously divine character is to worship not only a spatially, but a *temporally* fixed image of God. This sort of worship is a denial of God's freedom to reveal himself to the human in any form and at any time that God likes. Idolatry denies God's infinite freedom—and hence God's ability to affect the human being—for the sake of a fixed image of God" (23). Thus, Batnitzky alerts us to what is for Rosenzweig the critical aspect of fighting idolatry; the requirement to remain within time, subject to change, to an unknown future. In her opposition between Cohen and Rosenzweig, I would definitely put Benjamin in Rosenzweig's camp, but I would argue that Benjamin's own suspicion of the future being itself a potential source of idolatry puts them at odds over this question. Batnitzky intriguingly tells us that we must always "risk" idolatry in our quest for a future (188). For Benjamin, on the other hand, it's not so much the risk as the certainty of idolatry that he sees as constituting a basic aspect of political life. See also Moshe Halbertal and Avishai Margalit, *Idolatry*, trans. Naomi Goldblum (Cambridge: Harvard University Press, 1994); Hermann Cohen, *Religion of Reason: Out of the Sources of Judaism* (New York: Oxford University Press, 1995); Franz Rosenzweig, *The Star of*

Redemption (Madison: University of Wisconsin Press, 2005). I am grateful to Annika Thiem for her own illuminations of these questions.

3. Benjamin, "Critique of Violence," 252.

4. Although Benjamin discusses the Fall many times, this essay is one of the few in which he specifically mentions Eve (although only once and in a way that does not have a lot of significance for the overall essay).

5. Walter Benjamin, "On Language as Such and the Language of Man," in *Selected Writings*, 1:68. For an interpretation of this essay see Peter Fenves, "The Genesis of Judgment: Spatiality, Analogy, and Metaphor in Benjamin's 'On Language as Such and on Human Language,'" in *Walter Benjamin: Theoretical Questions*, ed. David S. Ferris (Stanford, CA: Stanford University Press, 1996), 75–93. See also a footnote in Werner Hamacher's "Afformative, Strike" regarding that writing: "Afformative, Strike," 136–38 n. 46.

6. Benjamin, "On Language as Such," 68.

7. Ibid., 69.

8. The things of the world retain their own "nameless language" for Benjamin even after the Fall. He speaks of the "communication of matter in magic communion." Ibid., 70.

9. Ibid.

10. Ibid., 71.

11. Ibid., 72.

12. Ibid.

13. Ibid.

14. Ibid., 71.

15. Ibid.

16. Ibid., 72.

17. Ibid., 71.

18. Ibid.

19. Benjamin, "Critique of Violence," 247.

20. Ibid.

21. For more on this, see Peter Fitzpatrick, *Modernism and the Grounds of Law* (New York: Cambridge University Press, 2001).

22. Benjamin, "Critique of Violence," 247.

23. For an overview of Benjamin's notion of myth see Winfried Menninghaus, "Walter Benjamin's Theory of Myth" in *On Walter Benjamin: Critical Essays and Recollections*, ed. Gary Smith (Cambridge: MIT Press, 1988), 292–325.

24. Benjamin, "Critique of Violence," 248.

25. Ibid.

26. Ibid.

27. Ibid., 249.

28. Ibid., 248.

29. Ibid., 249.

30. Ibid.

31. Tom McCall makes the interesting point that even the story of Korah is, in some sense, necessarily a myth: "The (Hebraic) Korah story can really only allegorize a pure violence purged of (Greek) mythic manifestations while remaining itself a convenient and striking—yet no less mythical—means to phenomenalize and

perform as mythic text Benjamin's own philosopheme of the pure." Tom McCall, "Momentary Violence" in Ferris, *Walter Benjamin: Theoretical Questions*, 93.

32. Benjamin, "Critique of Violence," 250.

33. Ibid.

34. Ibid.

35. Ibid.

36. When I presented this argument to a class that Bonnie Honig was then teaching at Northwestern, she pointed out that Korah himself may be exactly in the spirit of radical rebellion against authority that I am attributing to Benjamin himself. Korah was after all, as Honig pointed out, fighting for the right for each person to interpret God's authority as she saw fit. God answered that rebellion by burying Korah and his followers. Why then should we follow Benjamin in reading *this* of all stories as the prime instance of divine violence? This, I would say, is the price we pay for following Benjamin into this explicitly theological territory. Although God generally plays no role in Benjamin's politics except as a negative force, in the story of Korah, God is actually present. An all-knowing Deity will by definition be authoritative, absolute, and unquestionable; that comes with the territory. But despite the fact that this gives us, in the case of Korah, a troubling reading of that story, I would argue that the use of this story otherwise points us in the opposite direction, wherein we are given the means to defy the kinds of authorities that similarly bury and otherwise overwhelm such forms of rebellion.

37. Ibid.

38. This essay, which exists only as a fragment, was a commentary on an essay by Herbert Vorkwerk by the same name. Herbert Vorwerk, "Das Recht zur Gewaltanwendung," *Blätter fur religiösen Sozialismus*, ed. Carl Mennicke (Berlin, 1920), vol. 1, no. 4. Notice in the German title the same use of "Gewalt" as in "Kritik zur Gewalt" (the "Critique of Violence").

39. Walter Benjamin, "The Right to Use Force," in *Walter Benjamin: Selected Writing*, 1:231.

40. Ibid., 232.

41. Unfortunately, Benjamin's clear rejection of this vision comes in an essay he wrote called "Life and Force" that was published in the early 1920s and is now lost. Ibid., 234.

42. Ibid., 233. In this regard, I find Andrew Benjamin's distinction between religion and theology extremely useful. In his view, religion is part and parcel of phantasm. Theology supplies what he calls a "counter-measure" against it. Andrew Benjamin, *Working with Walter Benjamin* (Oxford: Oxford University Press, 2013).

43. Benjamin, "The Right to Use Force," 233.

44. Ibid.

45. Ibid., 233–34.

46. Benjamin, "Critique of Violence," 252.

47. Ibid., 250.

48. Walter Benjamin, "Zur Kritik der Gewalt," in *Gesammelte Schriften*, vol. 2.1 (Frankfurt am Main: Surkamp Verlag, 1980), 201. I am grateful to Marc de Wilde for pointing this out to me. I think this other translation not only strengthens the concept of moving away from mythic law but also shows the tortured, complex relationship we have with such law. We do not "ignore" the law, nor are we indif-

ferent to it; the law retains a great hold on us, and so we struggle with it, turning, painfully, away.

49. Benjamin, "Critique of Violence," 252.

50. See Alenka Zupančič, *Ethics of the Real: Kant, Lacan* (New York: Verso, 2000), 27.

51. Benjamin, "Critique of Violence," 241.

52. Ibid.

53. Ibid., 250.

54. Ibid., 252.

55. Benjamin, "Franz Kafka," 808.

56. Giorgio Agamben, *State of Exception*, trans. Kevin Attell (Chicago: University of Chicago Press, 2005), 59.

57. Simon Critchley, *The Faith of the Faithless: Experiments in Political Theology* (New York: Verso, 2012), 199–200. See also Samuel Weber, "Going Along for the Ride: Violence and Gesture: Agamben Reading Benjamin Reading Kafka Reading Cervantes," *Germanic Review* 81, no. 1 (Winter 2006): 65–83.

58. Agamben, *State of Exception*, 63.

59. Ibid.

60. Ibid.

61. Ibid., 64.

62. To be fair, as already noted, Benjamin doesn't always make this distinction clear either. Benjamin's lack of clarity on this point is something that I will return to in the conclusion.

63. This excellent question was put to me by Austin Sarat. For Benjamin the answer must be yes, but the Second Commandment does not serve much of the current Left, which is, as Jodi Dean shows, mired in a fascination with its own defeat (albeit challenged and excited by new activism, by Occupy Wall Street and the Maple Spring in North America, by even more recent events in Turkey and so forth). Rather it serves—and produces—a Left that has battled and subverted its own myriad forms of, and relationship to, idolatry. And this form of "leftism" would not necessarily be nice or kind, and certainly not "true." It could easily revert to fascism, to the "right wing" tilt that comes along with the phantasmagoria. See Jodi Dean, *The Communist Horizon* (New York: Verso, 2012).

64. I am once again indebted to Marc de Wilde for this insight.

65. Benjamin, "Critique of Violence," 239.

66. I think that in many crucial ways, Benjamin's treatment of the nonviolent general strike in the "Critique of Violence" is aligned with (although crucially not an example of) divine violence. In both instances, as noted, an action serves, not to produce new truths, but simply to remove false truths from the scene. In this way, both the general strike and acts of divine violence are instances of anti-idolatry (even as only the general strike is an example of following the Second Commandment, which is, of course, only directed toward human beings) and hence "nonviolent." I recognize that Benjamin muddies the waters by calling it divine "violence" in the first place. This may be an example of the problem of using language, with all its inherent potential for fetishism, to describe an antifetishist agenda (and the word "antifetishist" itself, as I suggested in the introduction, performs this problem as well).

67. Benjamin, "Critique of Violence," 246.

68. This is an operation that Benjamin performs that I will return to at various points in this book.

69. Perhaps more accurately, we knew we were striking, but we didn't know—couldn't really know—how the strike would transform us, take us out of the economy of violence into another political and anarchic realm of action.

70. Benjamin, *Origin*, 235.

71. "Unknowledge" might be a better word; a knowledge that unmakes (false) knowledges.

72. Benjamin, "Critique of Violence," 246.

73. In the conclusion, I will return to the discussion of whether we are capable, in the end, of eschewing violence completely.

74. Benjamin, "Critique of Violence," 250.

75. Benjamin, "Right to Use Force," 233.

76. See Saint Augustine, *City of God*, trans. Marcus Dods (New York: Modern Library, 1994).

77. Giorgio Agamben, *The Coming Community*, trans. Michael Hardt (Minneapolis: University of Minnesota Press, 1993), 53.

78. Walter Benjamin, "Letter to Gershom Scholem on Franz Kafka," in *Selected Writings*, 3:327.

79. A similar kind of failure can be spotted in the general strike Benjamin describes in the "Critique of Violence," which "fails" to be recognized as a normal political activity.

80. Benjamin, "Critique of Violence," 326–27.

81. Jacques Derrida, *Politics of Friendship*, trans. George Collins (New York: Verso, 1997), 27.

82. Benjamin, "Letter to Gershom Scholem," 327.

CHAPTER 2

1. Badiou, *Saint Paul*, 89.

2. For an excellent overview of Badiou and, in particular, a good sense of the political implications of his work, see Bruno Bosteels, *Badiou and Politics* (Durham, NC: Duke University Press, 2011). See also his *The Actuality of Communism* (New York: Verso, 2011).

3. Badiou, *Ethics*, 38. Badiou writes further that "at the core of the mastery of ethics is the power to determine who dies and who does not" (35). For an overview of this book, see Benjamin Noys, "Badiou's Fidelities: Reading the *Ethics*," *Communication & Cognition* 36, nos. 1–2 (2003): 31–44.

4. The irony here is that Kantianism—at least a certain view of Kantianism (to be described in the next two chapters)—is responsible for that false universal in most cases. For the purposes of this chapter, I will leave Kant as the straw man, a stand in for various Western metaphysical philosophies with an accompanying ethical stance that Badiou opposes. In the next chapter, I will try to complicate Kantianism itself.

5. Badiou, *The Communist Hypothesis*, 215. Badiou writes further that "*something*

whose value of existence was nil in the situation takes on a positive valence of existence" (221).

6. Once an event occurs, it ushers in a universal truth that is, in a sense, timeless, even as it didn't exist—even as a possibility—before the event.

7. Badiou, *Ethics*, 32.

8. Ibid., 41–42.

9. Ibid., 43.

10. Ibid., 46–47.

11. Ibid., 12.

12. Ibid., 45.

13. In the conclusion, I will revisit the question of Saint Paul, looking at Critchley's writing about it (and his own engagement with Badiou on the question) in his book *The Faith of the Faithless*.

14. Badiou, *Saint Paul*, 95. Badiou is hardly alone in his estimation of Paul among contemporary philosophers. In addition to Žižek's work (to be discussed further in this chapter) see Giorgio Agamben, *The Time That Remains: A Commentary on the Letter to the Romans*, trans. Patricia Dailey (Stanford, CA: Stanford University Press, 2005); see also Jacob Taubes, *The Political Theology of Paul* (Stanford, CA: Stanford University Press, 2003); Stanislas Breton, *The Radical Philosophy of Saint Paul* (New York: Columbia University Press, 2011). For Žižek's own reading of Badiou on Paul, see his "The Politics of Truth, or, Alain Badiou as a Reader of St. Paul," in *The Ticklish Subject: The Absent Centre of Political Ontology* (New York: Verso, 1999). See also Adam Kotsko, "Politics and Perversion: Situating Žižek's Paul," *Journal for Cultural and Religious Theory* 9, no. 2 (Summer 2008): 43–52.

15. Badiou, *Saint Paul*, 98. In this sense, Luther is not necessarily all that different from the heresy Simon Critchley describes as "mystical anarchism" (to be discussed in conclusion).

16. Ibid., 99.

17. Badiou, *Ethics*, 73.

18. Badiou, *Saint Paul*, 9.

19. Badiou, *Ethics*, 73.

20. Ibid., 85.

21. Ibid., 16.

22. Ibid., 47.

23. Ibid., 52.

24. Badiou, *Saint Paul*, 4.

25. Benjamin, "On Language as Such," 72.

26. Benjamin, *Origin*, 183.

27. Ibid.

28. Ibid.

29. Badiou, *Ethics*, 23.

30. Ibid.

31. I will make a similar argument, albeit one without any religious content, about Hart in chapter 4.

32. Badiou, *Saint Paul*, 4.

33. Ibid., 4–5.

34. Ibid., 33.
35. Ibid., 89.
36. Ibid., 87.
37. Ibid.
38. Ibid., 89.
39. Ibid., 87.
40. I discuss these distinctions, as well as the dark and hierarchical history of the treatment of love as a political concept, in *Love Is a Sweet Chain: Autonomy, Desire and Friendship in Liberal Political Theory* (New York: Routledge, 2001).
41. Ibid., 7–10.
42. Slavoj Žižek, *On Belief* (New York: Routledge, 2001), 89. See also Slavoj Žižek, *The Puppet and the Dwarf: The Perverse Core of Christianity* (Cambridge: MIT Press, 2003).
43. Žižek, *On Belief*, 89–90.
44. Ibid., 90.
45. Ibid., 90–91.
46. As Žižek goes on to assert, such a divine presence in ordinary flesh is not in and of itself our salvation. He asserts that Christ "does not do our work for us, he does not pay our debt, he 'merely' gives us a chance—with his death, he asserts our freedom and responsibility, i.e. he 'merely' opens up the possibility, for us." Ibid., 105.
47. Ibid., 130.
48. Ibid., 130–31.
49. Ibid., 130.
50. Benjamin, *Origin*, 183. Benjamin also tells us that it is "the offensive, the provocative quality of the gesture [to humanize Christ] which is baroque. Where man is drawn towards the symbol, allegory emerges from the depths of being to intercept the intention and triumph over it" (183).
51. Ibid.
52. See *Textual Conspiracies*, 257, for example.
53. Benjamin, *Origin*, 232–33.
54. Simon Critchley, no doubt, would call this the "faith of the faithless," the title of his book that I will engage with in the conclusion.
55. Badiou, *Saint Paul*, 87.
56. Ibid., 89.
57. If, in doing so, I turn Žižek and Badiou into Jews, I would simply cite Žižek himself in arguing, "Why not?"

CHAPTER 3

1. For an excellent reading of this essay by Kant, see Hent de Vries, *Religion and Violence: Philosophical Perspectives from Kant to Derrida* (Baltimore, MD: Johns Hopkins Press, 2001).
2. Immanuel Kant, *Critique of Judgment*, trans. Werner S. Pluhar (Indianapolis: Hackett, 1987), 135.
3. Susan Meld Shell, "Kant and the Jewish Question," *Hebraic Political Studies* 2, no. 1 (Winter 2007): 110.

4. Ibid., 112–13.

5. Ibid., 115.

6. I do this though very aware of Kant's reputation as the author of the understanding of law that the approach I am attributing to Benjamin is most set against. Yet Benjamin shows us that to recuperate a subject from the heart of what you oppose is (as we saw with his treatment of Jesus in the previous chapter) a way to perform what he calls an "unsurpassingly spectacular gesture" of subversion.

7. See Jean François Lyotard, *Lessons on the Analytic of the Sublime*, trans. Elizabeth Rottenberg (Stanford, CA: Stanford University Press, 1994); Zupančič, *Ethics of the Real*; Jacques Lacan, *The Ethics of Psychoanalysis*, trans. Dennis Porter (New York: Norton, 1997); Slavoj Žižek, *Tarrying with the Negative: Kant, Hegel and the Critique of Ideology* (Durham, NC: Duke University Press, 1993).

8. For other readings of Benjamin and Kant, see Rodolphe Gasché, "Objective Diversions: On Some Kantian Themes in Benjamin's 'The Work of Art in the Age of Mechanical Reproduction,'" in Benjamin and Osborne, *Walter Benjamin's Philosophy*.

9. Immanuel Kant, *Religion within the Limits of Reason Alone*, trans. Theodore M. Greene and Hoyt H. Hudson (New York: Harper & Row, 1960), 95 (henceforth *Religion*). Werner Hamacher briefly considers the relationship between Kant and Benjamin in his "Afformative, Strike," 122–23.

10. Kant, *Religion*, 97.

11. Ibid.

12. Ibid., 100.

13. Ibid., 103.

14. Ultimately, I am agnostic about whether Kant was truly a Christian or not. I'm not sure the answer really matters; it may well be that the Kingdom of God and the Kingdom of Ends amount to the same thing.

15. Kant, *Religion*, 100.

16. Ibid., 102.

17. Ibid.

18. This is an argument made by Moses Mendelssohn and, according to Kant, the key to the former's argument that Jews did not need to convert to Christianity.

19. Kant, *Religion*, 116.

20. Ibid., 117. Andrew Poe commented to me that he is not sure this represents such a break between the Third Critique and *Religion* after all. Kant might be indicating in the *Critique of Judgment* what the possibility for the Jewish law might be and then retroactively assessing it in *Religion*, from its failure to fulfill its own promise.

Kant also appears to backtrack from another observation in the Third Critique where he says that to obey God because of fear of hell or hope for heaven is not a moral reason to believe. *Critique of Judgment*, 352. In *Religion*, he tells us that "since no religion can be conceived of which involves no belief in a future life, Judaism . . . is not a religious faith at all" (117).

21. Kant, *Religion*, 127n.

22. Ibid., 152.

23. Ibid., 153.

24. Ibid., 157.

25. Ibid., 168.
26. Ibid., 119n.
27. Ibid.
28. Ibid.
29. Ibid., 157n.
30. Ibid., 100–101. The word "[helpful]" is in the original text.
31. Ibid., 101n.
32. Ibid.
33. Ibid.
34. Ibid., 130. Emphasis on "a sublime analogy" is mine; "[world of]" appears in brackets in original.
35. I suppose it could be said that this amounts to being instrumental toward instruments and ends oriented toward ends.
36. Kant, *Religion*, 98.
37. Ibid.
38. Ibid., 133.
39. Kant, *Critique of Judgment*, 135.
40. Ibid. Andrew Poe pointed out to me (as part of a larger project that he is working on tentatively entitled *Swarm: A Genealogy of Political Enthusiasm*) that enthusiasm here is contrasted—as in many of Kant's writings—against fanaticism. As he describes it, the conflict between older, Egyptian values and a new commitment to the moral law forms a tableau in which this contrast takes place. Enthusiasm is the correct response to the moral law; it is a recognition that the law itself remains beyond the scope of human subjects, even as the prospect of that law animates and produces the community of Levites (minus Korah and his followers). Fanaticism is precisely the failure to take the moral law as absent; hence it's an idolatrous position. As Poe points out, the Second Commandment is fraught because it reveals both the horror and the desire of idolatry. Enthusiasm must negotiate this difficult relationship.
41. Ibid. In a conversation about the sublime experience in Kant that I had with Shalini Satkunanandan, she stressed how the sublime experience bypasses any calculation on one's part; any benefits we anticipate in the experience becomes incidental to the event itself.
42. It's true that this particular object has no actual material presence but it still exists as a concept, as a term with some tangible representation (like the "Second Commandment"). Shalini Satkunanandan reminded me that the presence of the empirical need not always be bad precisely because, for Kant, you can see the moral law more clearly when it makes you go against natural dialectics or empirical decisions.
43. Kant, *Critique of Judgment*, 98.
44. Ibid., 105. I am indebted to Shalini Satkunandan for this insight.
45. Ibid., 106. Brackets are in the original.
46. Ibid., 112.
47. Ibid.
48. Ibid., 113.
49. Kant tells us that this harmony is simultaneously "subjectively purposive for reason, as the source of ideas" and nonpurposive as a pure aesthetic experience.

Ibid., 117. It produces an "abyss in which the imagination is afraid to lose itself" even as it also "conforms to reason's law" (115).

50. Ibid., 121.

51. Ibid., 127.

52. This servile model echoes, however dimly the more radical model in Benjamin where the objects of the world serve, not as our instruments, but as our allies in collectively overcoming our ensconcement in phantasms.

53. Kant, *Critique of Judgment*, 122–23.

54. Ibid., 135–36.

55. Benjamin, *Origin*, 160.

56. Ibid.

57. Ibid., 161.

58. Ibid., 177–78.

59. There is yet another way in which Kant and Benjamin approach a question in similar fashion but with different (or even opposite) senses of directionality: this involves Kant's notion of the two standpoints. For Kant: "We can enquire whether we do not take one standpoint when by means of freedom we conceive ourselves as causes acting a priori, and another standpoint when we contemplate ourselves with reference to our actions as affects which we see before our eyes." Immanuel Kant, *Groundwork of the Metaphysics of Morals*, trans. H. J. Paton (New York: Harper & Row, 1964), 118 (451). Benjamin's own version of the two standpoints (which were already considered in the introduction) are different from Kant's. In the *Origin of German Tragic Drama*, as already noted (and cited), Benjamin tells us: "Allegory, of course, thereby loses everything that was most peculiar to it: the secret, privileged knowledge, the arbitrary rule in the realm of dead objects, the supposed infinity of a world without hope. All this vanishes with this *one* about-turn, in which the immersion of allegory has to clear away the final phantasmagoria of the objective and, left entirely to its own devices, re-discovers itself, not playfully in the earthly world of things, but seriously under the eyes of heaven." *Origin*, 232.

Here we see that for Benjamin, one standpoint is our own, a material, finite view. The other is the standpoint of God, "the eyes of heaven." By giving the universal standpoint over to God and God alone, we ourselves are saved from that perspective and the false salvation it promises. This is not dissimilar to Kant's move toward the negative, but in this case, the result is, once again, opposite; whereas Kant uses the negative to propel himself (or rather, his subject) closer to God or to the noumenal realm, Benjamin uses that same operation to send us away from whatever phantasm passes as divine or noumenal (and hence, in a sense *toward* God in the sense of God as an aporia, a true negative that does nothing else for us but dispel its false representations). It is for this reason, as I have argued, that Kant's own move toward the sensual is also, in a sense, a move toward the noumenal/divine (at least when considered through a Benjaminian lens).

60. Benjamin, *Origin*, 217–18.

61. Ibid., 216.

62. Ibid., 224–25.

63. As Benjamin tells us, "Considered in allegorical terms, then, the profane world is both elevated and devalued." Ibid., 175.

64. Ibid., 232.

65. Here Andrew Poe made a very useful comment about Kant's "failure to protect" against idolatry. Given that, in his view, the negotiation with the Second Commandment is both horrible and full of desire, is there a danger that, in protection, the negotiation itself becomes impossible? In her wonderful engagement with Franz Rosenzweig's political theology, Leora Batnitzky tells us that "Rosenzweig emphasizes that idolatry is something that is always risked, particularly by those closest to God's revelation." Batnitzky, *Idolatry and Representation*, 188. Must we therefore "risk idolatry" by allowing the kind of dangers that Kant seems to court in his own concept of the sublime? Is Benjamin's prophylaxis against idolatry too severe? I would argue that in fact for Benjamin, we also are always risking idolatry by the very nature of our engagement with language and representation. There is no pure position for him from which to ensure that there is no risk of idolatry. Yet, for that very reason, we must remain aware of the ways that idolatry is constantly reasserting itself even as we struggle with it.

66. Kant, *Critique of Judgment*, 135–36.

67. Benjamin, *Origin*, 233. I will return to this idea of a "faithless leap" once more in the conclusion.

68. By contrast, we would have to call Kant's sublime a "leap of faith," at least in contrast with Benjamin.

69. Kant, *Religion*, 112. Shalini Satkunanandan reminded me that all forms of moral law are ultimately internal for Kant.

70. Ibid., 116.

71. Ibid., 113.

72. Ibid., 156.

73. Ibid., 113.

74. Ibid., 95.

75. Ibid., 114n.

76. As I argue at several points in this book, the term "positive" is not one that I seek to avoid entirely but rather reconceptualize. Rather than serving as an intuition of the divine, I see the positive, Benjamin's positive that is, as the ruin or remnant that remains after an object has served as a site of representational failure. This ultimately secular, deflated, and weak object is what we receive after our delusions have been subverted (at least for the moment).

77. Another way to ask this is this: if even Kant's reading of the Second Commandment is avowedly "sublime," does that mean that it is subject to the same stealthily idolatrous forms of representation that we see in Kant's larger philosophy? Or does this one law (as we see in Benjamin's case too) overcome, at least potentially, even its own inherent idolatry?

78. As when Benjamin tells us in the *Origin of German Tragic Drama* that "the language of the baroque is constantly convulsed by rebellion on the part of the elements which make it up" (207).

79. See Peter Fenves, *The Messianic Reduction: Walter Benjamin and the Shape of Time* (Stanford, CA: Stanford University Press, 2010).

80. Peter Fenves, *Late Kant: Towards Another Law of the Earth* (New York: Routledge, 2003), 2.

81. Ibid., 5.

82. Ibid., 158.

83. Ibid., 162.

84. Ibid., 162–63.

85. Ibid., 206 n. 3.

86. "The Paris of the Second Empire in Baudelaire," in Walter Benjamin, *The Writer of Modern Life: Essays on Charles Baudelaire*, ed. Michael W. Jennings, trans. Howard Eiland et al. (Cambridge: Belknap Press of Harvard University Press, 2006), 126.

87. Benjamin, "Franz Kafka," 798.

88. One place where Benjamin potentially reads Kant this way, or at least sees him as being thwarted by a certain form of materiality, comes when he writes: "On Baudelaire's 'Crépuscule du soir': the big city knows no true evening twilight. In any case, the artificial lighting does away with all transition to night. The same state of affairs is responsible for the fact that the stars disappear from the sky over the metropolis. Who ever notices when they come out? Kant's transcription of the sublime through 'the starry heavens above me and the moral law within me' could never have been conceived in these terms by an inhabitant of the big city." *The Arcades Project*, trans. Howard Eiland and Kevin McLaughlin (Cambridge: Belknap Press of Harvard University Press, 1999), 343. In other words, the physical presence of the big city with all of its lights obscures the transcendent moral law that Kant purports to intuit, freeing us from such things perhaps once and for all.

89. We can see another example of how to reread Kant along Benjaminian lines by looking at Kant's evocation of duty in the *Critique of Practical Reason* (thus spreading our inquiry beyond the Third Critique and later works). In his famous and, for Kant, strangely passionate declaration, he writes: "*Duty!* Thou sublime and mighty name that dost embrace nothing charming or insinuating, but requirest submission, and yet seekest not to move the will by threatening aught that would arouse natural aversion or terror, but merely holdest forth a law which of itself finds entrance into the mind, and yet gains reluctant reverence (though not always obedience), a law before which all inclinations are dumb, even though they secretly counterwork it; what origin is there worthy of thee, and where is it to be found the root of thy noble descent which proudly rejects all kindred with the inclinations; a root to be derived from which is the indispensable condition of the only worth which men can give themselves?" Immanuel Kant, *Critique of Practical Reason*, trans. T. K. Abbott (Amherst, NY: Prometheus Books, 1996), 108. Although he argues that there is nothing "charming" or "insinuating" in this call, Kant does seem to be quite charmed (and insinuated). He appears to be overcome (at least textually) by the power and, indeed, sublimity of this concept. In this way he might be indicating the idolatrous nature of this concept even while he formally seeks to deny it. If we read him in a dark, Benjaminian light, however, we can see this passage as a call that is purposefully misunderstood, misread, a failure (in the conclusion I will expand this concept through an exploration of the concept of misinterpellation). In the passage, Kant argues that he feels freed by the call of duty even as he is "subject to special laws." But it might be that he is freed by this call in another way, freed, that is, from the possibility of being delivered to duty. By answering the call of duty, he reveals through his own ecstatic response that it is an idol, thus dramatizing the ways in which an experience of the sublime offers a false sense of transcendence. In achieving *this* form of freedom, Kant in a sense does respond to "the call" he

receives. This is the call to a different type of failure, a different relationship with transcendence (i.e., none whatsoever, what happens when it turns out that transcendence can never be achieved). In his response to the call, a different sort of "duty" also arises, a duty that is truly his own, not produced out of any apprehension of higher power (i.e., once again the "burden" of a freedom that is purely and only his own).

90. Kant, *Religion*, 112.

91. Shalini Satkunanandan speaks of the burden of freedom in Kant. The anarchism I see as being possible through a Benjaminian reading of his work is similarly burdened. In her analysis of the *Groundwork*, Satkunanandan writes: Autonomy here is literally being oneself a law to oneself. The will's object here is 'itself as giving universal law.' Thus the supreme principle of morality and the principle of autonomy are in an identity. In addition to paving the way for a self-grounding ground for *Sitten* [morals], Kant's proof of the identity of freedom and obligation shows me that under the sway of the natural dialectic I not only flee from my duty, I *also* flee from my freedom. My freedom, moreover, is lawful—it is not doing whatever I please. I already knew my duty was a burden; now I see that my freedom is as well." Shalini Satkunanandan, "The Extraordinary Categorical Imperative," *Political Theory* 39, no. 2 (2011): 245.

92. Benjamin, *Origin*, 161.

93. Kant, *Religion*, 96.

94. This raises questions about the temporality of law. Are we, like Arendt's promisers, forming ourselves in our own future? I think a Benjaminian temporality would not quite work this way because, as I'll argue further in the conclusion, the practice of law in an anarchist context shouldn't be seen as a long steady movement in one direction but rather as a series of instances in which any one moment is as related to any other as it is to the instances that follow after it (such a view, as I will argue, would have a major impact, for instance, on the notion of precedent).

95. Kant, *Religion*, 96.

96. Ibid.

97. Ibid.

98. Kant goes on in that same paragraph to argue that we can't deny that the church may "perhaps be a special divine arrangement" (i.e., that perhaps the church got it right). Ibid.

99. In thinking about the nature of such a law, Kant also helps us to think about what our relationship to the law might be. In *Religion*, he writes that "the highest goal of moral perfection of finite creatures—a goal to which man can never completely attain—is love of the law" (136). If love is the way for finite beings such as ourselves to engage with law, what kind of love are we talking about (and, hence, what kind of law)? As I've argued several times already, the concept of love itself brings in a plethora of idolatry; it has been evoked by thinkers ranging from Augustine to Negri and is often a way to smuggle in or smooth over various hierarchies and forms of dominance in the name of such a sweet-sounding emotion. If we subject Kant to a Benjaminian lens, I would say that to love the law must mean to love it *after* it has been exposed as delusion, after its promise to deliver us and save us has been proven empty. If we can still love the law after it has been stripped of the false authority given to it by delusion, that kind of love is the appropriate way to

think about the law. Only such a deflated, anti-idolatrous love would be appropriate for the kind of law we are talking about here. But I think the term is so loaded, has so many bad associations and misuses, that it would be better just to forget about it and leave love out of politics altogether.

100. This is the one law that keeps coming back to us, by virtue of the fact that its operation is central to the very concept of law; it is the one thing that continually survives its own unmaking.

CHAPTER 4

1. Meyer, *The Justice of Mercy*, 9.
2. Ibid.
3. Ibid.
4. Ibid., 10.
5. Ibid., 11.
6. Ibid., 12.
7. Ibid.
8. Ibid.
9. Ibid., 13.
10. Meyer's own interest is in the effect such an understanding of law has on the way courts actually operate. Thus, in criminal law, "We have come to care more about mens rea [i.e., state of mind] than result, with desert primarily defined in terms of culpability rather than the extent of harm caused" (ibid., 14). Constitutional law has to be fomented on a "rational basis" and tort law is based on the idea of a "reasonable person" and what she would and would not do in terms of notions of responsibility and harm. Meyer notes that grace and mercy are (wrongly) seen as "cop-out[s]," contaminations of the purity of law with human weakness and a false and misguided sense of decency (15). Summarizing this phenomenon, Meyer tells us: "Our kanticism is a powerful dream of humanity as only a little lower than the angels, and that lends law both nobility and authority" (15).
11. See, for example, Ronald Dworkin, *Taking Rights Seriously* (Cambridge: Harvard University Press, 1977) and also his *Law's Empire* (Cambridge: Harvard University Press, 1986).
12. H. L. A. Hart, *The Concept of Law*, 2nd ed. (New York: Oxford University Press, 1961), 252n.
13. For this and many other insights, I am very grateful to Darien Shanske. See H. L. A. Hart, "Positivism and the Separation of Law and Morals," *Harvard Law Review* 71 (1958): 593–629.
14. Or perhaps "Kanticism" since the occlusion is, of course, a deformation of the original philosophy that formed it.
15. Hart, *The Concept of Law*, 20.
16. Ibid., 135. Hart appears to reject morals as having an "open texture" of their own (168). Unlike the law (and as with language), in the case of morals such an open texture is confounding and dangerous in Hart's view. Thus, Hart asks about morals in general: "Are they immutable principles which constitute part of the fabric of the Universe, not made by man, but awaiting discovery by the human intellect? Or are they expressions of changing human attitudes, choices, demands, or feelings?" (168).

Such a concern is a consequence of the fact that Hart has not committed, as Benjamin has, to a full iconoclasm. For Benjamin, as we have already seen several times, we do not have to choose between moral codes; they are idolatrous one and all.

17. Ibid., 11.

18. Ibid., 11–12.

19. Ibid., 12.

20. Ibid., 147.

21. Ibid., 133.

22. Ibid., 152.

23. Ibid., 154.

24. Ibid., 134.

25. Ibid., 159.

26. Ibid., 193.

27. Ibid., 195.

28. Ibid., 194–98.

29. See Thomas Hobbes, *Leviathan*, ed. Richard Tuck (New York: Cambridge University Press, 1996); Thomas Hobbes, *Man and Citizen (De Homine and De Cive)*, ed. Bernard Gert (Indianapolis: Hackett, 1991).

30. Hart, *The Concept of Law*, 194–95.

31. Ibid., 195.

32. Ibid., 196.

33. Kant does this too when he famously writes "If cinnabar were one moment red, the next moment black, one moment light, the next moment heavy, if human beings one moment changed into one animal shape, the next moment into a different animal shape, if on the longest day the country were one moment covered with fruit, the next moment with ice and snow, then my empirical imagination would not even be able to think of the heavy cinnabar in connection with the representation of the color red." Immanuel Kant, *Critique of Pure Reason: A Revised and Expanded Translation Based on Meiklejohn*, trans. Vasilis Politis (London: J.M. Dent and Sons, 1993), 123. As already noted in the previous chapter, Kant also demonstrates a Hart-like sensibility whenever he refers to rational creatures besides human beings (which he does quite consistently). He says, for example (also in the *Critique of Pure Reason*): "I should not hesitate to stake my all on the truth of the proposition . . . that, at least, some one of the planets, which we see, is inhabited" (529).

34. Hart, *The Concept of Law*, 206.

35. Hart, "Positivism," 607–8.

36. Hart, *The Concept of Law*, 198.

37. Ibid., 192.

38. Ibid., 192–93.

39. Ibid., 201.

40. Ibid., 202.

41. Ibid., 6.

42. Ibid., 201.

43. Hart, "Positivism," 613.

44. Ibid.

45. Ibid., 616–17.

46. Hart, *The Concept of Law*, 211. See also "Positivism," 598.

47. Hart, *The Concept of Law*, 211.

48. Ibid. In his debate with Fuller, Hart returns to this theme of anarchy and its risks. There he writes: "Bentham had in mind the anarchist who argues thus: 'This ought not to be the law, therefore it is not and I am free not merely to censure but to disregard it.' On the other hand he thought of the reactionary who argues: 'This is the law, therefore it is what it ought to be,' and thus stifles criticism at its birth. . . . There are therefore two dangers between which insistence on this distinction will help us to steer: the danger that law and its authority may be dissolved in man's conceptions of what law ought to be and the danger that the existing law may supplant morality as a final test of conduct and so escape criticism." "Positivism," 598.

49. Joseph Raz, *The Authority of the Law: Essays on Law and Morality* (Oxford: Clarendon Press, 1979), 70.

50. More commonly he tells us, "In [cases where law is not unsettled, not offering a "gap"] judges are typically said to apply the law, and since it is source-based, its application involves technical, legal skills in reasoning from those sources and does not call for moral acumen." Ibid., 49–50.

51. Raz resists the "attempt to routinize [civil disobedience] and make it a regular form of political action to which all have a right. Its exceptional character lies precisely in the reverse of this claim, in the fact that it is (in liberal states) one type of political action to which one has no right." Ibid., 275.

52. Ibid., 276. Speaking on behalf of this argument, Raz writes that "no man shall be liable for breach of duty if his breach is committed because he thinks that it is morally wrong for him to obey the law on the ground that it is morally bad or wrong totally or in part" (276).

53. Ibid.

54. Ibid., 288.

55. Scott J. Shapiro, *Legality* (Cambridge: Harvard University Press, 2011), 194. For other legal positivists, see, for example, Jules Coleman, *Markets, Morals and the Law* (New York: Cambridge University Press, 1988) as well as his *The Practice of Principle: In Defense of a Pragmatist Approach to Legal Theory* (New York: Oxford University Press, 2000). See also Leslie Green, *The Authority of the State* (Oxford: Clarendon Press, 1990), which makes more concessions to moral reasoning.

56. Shapiro, *Legality*, 194.

57. Ibid., 119.

58. Ibid., 281. Shapiro goes on to write: "The law is completely determinate, then, when it regulates every action under every possible description. The law will be indeterminate, in turn, whenever the law does not regulate some action under some possible description. This will occur in a number of situations, including when the action falls within the penumbra of some rule but not the core of a more specific rule, the core of a morally loaded rule but not the core of a more morally specific rule, or the core of two inconsistent rules when there is no rule that resolves such conflicts. Since actions inevitably fall within one of these categories, it follows that the law will never be completely determinate" (281).

59. Ibid., 257. Here Shapiro cites the case *McCulloch v. Maryland*, which estab-

lished the constitutional principle of implied powers, not previously specified, for the federal government.

60. Ibid.

61. Ibid.

62. Ibid., 256.

63. Benjamin, "Critique of Violence," 236.

64. Ibid.

65. Ibid.

66. Ibid., 237.

67. This may explain why Hart engages in a "minimum content of natural law" and why Joseph Raz, his more recent disciple, sees some commonality with natural law theory as well. Raz, *Authority of the Law*, 39. As Benjamin describes it, positive law is a response to the dangers of violence that come from political actors following their own moral creeds ("natural law"). This view is consistent with Hart, who, as we saw, worried about the "danger of anarchy" that would ensue if laws could be followed by choice rather than by command. Benjamin writes of this dilemma: "This legal system tries to erect, in all areas where individual ends could be usefully pursued by violence, legal ends that can be realized only by legal power . . . it follows that the law sees violence in the hands of individuals as a danger undermining the legal system." "Critique of Violence," 238.

68. Positive law and legal positivism are not exactly the same thing, although I am using the terms fairly interchangeably. One can say that there are various kinds of legal theories including positive and natural law. This does not commit one to any particular opinion. To say that one is a legal positivist means that one would argue that only positive law is really law. Yet Benjamin's use of the term positive law evokes this very belief, and thus, although he speaks of positive law where Hart speaks of legal positivism, I believe that they are addressing the same phenomenon. I owe thanks to Darien Shankse for help with the distinction between positive law and legal positivism.

69. Benjamin, "Critique of Violence," 241–42.

70. Ibid., 243.

71. Throughout this book and especially as we reach the end, I've been using a language that sounds as if these changes are once and for all. In fact, from a Benjaminian perspective, this is unlikely insofar as the phantasmagoria does not vanish but simply recedes or is disrupted. I use this language nonetheless for largely rhetorical reasons, to give the reader a sense of real possibility even if that possibility may be intermittent and temporary rather than ongoing and enduring.

72. Benjamin, "Critique of Violence," 241.

73. Badiou, *Saint Paul*, 89.

74. This is akin perhaps to Marx's "negation of the negation." Karl Marx, *Capital*, vol. 1 (New York: Penguin Classics, 1990), 929 (chapter 32).

75. In a previous book, *Divine Violence*, I argued that Carl Schmitt presents us with a false choice between dictatorship and anarchy where anarchy itself is simply to "decide against the decision." I see this choice between formalism and rules skepticism as another false choice, a version of what Schmitt himself suggests (albeit a more benign version of Schmitt's choice, to be sure).

CHAPTER 5

1. Apparently, Toussaint Louverture wrote his own name without the apostrophe that is used in French (L'Ouverture). Mostly I will just refer to him as "Toussaint," adopting the style of C. L. R. James. In contemporary Creole, his name is rendered Tousen Louvèti. In terms of other nomenclature, in general, I prefer the admittedly awkward term "ex-slaves" to "the Haitian people" or "the Haitian masses." The latter terms suggest idolatrous forms of identity that often and easily coalesce around some sense of grouping. The term "ex-slaves" resists that coalescence by reminding us of the struggle against slavery itself rather than the identity or identities that follow in the wake of that struggle. In general, it is hard to speak on behalf of the ex-slaves who themselves rarely wrote anything. While we have the memoires of Toussaint Louverture and other leaders, we don't have much corresponding documentation for the ordinary ex-slaves themselves. Caroline Fick notes that "to date, very little research, at least from the standpoint of primary archival sources, has been devoted specifically to the mass of black slave laborers who participated in this revolution on their own terms and with interests and goals embodying their own needs and aspirations, often at variance with, if not in direct opposition to, the path being staked out by those in positions of leadership or control." Carolyn E. Fick, *The Making of Haiti: The Saint Domingue Revolution from Below* (Knoxville: University of Tennessee Press, 1990), 1. Most of the sources she turns to as well as others who focus on the lives of ordinary former slaves come from writings by leaders, foreign visitors, later historians, and other sources. The absence of direct narratives from the ex-slaves themselves is an aporia at the heart of the radical nature of this revolution. Authors like Fick, Dubois, and James seek to engage with that aporia, but we should always bear in mind that to some extent the figures they are talking about have not been allowed their own voice. David Patrick Geggus also gives a good overview of the sources about the revolution and slave narratives. See David Patrick Geggus, *Haitian Revolutionary Studies* (Bloomington: Indiana University Press, 2002).

2. Laurent Dubois and John D. Garrigus, *Slave Revolution in the Caribbean 1789–1804: A Brief History with Documents* (New York: Bedford / St. Martin's, 2006), 8. See also John Garrigus, *Before Haiti: Race and Citizenship in French Saint-Domingue* (New York: Palgrave, 2006).

3. Dubois and Garrigus, *Slave Revolution*, 8.

4. C. L. R. James, *The Black Jacobins: Toussaint L'Ouverture and the San Domingo Revolution*, 2nd ed. (New York, Vintage Books, 1989), 26.

5. Ibid., 120.

6. Dubois and Garrigus, *Slave Revolution*, 18.

7. Such a stance explains why at various points in his resistance Toussaint turned to both the Spanish and the British—the enemies of France at that time—to seek the permanent abolishment of slavery (although both refused him).

8. Illan rua Wall, *Human Rights and Constituent Power: Without Model or Warranty* (New York: Routledge/GlassHouse, 2011) 17.

9. Ibid. See also Fick, *The Making of Haiti*, 111; Laurent Dubois, *Avengers of the New World: The Story of the Haitian Revolution* (Cambridge: Belknap Press of Har-

vard University Press, 2004), 102–3. The original text comes from Althéa de Peuch Parham, *My Odyssey: Experience of a Young Refugee from Two Revolutions, by a Creole of Saint-Domingue* (Baton Rouge: Louisiana State University Press, 1959). Fick also writes a good overview (in French) in "La revolution de Saint-Domingue: De l'insurrection du 22 août 1791 à la formation de l'État haïtien," in *L'insurrection des esclaves de Saint-Domingue*, ed. Laënnec Hurbon (Paris: Éditions Karthala, 2000). Other essays in that volume are also helpful for specific information about the Haitian slaves and their customs, beliefs, and practices. For a well-known account that is a bit closer to the contemporary period of the revolution see Thomas Madiou, *Histoire d'Haiti*, vol. 2, *1799–1803* (Port au Prince, Haiti: Editions Henri Deschamps, 1989).

10. Wall, *Human Rights*, 18.

11. Ibid.

12. Benjamin, "Concept of History," 390.

13. I should make it clear here that a *"weak* messianic power" should be taken as referring, not to a power that people possess themselves (so that they are acting as messiahs), but rather a messianic power—the power of divine violence—that allows human beings their own ability to resist and act (however "weakly").

14. James, *Black Jacobins*, 281.

15. Ibid., 281–82.

16. This is not the only time that Toussaint speaks of France as a parent figure. In his memoir he writes of his battle with General Leclerc (and the fact that France—and Napoleon—inexplicably favored Leclerc over Toussaint himself): "If two children fight together, doesn't their father or their mother have to stop them, decide who is the aggressor, punish one or both in the case that they are both wrong?" Toussaint L'Ouverture, *Mémoires du general Toussaint Louverture* (Guitalens-L'Albarede, France: Editions La Girandole, 2009), 128. This and all subsequent translations from the *Mémoires* are my own. See also Gerard M. Laurent, ed., *Toussaint Louverture: A travers sa corresondance (1794–1798)* (Madrid: Industrias Graficas, España, 1953); Toussaint Louverture, *Lettres à la France: Idées pour la liberation du people noir d'Haïti* (Bruyères-le-Châtel, France: Nouvelle Cité, 2011).

17. James, *Black Jacobins*, 281.

18. Ibid.

19. Ibid., 290.

20. Ibid., 283.

21. Ibid., 278.

22. Fick, *The Making of Haiti*, 209.

23. Ibid., 213–14.

24. Toussaint, *Mémoires*, 99.

25. Ibid., 84.

26. Ibid., 69.

27. Ibid., 101.

28. Ibid., 140.

29. For an account of some of the voices that came out of Haiti at that time—voices that are not limited to the slave narrative, which is usually hegemonic—see Deborah Jenson, *Beyond the Slave Narrative: Politics, Sex and Manuscripts in the Haitian Revolution* (Liverpool: Liverpool University Press, 2011). See also (in a more

general sense) Siba N. Grovogui, "No More, No Less: What Slaves Thought about Their Humanity," in *Silencing Human Rights: Critical Engagements with a Contested Project*, ed. Gurminder K. Bhambra and Robbie Shilliam (New York: Palgrave, 2008), 43–60.

30. Dubois and Garrigus, *Slave Revolution*, 18.

31. James, *Black Jacobins*, 81.

32. Ibid., 82.

33. For an alternative (and much more radical) view of marronage see Neil Roberts, "State, Power, Anarchism," *Perspectives on Politics* 9, no. 1 (March 2011): 84–88. See also his "Marronage between Past and Future: Requiem for Édouard Glissant," *C.L.R. James Journal* 18, no. 1 (Fall 2012): 5–6, special issue on the work of Édouard Glissant, edited by John Drabinski and Marisa Parham; Eugene D. Genovese, *From Rebellion to Revolution: Afro-American Slave Revolts in the Making of the Modern World* (Baton Rouge: Louisiana State University Press, 1979). See also Jimmy Casas Klausen, *Fugitive Rousseau: Slavery, Primitivism, and Political Freedom* (New York: Fordham University Press, 2014).

34. Fick, *The Making of Haiti*, 49.

35. Fick also writes: "Here in Saint Domingue, the whole situation had radically changed; the colonial context in which colonists could try to reassure themselves by seeing armed maroon bands as entities outside of the plantations—troublesome, to be sure, but not enough to threaten the foundations and institutional viability of slavery—had now fallen into a million pieces and reposed, literally, on little more than a pile of ashes." Ibid., 106.

36. For Fick, the interpretation of the events in France did have an intellectual component, especially among those slaves and domestics who were more integrated into the life of French plantation owners. She writes, "When news of the French Revolution reached the colony, slaves heard talk of liberty and equality, and they interpreted these ideals in their own way. Domestics listened to their masters argue over independence while they perfunctorily served them their meals and drinks. Some had even traveled to France with masters who could not do without their servants. They were exposed to new ideas, to the principles upon which their revolution was being built." Ibid., 86.

37. Ibid., 107.

38. Ibid., 208.

39. James, *Black Jacobins*, 242.

40. Fick, *The Making of Haiti*, 209–10.

41. Ibid., 180.

42. Ibid., 168.

43. For Fick this is the one good legacy of the Haitian Revolution that survives to this day, besides Haitian independence and the end of slavery. Unlike the large-scale latifundia plantation systems that persist in one form or another in many other Caribbean former slave societies, Haiti today is marked mainly by the same small-scale farming that was set up during revolutionary times. Ibid., 249–50.

44. Ibid., 247.

45. Ibid. Fick also tells us that, rather than forming a collective and organized movement, these "constituted, rather, the generalized, spontaneous, and inarticulate expression of discontent in reaction to a system that had little to do with the

freedom these ex-slaves had fought for, but now were not allowed to define. It was this personal attachment to the land and the active imposition of their own will upon its cultivation and utilization that would transform their past identity as slaves into that of free persons. And it was this that the new regime deprived them of" (182). In her consideration of their economic and political practices, Fick focuses on the period of transition from a full slave to a "semi-wage, semi-sharecropping labor system" from the end of 1793 to the middle of 1794, arguing that this period "offers a unique opportunity to discern, through their acts of resistance to the new system and thus from their own vantage point, what that freedom meant to them" (168). She also writes of this period: "On some plantations the workers had, in effect, taken over the land for their own purposes. As they were organized in brigades, each group would cultivate that portion of the land assigned to it, and the workers would then sell the products that were superfluous to their needs" (169).

46. Dubois, *Avengers*, 108–9. See also John Thornton, "I Am the Subject of the King of Kongo: African Political Ideology and the Haitian Revolution," *Journal of World History* 4 (Fall 1993): 186.

47. Fick, *The Making of Haiti*, 150.

48. Ibid., 215.

49. James, *Black Jacobins*, 361–62.

50. One author who discusses this is David Scott. See his *Conscripts of Modernity: The Tragedy of Colonial Enlightenment* (Durham, NC: Duke University Press, 2004). Scott's claim is that the slaves and their revolution are entirely caught up in modernity, not something apart. For an excellent engagement with Scott, one that engages some of Scott's key assumptions, see Kevin Olson, "Conscripted by Modernity? Sovereign Imaginaries for the Haitian Revolution," unpublished manuscript.

51. Badiou, *Saint Paul*, 89.

52. See for example, Jean-Jacques Rousseau, *The Social Contract*, trans. Maurice Cranston (New York: Penguin Classics, 1968), 142–43.

53. Benjamin, "Concept of History," Thesis XII, 394. I am indebted to Marc de Wilde for this connection and insight.

54. Ibid.

55. Michel-Rolph Trouillot helps us think more about the unthinkability, the true impossibility of the Haitian Revolution in his article "Des Journaux de planteurs à l'Académie: La revolution haïtienne comme histoire impensable," *Le Journal de l'Histoire caraibéene* 25, nos. 1–2: 81–85.

56. Respectively, Wall, *Human Rights*, 16; and Sibylle Fischer, *Modernity Disavowed: Haiti and the Cultures of Slavery in the Age of Revolution* (Durham, NC: Duke University Press, 2004), 3. To be sure, not everyone forgot about Haiti; American slaves for one, recalled and treasured the victory of the Haitian slaves over European powers, as did, of course, the Haitians themselves. In terms of other authors who deal with the silencing of the Haitian Revolution, Fischer's *Modernity Disavowed* is an excellent source. She describes this silencing as itself part and parcel of modernity. She also discusses the resistance of "a radically heterogeneous, transnational cultural network [that] emerged whose political imaginary mirrored the global scope of the slave trade and whose projects and fantasies of emancipation converged, a least for a few years, around Haiti" (1). Another good source that

details the silencing of the Haitian Revolution is the justifiably well-known book by Michel-Rolph Trouillot, *Silencing the Past: Power and the Production of History* (Boston: Beacon Press, 1995). Susan Buck-Morss's *Hegel, Haiti and Universal History* (Pittsburgh: University of Pittsburgh Press, 2009) is, in its own way, an answer to that silencing. She convincingly reads Hegel's discussion of the master/slave relationship in his *Phenomenology of Spirit* as an unspoken response to the Haitian Revolution.

57. This is a project I am currently working on, a book, tentatively entitled *When Anarchism Was Young: Retrieving Early Twentieth-Century Spanish Radicalism as a Way of Life*.

CONCLUSION

1. Once again, Neil Roberts in "State, Power, Anarchism" provides an interesting and different perspective on marronage, as does Jimmy Casas Klausen in *Fugitive Rousseau*.

2. Benjamin, "Critique of Violence," 244, and "Zur Kritik der Gewalt," 191.

3. Benjamin, "Critique of Violence," 246.

4. Critchley, *Faith of the Faithless*, 197.

5. Ibid., 199.

6. For an account of Agamben's relationship to Benjamin (reading both through a Kantian lens) see Benjamin Morgan, "Undoing Legal Violence: Walter Benjamin and Giorgio Agamben's Aesthetic of Pure Means," *Journal of Law and Society* 34, Issue 1 (March 2007): 46–64. One of the main works in which Agamben treats Benjamin's legal work is *State of Exception*. For an excellent gloss on that reading see Weber, "Going Along for the Ride"; see also Vivian Liska, "The Legacy of Benjamin's Messianism: Giorgio Agamben and Other Contenders," in Goebel, *Companion to Walter Benjamin*.

7. Benjamin, "Critique of Violence," 250.

8. Critchley, *Faith of the Faithless*, 203.

9. Ibid., 128.

10. Ibid.

11. In general, while I am in agreement with many of his criticisms of both Agamben and Žižek, I find myself more in sympathy with them than Critchley is. His claim that Agamben has abandoned law may be partially right, but only partially. Agamben's numerous and important turns to Jewish law and texts are indicative of a more complicated relationship than Critchley lets on. And Žižek, for all his "obsessions" (Critchley's words), is a brilliant reader. Calling someone a fantasist (as Critchley basically does with both Žižek and Agamben) is too easy; as Benjamin shows, we are all fantasists in our way. The point is to redeem those interstitial readings that coexist with that phantasm. Rather than dismiss Žižek outright, as Critchley does, I read him in this spirit.

12. To the extent that there is anything that could be considered "old school" about Žižek.

13. Critchley, *Faith of the Faithless*, 210–11.

14. Ibid., 212.

15. Slavoj Žižek, *Violence: Six Sideways Reflections* (London: Profile, 2008), 201.

16. Ibid.

17. Ibid., 202. Saul Newman also disagrees with Agamben on this point. See Saul Newman, *The Politics of Postanarchism* (Edinburgh: University of Edinburgh Press, 2009).

18. Critchley, *Faith of the Faithless*, 220.

19. Žižek, *Violence*, 202.

20. Critchley, *Faith of the Faithless*, 236.

21. Ibid., 217–18. He also equates divine violence with Levinas's notion of essential violence, whereby "to welcome the other is to unseat the archic assurance of our place in the world, our sovereignty. Thus, to open oneself to the experience of transcendence, to the pacific itself, is violence" (223).

22. Critchley, *Faith of the Faithless*, 220.

23. Ibid., 220–21.

24. If so, the sense that human imperfection offers a safe barrier between the human and the divine is akin to what we already saw with Kant and Hart, a sense of being "idol proof" that potentially allows more, rather than less, idolatry to occur.

25. Benjamin, "Critique of Violence," 250.

26. Benjamin, "Zur Kritik der Gewalt," 200. Andrew Benjamin points out that "divine violence is a poor translation for 'göttliche Gewalt'," which is better translated as "God's violence." Were this translation the norm, it would be much harder to confuse human and divine agency.

27. Benjamin, "Critique of Violence," 250.

28. Ibid.

29. Ibid. and "Kritik der Gewalt," 200.

30. Critchley, *Faith of the Faithless*, 221.

31. Ibid., 243.

32. Ibid., 237. Bonhoeffer also speaks, more troublingly from a Benjaminian perspective, of a "free responsibility of the one who acts, a responsibility not bound by any law" (236).

33. Ibid., 222.

34. Ibid., 214.

35. In an earlier book I wrote on Hobbes, I argue that for Hobbes, too, language provides a more democratic (or anarchist) set of determinations about meaning, one that the sovereign mostly has to adjust to despite Hobbes assertion that the sovereign is the "great decider." See *Subverting the Leviathan: Reading Thomas Hobbes as a Radical Democrat* (New York: Columbia University Press, 2007).

36. Cited in Critchley, *Faith of the Faithless*, 215.

37. Benjamin, "Critique of Violence," 239.

38. Critchley, *Faith of the Faithless*, 243. Fascinatingly for my own purposes, Critchley suggests that "Žižek then translates divine violence into Kantian categories as 'the direct intervention of the noumenal into the phenomenal.' Divine violence becomes equated with the Kantian sublime as the violent transgression of human finitude. For Kant, the sublime is an emotion that places human beings in the fundamental tension between infinity (*Unendlichkeit*) and finitude (*Endlichkeit*), between immanence and transcendence, between representation and that which exceeds it" (241–42).

39. Ibid., 243.

40. In writing this, I am cognizant of the fact that, as I've already noted, Benjamin can see a very broad program of resistance such as the revolutionary general strike as being "nonviolent," but Benjamin does not give us enough information here to tell whether in his view such "nonviolence" is all that we need to unmake the state and its apparatuses of violence. Clearly for Benjamin there is an entire nonviolent realm, but in the direct engagement with mythic violence, it is not clear that for him nonviolence is always an option. I will argue this point further a bit later in the chapter.

41. In terms of Benjamin's own writings on the subject, it is interesting to note that while his notion of *Gewalt* translates both as "force" and as "violence," in ordinary spoken German "violence" is given a slightly different term. While the term *Gewalt* is used in German to refer to "violence," it is usually meant as the violence done by natural or large forces (like a volcano). If one is referring to the violence of a street gang or the like, one uses the longer term *Gewaltaetigkeit* (i.e., "doing violent deeds"). This does not mean that Benjamin's notion of violence excludes the kinds of human-on-human crimes that we normally attribute to the English term "violence." but it does suggest that he has something else in mind, something more connected to legal and state power, a kind of violence that is normally not recognized as such but which is once again (as the "Critique of Violence" attests) the true danger to human beings. I am indebted to Angelika von Wahl for these insights.

42. Žižek, *Violence*, 203.

43. Ibid., 205. To be fair, Žižek tells us that we should *"love with hatred"* (204).

44. Critchley, *Faith of the Faithless*, 250.

45. Louis Althusser, "Ideology and Ideological State Apparatuses," in *Lenin and Philosophy and Other Essays* (New York: Monthly Review Press, 1972), 118. For an important reading of Althusser and interpellation theory see Judith Butler, *The Psychic Life of Power: Theories of Subjection* (Stanford, CA: Stanford University Press, 1997).

46. Frantz Fanon, *Black Skin, White Masks*, trans. Charles Lam Markmann (New York: Grove Press, 1967), 109.

47. I would love to be able to say that I came up with the term, but in fact it comes from Mark Antaki, when we were discussing an earlier book of mine (*Textual Conspiracies*). I am grateful to him for his gift of this helpful neologism (since then, I've also seen it bandied about here and there, so it might have several originators, as is quite appropriate for such a term).

48. Althusser, "Ideology," 118. For an interesting discussion of Althusser's interpellation theory, see Charles Barbour, *The Marx Machine* (New York: Lexington Books, 2012), 62.

49. Althusser, "Ideology," 118.

50. Benjamin, "Franz Kafka," 808.

51. Franz Kafka, "Abraham," in *Parables and Paradoxes*, 41. Benjamin's discussion of Kafka and the Second Commandment immediately follows his consideration of this parable in "Frank Kafka: On the Tenth Anniversary of His Death."

52. Franz Kafka, "Abraham," 43–45.

53. Ibid., 43.

54. Althusser, "Ideology," 116–18.

55. Benjamin, "Concept of History," 397.

56. Benjamin, "Critique of Violence," 241.

57. Rousseau, *The Social Contract*, 54.

58. Badiou, *Saint Paul*, 89.

59. Ibid., 87.

60. Kant, *Groundwork*, 114 (447).

61. In fact it's even more complicated than that because, as I have argued in *Textual Conspiracies*, it is really a case of *mis*recognition (not meant in the Althusserian sense) or "recognizing our misrecognition." *Textual Conspiracies*, 246–48.

62. I don't say this to make the facetious argument that modern subjects of the phantasmagoria have it as bad as the Haitian slaves but rather that the radical kernel of resistance to phantasms offered by the example of the slave revolution in Haiti also serves the modern subject.

63. Insofar as the subjects of the Second Commandment remain fallen and guilty—even despite our obedience to this one law—our relationship to the Second Commandment will still feel like a choice; the sense of agency that we receive from our obedience almost inevitably includes the very basis for that agency. This is why there is always the danger that the Second Commandment itself can become an idol, and, further, why the Second Commandment must always be applied even to itself.

64. Hart, *The Concept of Law*, 19.

65. Ibid., 35–36. See Hans Kelsen, *General Theory of Law and State* (Clark, NJ: Lawbook Exchange, 2007).

66. Hart, *The Concept of Law*, 6–9.

67. Ibid., 8.

68. I engage in this thought exercise with some trepidation, for it involves, first of all interfering with the "autonomy" of this community by projecting what they would and would not do (this is exactly what Benjamin says not to do!). If this community is to be its own authors, then it should not have interference from this author or any other. More prosaically, it's always a risk to talk about how a better form of politics would actually work simply because it immediately takes on connotations of utopianism and unworkability. Insofar as it is, of necessity, a flawed, partial explanation, to get into details like this always threatens to lose the baby (the principles being considered) with the bathwater (the examples being proffered).

69. I can imagine that with this statement, I have lost a bunch of my fellow anarchists for whom nothing should be decisive and determinist, even within the shifting context of anarchist forms of obligation. But I can't see how it would work otherwise; it is human decision that Benjamin's notion of divine violence permits, and decisions must be real, meaningful, and yes, binding. If a community—however defined—"decided" to do something, but whoever didn't feel like doing it anymore didn't have to, it wouldn't be a decision, just a suggestion. Maybe there is some value to thinking further about such a society, but anarchism as a practice has rarely been of this sort and, I think, for a good reason; it comes too close to what Benjamin calls a "childish anarchism," or what Critchley calls "mystical anarchism," an anarchism, that is, where there is no law at all (or rather, there is law but it is not followed). If there is to be law, as I have argued strenuously in this book, it must have some expression, some substance, some bearing on the way a community lives. And, at any rate, this law, this decision of a community, would not bind in the same

way as mythic law; it would not have that force of false authority to make it impregnable. It would just be a decision, one that could readily be challenged and unmade.

70. I am intrigued by various experiments with this kind of question in actual contemporary anarchist communities; there are, for example practices wherein there are multiple models of behavior at any given time and they coexist as best they can (so that only those who want to be bound by a rule are so bound). I think, however, that even this model includes a loose obligation since there will be, at any given time, lots of people bound by lots of (albeit different) rules.

71. For more on the performativity of bindingness see Karen Feldman, *Binding Words: Conscience and Rhetoric in Hobbes, Hegel and Heidegger* (Evanston, IL: Northwestern University Press, 2006).

72. Klausen, *Fugitive Rousseau*, 323.

73. There is also always the possibility of a kind of limited internal exit. Klausen engages with Albert Hirschmann's famous *Exit, Voice, and Loyalty*, in order to rethink about exit as a possibly radical strategy as well. Exit may not have to be physical; rather, communities could persist within communities. See Albert Hirschmann, *Exit, Voice, and Loyalty: Responses to Decline in Firms, Organizations, and States* (Cambridge: Harvard University Press, 1970).

74. Also, I would add, given that nearly every liberal author who discusses law warns us against "anarchy," the price of not following the laws as they are currently conceived, this alone might cause us to take the question of anarchism more seriously. Although they paint anarchy in terms of total lawlessness, a free-for-all, when we move through this projection, we see something else, an actual alternative, a way out of "fate."

75. Critchley, *Faith of the Faithless*, 178.

76. Ibid.

77. Ibid., 181.

78. Benjamin, *Origin*, 233. I discuss this at some length in the concluding chapter of *Textual Conspiracies*.

79. And here I cannot help but think of Robyn Marasco's forthcoming book *The Highway of Despair: Critical Thinking after Hegel*. The despair she finds is that book is the same necessary letdown, the giving up on hope for phantasmic rescues that precedes the possibility of political action.

80. Benjamin, "Critique of Violence," 252.

Bibliography

Agamben, Giorgio. *The Coming Community*. Minneapolis: University of Minnesota Press, 1993.

Agamben, Giorgio. *State of Exception*. Chicago: University of Chicago Press, 2005.

Agamben, Giorgio. *The Time That Remains: A Commentary on the Letter to the Romans*. Trans. Patricia Dailey. Stanford, CA: Stanford University Press, 2005.

Althusser, Louis. "Ideology and Ideological State Apparatuses." In *Lenin and Philosophy and Other Essays*. Monthly Review Press, 1972.

Arendt, Hannah. *On Revolution*. New York: Penguin Books, 1986.

Augustine (Saint). *City of God*. Trans. Marcus Dods. New York: Modern Library, 1994.

Badiou, Alain. *The Communist Hypothesis*. Trans. David Macey and Steve Corcoran. New York: Verso, 2010.

Badiou, Alain. *Ethics: An Essay on the Understanding of Evil*. Trans. Peter Hallward. New York: Verso, 2001.

Badiou, Alain. *Saint Paul: The Foundation of Universalism*. Trans. Ray Brassier. Stanford, CA: Stanford University Press, 2003.

Barbour, Charles. *The Marx Machine*. New York: Lexington Books, 2012.

Batnitzky, Leora. *Idolatry and Representation: The Philosophy of Franz Rosenzweig Reconsidered*. Princeton: Princeton University Press, 2000.

Benjamin, Andrew. *Working with Walter Benjamin: Recovering a Political Philosophy*. Oxford: Oxford University Press, 2013.

Benjamin, Walter. *The Arcades Project*. Trans. Howard Eiland and Kevin McLaughlin. Cambridge: Belknap Press of Harvard University Press, 1999.

Benjamin, Walter. "Critique of Violence." In *Walter Benjamin: Selected Writings*, ed. Marcus Bullock and Michael W. Jennings, vol. 1, *1913–1926*. Cambridge: Belknap Press of Harvard University Press, 1996.

Benjamin, Walter. "Franz Kafka: On the Tenth Anniversary of His Death." In *Walter Benjamin: Selected Writings*, ed. Marcus Bullock and Michael W. Jennings, vol. 2, *1927–1934*. Cambridge: Belknap Press of Harvard University Press, 1999.

Benjamin, Walter. "Letter to Gershom Scholem on Franz Kafka." In *Walter Benjamin: Selected Writings*, ed. Marcus Bullock and Michael W. Jennings, vol. 3, *1935–1938*. Cambridge: Belknap Press of Harvard University Press, 2002.

Benjamin, Walter. "On Language as Such and the Language of Man." In *Walter Benjamin: Selected Writings*, ed. Marcus Bullock and Michael W. Jennings, vol. 1, *1913–1926*. Cambridge: Belknap Press of Harvard University Press, 1996.

Benjamin, Walter. "On the Concept of History." In *Walter Benjamin: Selected Work*, ed. Marcus Bullock and Michael W. Jennings, vol. 4, *1938–1940*. Cambridge: Belknap Press of Harvard University Press, 2003.

Benjamin, Walter. *The Origin of German Tragic Drama*. Trans. John Osborne. New York: Verso, 1998.

Benjamin, Walter. "The Paris of the Second Empire in Baudelaire." In *The Writer of Modern Life: Essays on Charles Baudelaire*, ed. Michael W. Jennings, trans. Howard Eiland et al. Cambridge: Belknap Press of Harvard University Press, 2006.

Benjamin, Walter. "The Right to Use Force." In *Walter Benjamin: Selected Writings*, ed. Marcus Bullock and Michael W. Jennings, vol. 1, *1913–1926*. Cambridge: Belknap Press of Harvard University Press, 1996.

Benjamin, Walter. "Zur Kritik der Gewalt." In *Gesammelte Schriften*, vol. 2.1. Frankfurt am Main: Surkamp Verlag, 1980.

Bensaïd, Daniel. *Walter Benjamin. Sentinelle messianique: À la gauche du possible*. Paris: Les prairies ordinaires, 2010.

Birnbaum, Antonia. *Bonheur justice, Walter Benjamin: Le détour grec*. Paris: Éditions Payot & Rivages, 2008.

Bosteels, Bruno. *The Actuality of Communism*. New York: Verso, 2011.

Bosteels, Bruno. *Badiou and Politics*. Durham: Duke University Press, 2011.

Breton, Stanislas. *The Radical Philosophy of Saint Paul*. New York: Columbia University Press, 2011.

Britt, Brian. *Walter Benjamin and the Bible*. New York: Continuum, 1996.

Buck-Morss, Susan. *Hegel, Haiti and Universal History*. Pittsburgh: University of Pittsburgh Press, 2009.

Butler, Judith. *The Psychic Life of Power: Theories of Subjection*. Stanford, CA: Stanford University Press, 1997.

Castle, Terry. "Phantasmagoria: Spectral Technology and the Metaphorics of Modern Reverie." *Critical Inquiry* 15, no. 1 (Autumn 1988): 26–61.

Cohen, Hermann. *Religion of Reason: Out of the Sources of Judaism*. New York: Oxford University Press, 1995.

Cohen, Margaret. "Benjamin's Phantasmagoria: The *Arcades Project*." In *The Cambridge Companion to Walter Benjamin*, ed. David S. Ferris. New York: Cambridge University Press, 2004.

Coleman, Jules. *Markets, Morals and the Law*. New York: Cambridge University Press, 1988.

Coleman, Jules. *The Practice of Principle: In Defense of a Pragmatist Approach to Legal Theory*. New York: Oxford University Press, 2000.

Critchley, Simon. *The Faith of the Faithless: Experiments in Political Theology*. New York: Verso, 2012.

Dean, Jodi. *The Communist Horizon*. New York: Verso, 2012.

Derrida, Jacques. *Dissemination*. Trans. Barbara Johnson. New York: Continuum, 2004.

Derrida, Jacques. "Force of Law: The 'Mystical Foundation of Authority.'" In *Acts of Religion*, ed. Gil Anidjar. New York: Routledge, 2001.

Derrida, Jacques. *Politics of Friendship*. Trans. George Collins. New York: Verso, 1997.

de Vries, Hent, *Religion and Violence: Philosophical Perspectives from Kant to Derrida*. Baltimore, MD: Johns Hopkins University Press, 2001.

de Wilde, Marc. "Benjamin's Politics of Remembrance: A Reading of 'Über den Begriff der Geschichte.'" In *A Companion to the Works of Walter Benjamin*, ed. Rolf J. Goebel. Rochester, NY: Camden House, 2009.

de Wilde, Marc. "Walter Benjamin's Other Law." In *Law's Environment: Critical Legal Perspectives*, ed. U. de Vries and L. Francot. The Hague: Eleven, 2011. 137–54.

Dubois, Laurent. *Avengers of the New World: The Story of the Haitian Revolution*. Cambridge: Belknap Press of Harvard University Press, 2004.

Dubois, Laurent, and John D. Garrigus. *Slave Revolution in the Caribbean 1789–1804: A Brief History with Documents*. New York: Bedford / St. Martin's, 2006.

Dworkin, Ronald. *Law's Empire*. Cambridge: Harvard University Press, 1986.

Dworkin, Ronald. *Taking Rights Seriously*. Cambridge: Harvard University Press, 1977.

Fanon, Frantz. *Black Skin, White Masks*. Trans. Charles Lam Markmann. New York: Grove Press, 1967.

Feldman, Karen. *Binding Words: Conscience and Rhetoric in Hobbes, Hegel and Heidegger*. Evanston, IL: Northwestern University Press, 2006.

Fenves, Peter. "The Genesis of Judgment: Spatiality, Analogy, and Metaphor in Benjamin's 'On Language as Such and on Human Language.'" In *Walter Benjamin: Theoretical Questions*, ed. David S. Ferris. Stanford, CA: Stanford University Press, 1996. 75–93.

Fenves, Peter. *Late Kant: Another Law of the Earth*. New York: Routledge, 2003.

Fenves, Peter. *The Messianic Reduction: Walter Benjamin and the Shape of Time*. Stanford, CA: Stanford University Press, 2010.

Fick, Carolyn E. *The Making of Haiti: The Saint Domingue Revolution from Below*. Knoxville: University of Tennessee Press, 1990.

Fick, Carolyn E. "La revolution de Saint-Domingue. De l'insurrection du 22 août 1791 à la formation de l'État haïtien." In *L'insurrection des esclaves de Saint-Domingue*, ed. Laënnec Hurbon. Paris: Éditions Karthala, 2000.

Fischer, Sibylle. *Modernity Disavowed: Haiti and the Cultures of Slavery in the Age of Revolution*. Durham: Duke University Press, 2004.

Fitzpatrick, Peter. *Modernism and the Grounds of Law*. New York: Cambridge University Press, 2001.

Garrigus, John. *Before Haiti: Race and Citizenship in French Saint-Domingue*. New York: Palgrave, 2006.

Gasché, Rodolphe. "Objective Diversions: On Some Kantian Themes in Benjamin's 'The Work of Art in the Age of Mechanical Reproduction.'" In *Walter Benjamin's Philosophy: Destruction and Experience*, ed. Andrew Benjamin and Peter Osborne. New York: Routledge, 1994.

Geggus, David Patrick. *Haitian Revolutionary Studies*. Bloomington: Indiana University Press, 2002.

Genovese, Eugene D. *From Rebellion to Revolution: Afro-American Slave Revolts in the Making of the Modern World*. Baton Rouge: Louisiana State University Press, 1979.

Green, Leslie. *The Authority of the State*. Oxford: Clarendon Press, 1990.

Grovogui, Siba N. "No More, No Less: What Slaves Thought about their Humanity." In Gurminder K. Bhambra and Robbie Shilliam, eds. *Silencing Human Rights: Critical Engagements with a Contested Project*. New York: Palgrave, 2008. 43–60.

Halbertal, Moshe, and Avishai Margalit. *Idolatry*. Trans. Naomi Goldblum. Cambridge MA: Harvard University Press, 1994.

Hamacher, Werner. "Afformative, Strike: Benjamin's 'Critique of Violence.'" In *Walter Benjamin's Philosophy. Destruction and Experience*, ed. Andrew Benjamin and Peter Osborne. New York: Routledge, 1994. 110–38.

Hart, H. L. A. *The Concept of Law*. 2nd ed. New York: Oxford University Press, 1961.

Hart, H. L. A. "Positivism and the Separation of Law and Morals." In *Harvard Law Review* 71 (1958): 593–629.

Hirschmann, Albert. *Exit, Voice, and Loyalty: Responses to Decline in Firms, Organizations, and States*. Cambridge: Harvard University Press, 1970.

Hobbes, Thomas. *Leviathan*. Ed. Richard Tuck. New York: Cambridge University Press, 1996.

Hobbes, Thomas. *Man and Citizen (De Homine and De Cive)*. Ed. Bernard Gert. Indianapolis: Hackett, 1991.

Hurbon, Laënnec, ed. *L'insurrection des esclaves de Saint-Domingue*. Paris: Éditions Karthala, 2000.

James, C. L. R. *The Black Jacobins: Toussaint L'Ouverture and the San Domingo Revolution*. 2nd ed. New York, Vintage Books, 1989.

Jenson, Deborah. *Beyond the Slave Narrative: Politics, Sex and Manuscripts in the Haitian Revolution*. Liverpool: Liverpool University Press, 2011.

Kafka, Franz. "Abraham" and "The Invention of the Devil." In *Parables and Paradoxes: Bilingual Edition*. New York: Schocken Books, 1961.

Kant, Immanuel. *Critique of Judgment*. Trans. Werner S. Pluhar. Indianapolis: Hackett, 1987.

Kant, Immanuel. *Critique of Pure Reason: A Revised and Expanded Translation Based on Meiklejohn*. Trans. Vasilis Politis. London: J.M. Dent and Sons, 1993.

Kant, Immanuel. *Critique of Practical Reason*. Trans. T. K. Abbott. Amherst, NY: Prometheus Books, 1996.

Kant, Immanuel. *Groundwork of the Metaphysics of Morals*. Trans. H. J. Paton. New York: Harper & Row, 1964.

Kant, Immanuel. *Religion within the Limits of Reason Alone*. Trans. Theodore M. Greene and Hoyt H. Hudson. New York: Harper & Row, 1960.

Kelsen, Hans. *General Theory of Law and State*. Clark, NJ: Lawbook Exchange, 2007.

Klausen, Jimmy Casas. *Fugitive Rousseau: Slavery, Primitivism, and Political Freedom*. New York: Fordham University Press, 2014.

Kotsko, Adam. "Politics and Perversion: Situating Žižek's Paul." *Journal for Cultural and Religious Theory* 9, no. 2 (Summer 2008): 43–52.

Lacan, Jacques. *The Ethics of Psychoanalysis*. Trans. Dennis Porter. New York: Norton, 1997.

Laurent, Gerard M., ed. *Toussaint Louverture: A travers sa corresondance (1794–1798)*. Madrid: Industrias Graficas, España, 1953.

Liska, Vivian. "The Legacy of Benjamin's Messianism: Giorgio Agamben and Other Contenders." In *A Companion to the Works of Walter Benjamin*, ed. Rolf J. Goebel. Rochester, NY: Camden House, 2009.

L'Ouverture, Toussaint. *Lettres à la France: Idées pour la liberation du people noir d'Haïti*. Bruyères-le-Châtel, France: Nouvelle Cité, 2011.

L'Ouverture, Toussaint. *Mémoires du general Toussaint Louverture*. Guitalens-L'Albarede, France: Editions La Girandole, 2009.

Lyotard, Jean François. *Lessons on the Analytic of the Sublime*. Trans. Elizabeth Rottenberg. Stanford, CA: Stanford University Press, 1994.

Madiou, Thomas, *Histoire d'Haiti*. Vol. 2, *1799–1803*. Port au Prince, Haiti: Editions Henri Deschamps, 1989.

Martel, James. *Divine Violence: Walter Benjamin and the Eschatology of Sovereignty*. New York: Routledge/GlassHouse, 2011.

Martel, James. *Love Is a Sweet Chain: Autonomy, Desire and Friendship in Liberal Political Theory*. New York: Routledge, 2001.

Martel, James. "Nothing Exists Except an Earthenware Pot: Resisting Sovereignty on Robinson's Island." *Societies* 2, no. 4 (2012): 372–87.

Martel, James. *Subverting the Leviathan: Reading Thomas Hobbes as a Radical Democrat*. New York: Columbia, 2001.

Martel, James. *Textual Conspiracies: Walter Benjamin, Idolatry and Political Theory*. Ann Arbor: University of Michigan Press, 2011.

Marx, Karl. *Capital*. Vol. 1. New York: Penguin Classics, 1990.

McCall, Tom. "Momentary Violence." In *Walter Benjamin: Theoretical Questions*, ed. David S. Ferris. Stanford, CA: Stanford University Press, 1996.

Menninghaus, Winfried. "Walter Benjamin's Theory of Myth." In *On Walter Benjamin: Critical Essays and Recollections*, ed. Gary Smith. Cambridge: MIT Press, 1988. 292–325.

Meyer, Linda Ross. *The Justice of Mercy*. Ann Arbor: University of Michigan Press, 2010.

Morgan, Benjamin. "Undoing Legal Violence: Walter Benjamin and Giorgio Agamben's Aesthetic of Pure Means." *Journal of Law and Society* 34, no. 1 (March 2007): 46–64.

Newman, Saul. *The Politics of Postanarchism*. Edinburgh: University of Edinburgh Press, 2009.

Noys, Benjamin. "Badiou's Fidelities: Reading the Ethics." *Communication & Cognition* 36, nos. 1–2 (2003): 31–44.

Olson, Kevin. "Conscripted by Modernity? Sovereign Imaginaries for the Haitian Revolution." Paper submitted for the Western Political Science Association, March, 2013.

Parham, Althéa de Peuch. *My Odyssey: Experience of a Young Refugee from Two Revolutions, By a Creole of Saint-Domingue*. Baton Rouge: Louisiana State University Press, 1959.

Poe, Andrew. "Swarm: A Genealogy of Political Enthusiasm." Manuscript being prepared for publication.

Raz, Joseph. *The Authority of Law: Essays on Law and Morals.* Oxford: Clarendon Press, 1979.

Roberts, Neil. "Marronage between Past and Future: Requiem for Édouard Glissant." *C.L.R. James Journal* 18, no. 1 (Fall 2012): 5–6. Special issue on the work of Édouard Glissant, edited by John Drabinski and Marisa Parham.

Roberts, Neil. "State, Power, Anarchism." *Perspectives on Politics* 9, no. 1 (March 2011): 84–88.

Rose, Gillian. "Walter Benjamin: Out of the Sources of Modern Judaism." In *The Actuality of Walter Benjamin,* ed. Laura Marcus and Lynda Nead. London: Lawrence & Wishart, 1998. 85–117.

Rosenzweig, Franz. *The Star of Redemption.* Madison: University of Wisconsin Press, 2005.

Rousseau, Jean-Jacques. *The Social Contract.* Trans. Maurice Cranston. New York: Penguin Classics, 1968.

Satkunanandan, Shalini. "The Extraordinary Categorical Imperative." *Political Theory* 39, no. 2 (2011): 234–60.

Scott, David. *Conscripts of Modernity: The Tragedy of Colonial Enlightenment.* Durham: Duke University Press, 2004.

Shapiro, Scott J., *Legality.* Cambridge: Harvard University Press, 2011.

Shell, Susan Meld. "Kant and the Jewish Question." *Hebraic Political Studies* 2, no. 1 (Winter 2007): 101–36.

Taubes, Jacob. *The Political Theology of Paul.* Stanford, CA: Stanford University Press, 2003.

Thornton, John. "'I Am the Subject of the King of Kongo': African Political Ideology and the Haitian Revolution." *Journal of World History* 4 (Fall 1993): 181–214.

Trouillot, Michel-Rolph. "Des Journaux de planteurs à l'Académie: La revolution haïtienne comme histoire impensable." *Le Journal de l'Histoire caraibéene* 25, nos. 1–2: 81–85.

Trouillot, Michel-Rolph. *Silencing the Past: Power and the Production of History.* Boston: Beacon Press, 1995.

Vorwerk, Herbert. "Das Recht zur Gewaltanwendung." *Blätter fur religiösen Sozialismus,* ed. Carl Mennicke. Berlin, 1920, vol. 1, no. 4.

Wall, Illan rua. *Human Rights and Constituent Power: Without Model or Warranty.* New York: Routledge/GlassHouse, 2011.

Weber, Samuel. "Going Along for the Ride: Violence and Gesture: Agamben Reading Benjamin Reading Kafka Reading Cervantes." *Germanic Review* 81, no. 1 (Winter 2006): 65–83.

Žižek, Slavoj. *On Belief.* New York: Routledge, 2001.

Žižek, Slavoj. *The Puppet and the Dwarf: The Perverse Core of Christianity.* Cambridge: MIT Press, 2003.

Žižek, Slavoj. *Tarrying with the Negative: Kant Hegel and the Critique of Ideology.* Durham: Duke University Press, 1993.

Žižek, Slavoj. *The Ticklish Subject: The Absent Centre of Political Ontology.* New York: Verso, 1999.

Žižek, Slavoj. *Violence: Six Sideways Reflections.* London: Profile, 2008.

Zupančič, Alenka. *Ethics of the Real: Kant, Lacan.* New York: Verso, 2000.

Index